Social Welfare
in Third World
Development

Social Welfare in Third World Development

Howard Jones

St. Martin's Press   New York

First published in the United States of America in 1989

Printed in Hong Kong

ISBN 0-312-03749-X

Library of Congress Cataloging-in-Publication Data
Jones, Howard, 1918–
    Social welfare in Third World development/Howard Jones.
      p.   cm.
    ISBN 0–312–03749–X : $39.95 (est.)
    1. Human services—Developing countries.   2. Developing countries—
  Social conditions.   I. Title.
HV525.J66   1989
361.9172′4—dc20   89-10782
                                             CIP

To my wife, Bess, who has contributed so much over many years
not only to this, but also to my other books

Contents

List of Tables

List of Figures

List of Exhibits

Acknowledgements

This book owes much to individuals who have read particular chapters or have discussed parts of its subject matter with me. I should like particularly to mention Mr M. J. Shepperdson of University College, Swansea and Dr Paul Romaya and Ms H. R. Snee of the then University of Wales Institute of Science and Technology (now the University of Wales College of Cardiff).

My further debt to those who have contributed to the scientific literature on these subjects is obvious – particularly to those whose work I have quoted directly. I hope due acknowledgement of this has been made at appropriate places in the text.

In addition the author and publishers wish to acknowledge kind permission given by the following for the inclusion of copyright material:

Center for International Studies, Cornell University, for Figure 3.2, originally published in M. J. Esman, *The Landless and Near-Landless in Developing Countries*.
UNESCO for extracts from the *UNESCO Statistical Yearbooks*, 1984, 1986, 1987 and 1988, *Trends and Projections of Enrolment by Level of Education and by Age: 1960–2000 (as assessed in 1982)*, and for Table 8.1, originally published in *The Experimental World Literacy Programmes: a Critical Assessment*.
United Nations for material from *World Population Trends and Policies: 1981 Monitoring Report*, vol. I *Population Trends*; *World Population Trends and Policies, Population and Development Interrelations and Population Policies: 1983 Monitoring Reports*, vol. I *Population Trends* (1984); *World Population Prospects: Estimates and Projections as Assessed in 1984*

(1986); and Figures 10.1 and 12.1 from the *United Nations Chronicle*.

United Nations World Population Fund and the *New Internationist* Magazine for Figures 3.1, 3.3 and 12.2, originally published in the *World Population Report*, 1988.

World Bank for Figures 1.1, 1.2, 6.1 and 7.1, originally published in the *World Development Report*, 1988, and for statistical material from that and earlier World Development Reports, copyright 1988 by the International Bank for Reconstruction and Development/The World Bank, reprinted by permission of Oxford University Press.

World Health Organisation for Tables 5.3, 6.1 and 6.2, originally published in the *Sixth Report on the World Health Situation* 1980, and *Evaluation of the Strategy for Health for All: The Seventh Report on the World Health Situation*, 1987. An update note was based on the *World Health Statistics Annual*, 1983.

Penguin Books Ltd for Table 7.5, originally published in Blaug, Layard and Woodhally (1969) *The Causes and Consequences of Graduate Unemployment in India*.

Every effort has been made to trace all the copyright-holders, but if any have been inadvertently overlooked the publishers will be pleased to make the necessary arrangement at the first opportunity.

Finally may I express my gratitude to the academics, planners and social welfare professionals in the various countries which I have been privileged to visit and work in over the last twenty years; and also to the ordinary people of those countries, the real victims of underdevelopment, who gave me the motivation and the first-hand knowledge I needed to write this book.

HOWARD JONES

Introduction

The developing or underdeveloped countries, or the Third World, include most of the world's population and cover the larger part of the earth's surface but enjoy only a fraction of its wealth. Millions die from preventable disease or starvation, while many of those who survive remain malnourished and illiterate for the rest of their lives. Even in the countries which have been able to make progress large minorities still languish in absolute poverty (Ahluwalia and Carter, 1981). The rest are caught in an underdevelopment trap from which there seems little chance of escaping.

This book is concerned with the kind of policies which Third World governments need to adopt if they are to cope with the grievous social problems confronting them. It must therefore cover a very wide field, and if it is to be of any practical use must also be very specific, with much necessary detail. Amid so many trees it may not be easy to discern the shape of the wood itself. This introduction must therefore first spell out the guiding principles, the presuppositions implicit throughout the work.

These assumptions arise mainly from the fact that the problems to be solved are so different from those of the industrialised countries. Social policies also therefore need to be of a very different character – seeming unorthodox to those accustomed to the way in which these issues are examined in a predominantly European and American social welfare literature. Seven inter-related principles are involved:

1. Poverty is the central problem. Most Third World countries are poor, and their peoples subject to many different forms of deprivation: powerlessness, hunger, urban squalor, landlessness,

illiteracy, avoidable ill health, familial deprivation, the exploitation of women and so on. Most of the poverty in underdeveloped countries is concentrated in the rural areas where most of the people live.

2. The various aspects of poverty interact. Inequality in education perpetuates inequalities in status and 'life chances'. Squalid living conditions adversely affect health and life expectancy. Loss of land rights exacerbates the problem of poverty in all its forms. Uncontrolled fertility, itself partly the result of the despair engendered by deprivation, results only in a further deepening of that deprivation. Inequalities of power stand in the way of any steps towards greater social justice. The interconnections are endless.

3. The underdevelopment of Third World countries, resulting from an unjust international economic order, is the main cause of poverty, causing per capita economic growth to be at best static, and in the poorest countries to be actually declining. What resources there are, are also inequitably distributed. Therefore, although national economic plans to stimulate growth and achieve a more equitable distribution of its rewards are necessary, a reordering of international economic relationships is also important if either endeavour is to be successful.

4. The substantial returns obtained from investments in 'human capital' mean that social welfare provision aimed at the reduction of poverty, far from being a luxury for such poor countries, can make its own substantial contribution to economic growth.

5. The emphasis on growth must not be allowed to obscure the importance for policy of non-economic objectives. Development is more than growth; it should be social development: progress should also be made towards social justice and an improvement in the quality of life.

6. Both economic and social welfare policy must be appropriate to local economic circumstances, but also to a country's cultural, geographical and demographic circumstances. A major obstacle to such indigenisation is the cultural dominance of the industrialised North, arising from and serving the latter's economic dominance, and therefore helping to preserve the condition of underdevelopment.

7. The most valuable indigenous social welfare resource available to the underdeveloped country is the traditional system of mutual aid based on the family. This is suffering attrition, but its survival, at least for the foreseeable future, is necessary if the problems resulting from widespread poverty are to be alleviated.

Meaning of Development

The term 'development' is often used as if it were synonymous with economic development or 'growth'. It is used here to mean 'social development', a much broader concept (Seers, 1969; cf. Little, 1982, p. 6). This excludes situations, sadly not uncommon, in which a country's gross national product (GNP) is increasing but little or none of it finds its way either into the hands of the poor or into socially desirable forms of public expenditure such as education, public health and hygiene, housing or family welfare. The debate about development cannot avoid being concerned with value-laden issues like these (Little, 1982, pp. 6ff).

To talk of 'developing countries' is to imply that such advances are actually taking place, but, even using the narrow criterion of economic growth as the measure of development, the facts give the lie to this. This was acknowledged by the Independent Commission on International Development Issues, in the *Brandt Report* (Brandt, 1980), which, while calling for more international aid, also made proposals for modest changes in international financial and economic relationships to foster growth in the underdeveloped countries.

This Report led directly to a Summit meeting of North–South leaders at Cancum in 1981, and stimulated a great deal of discussion. But neither it nor a second *Brandt Report*, (Brandt, 1983) have had much practical effect. They did, however, foreshadow the demand from the poor countries for a New International Economic Order, a demand which the worsening plight of those countries amply justifies. Thus the *1988 World Development Report* (World Bank, 1988, pp. 222–3) estimates that the annual average per capita growth in GNP of 'low-income' Third World countries, for the period 1965–86 (excluding the better performing economies of India and China) was only 0·5 per cent. No fewer than twelve of the countries in this group had negative growth over this period. Bearing in mind the level of need and a growth rate over four times as large in the already prosperous North this is bad enough, but things do not seem likely to improve much. Growth figures for the low-income countries in 1986 and 1987 show a steady decline, which hardly lends support to the claim by the Bank that 1985–95 would be a decade of opportunity (World Bank, 1986, p. 44).

In the better-off, the so-called 'middle-income developing countries', projected per capita growth rates are falling even faster. The annual average for 1965–86 is not high, at 2·6 per cent, but even this figure masks wide disparities between high-performing South Asian countries such as Singapore, Hong Kong and South Korea, and other 'middle-income' countries, six of them with zero growth (World Bank, 1988, pp. 222–3). It should also be noted, having in mind the distinction between growth and development referred to above, that internal economic inequalities within these 'middle-income' countries remain great. Among 23 such countries for which the World Bank had figures in 1988, the bottom 20 per cent of households shared on average only 4·4 per cent of household incomes, while the top 20 per cent monopolised 51·9 per cent (World Bank, 1988, pp. 272–3).

This situation is often reflected in regional inequalities. For instance, in 1979 in the impoverished north-east of Brazil (a middle-income country) 'the average per capita income was about 40% of the national average' (World Bank, 1982, pp. 25). But this is not the whole story. Even such neglected areas have their submerged minorities, suffering a degree of deprivation and misery equal to that endured by the many in the poorest countries.

In evaluating the significance of figures such as these one must allow for differences in baselines, whether between Third World countries and the industrialised world, or within the Third World between low-income and middle-income countries. Even if growth rates were comparable it would, of course, for the poorer countries, be a percentage of a lower GNP. For example, the average growth rate of 3·7 per cent for China and India produced an increase in per capita income of just $11·1, whereas the apparently lower growth of 2·3 per cent for the industrialised countries meant an increase of $298. The increase for the other low income countries was $1 (World Bank, 1988, pp. 222–3).

Growth and Welfare

There is reason to believe that certain patterns of economic growth actually widen the gap within a country between rich and poor. Adverse consequences are particularly likely for the rural poor (Griffin and Khan, 1982). There is general agreement with what is called the Kuznets hypothesis: that the initial effect of growth will be to increase inequality, this trend only being reversed when a certain minimum per capita level of GNP has been reached (Ahluwalia and Carter, 1981, pp. 464–9; Adelman and Morris, 1973). On this basis, the tide never would turn for the poorest countries.

Ahluwalia and Carter (1981, p. 485) argue that growth can nevertheless raise the incomes of the most deprived families, even if (as predicted by the Kuznets hypothesis) it is at a slower rate than the average for a country as a whole, and therefore causes inequalities to increase. They estimate that, if there had been accelerated growth from 1975 onwards, a 30 per cent reduction in absolute poverty could have been achieved by the year 2000 (ibid, p. 489). Of course this prediction could easily be falsified by government policies which exploited the poor – for example, by discriminating against the rural areas in the interest of industrialisation and the towns, or could be tilted in the other direction by more active attempts by government to improve the position of the poorest.

But suppose, in spite of Kuznets, that policies are adopted also to reduce inequality. Some argue that there then has to be a trade-off in growth. Two main reasons are offered for this (ibid., p. 486): first that redistribution reduces the surplus available to the better-off for saving and therefore investment; secondly that it reduces the reward for success and so weakens incentives for effort. There could also be a third factor. Redistribution could take the form of directing the growth process itself into channels which benefit the poor. Thus the government could '(a) increase linkage of the poor to the faster growing segments of the economy so as to increase the flow of indirect benefits; and (b) provide much greater direct support to productive activities upon which the poor are heavily dependent and which have a potential for effective expansion' (ibid, p. 486). Free-market economists like the neo-classicists (see Chapter 1) would see this as clumsy interference with the efficient allocation of resources through the price mechanism, bound to exact its economic toll.

On the first point about savings it will perhaps suffice for the moment to point out that the surplus income of the better-off is not necessarily saved. Experience shows that much of it may be spent on imported consumer luxuries. Poor countries cannot afford to expend their precious foreign credits in this way; they are needed to acquire the sinews of development: fertilisers, raw materials, machinery, technology and so on. These in the long run will be the means by which future savings and investment can be generated.

The second argument, about the need for incentives, often seems to be used as if it applied only to the capitalists. What is rarely understood is the need to provide incentives to motivate the masses. The spirit of enterprise and creativity which broadly-based economic growth requires cannot be expected from a people who are sunk in the hopeless apathy which poverty breeds.

Finally there is the efficacy of the free market as compared with the conscious direction of investment. This raises important issues requiring closer examination, but for the time being it is probably worthwhile pointing to the achievements of Taiwan and Korea, the so-called 'baby tigers' of postwar development. Their success stems not from adherence to free-market principles, but from government intervention to create a small-farm agriculture and labour-intensive export-led industrialisation.

Human Capital

The charge that redistribution involves a significant trade-off against growth is levelled particularly against the social services. For instance, they are said to sap the independence and energy of recipients. Where this does not simply call attention to the need for more intelligent methods of service delivery, it is a variation on the theme of incentives – which can have little meaning for the very poor. However there is another argument: that welfare expenditure is a luxury, and that only economically successful countries can afford it. In line with this belief, donors of official aid are much more willing to provide finance for what they call 'productive investment'.

Opposition to this naive proposition comes from two directions: convergence theory, and the concept of 'human capital'. The general hypothesis put forward by convergence theorists (Rimlinger, 1971; Mishra, 1973, 1976) is that social structure is related to the level of industrialisation achieved by a country rather than to its political ideology. In particular attempts were made to show that, in spite of the conflicting political positions of the United States and the Soviet Union, they were 'converging' socially, as they responded in similar ways to the requirements of an industrial economy. Some aspects of *perestroika* in the USSR and the New Economic Regions in China might be seen as examples of this.

If the convergence hypothesis is true, it follows that welfare systems would also be correlated with the progress made in industrialisation. None of the research on this has included Third World countries, except for Israel (Mishra, 1973) which might be considered so on some definitions. This is a pity, as countries with such severely restricted industrialisation could have provided a control against which the hypothesis might be tested. The prediction would be that industrialised countries as a group would have more advanced state welfare systems than the countries of the Third World.

If this simply meant that the greater affluence of the more industrialised countries enabled them to make better social provision, it would not be a very striking discovery. Mishra (1976, p. 31) seems to be implying the very opposite of this: that welfare provision actually facilitates economic development. This seems also to be the view of the World Bank (though expressed less enthusiastically than heretofore), and of various writers who argue for the contribution which a 'basic needs' policy can make to growth (Streeten *et al.*, 1981, pp. 96ff, 1984; Quibria, 1982). According to this view, better health and nutrition mean a more vigorous people; and education gives them the knowledge and skills they need in order to achieve growth. There is also a gain in grasp and vision. Raise the people just a little and further progress begins to seem possible to them. Investment in human capital may prove to be even more profitable than that in more tangible assets. It must be seen, of course, as a long-term policy, needing time to produce its effects.

The evidence for these statements will be presented in the chapters which follow, making a case for welfare expenditure even by poor countries. Comparing poor but socialistically-minded countries like Cuba or China with, say, the United States, it becomes clear that growth and welfare are not necessarily opposed to each other. Yet optimism about the role of welfare expenditure in stimulating growth must be moderated by the recognition that a country's development will be determined in the first place, not by the hard work and enterprise of its people, but by domestic economic policies, and by global factors calling for global structural solutions. And there can be no doubt that prosperity does enable a country to afford better services. Truisms do, after all, have to contain some truth. It makes most sense to think of the relationship between welfare and growth as a reciprocal one.

1

The Economic Debate

The problems of the underdeveloped countries are not, as we have seen, exclusively economic. They are partly due to the failure of political leaders – failures which perhaps result from weakness or ignorance, or sometimes from outright exploitation, either by them or the powerful local interests whom they represent. But although a higher GNP will not solve all of a country's social problems, it is inseparable from them.

Balance of Payments Problems

The balance of payments looms very large here. If it is adverse, steps may have to be taken to try to increase exports in what is clearly an unfavourable trading environment, distorting the internal economy in the process. It may become necessary to restrict imports, perhaps by means of tariffs or other protectionist measures. In particular it becomes difficult to afford the imports vital for development, let alone those required for the satisfaction of consumer needs. And the country's internal resources are drained to service the loans needed to plug the gap. Growth is inevitably affected and social problems multiply.

The current balance of payments crisis in the South has a long history. During the boom years of the fifties and sixties satisfactory rates of economic growth were being achieved, especially by the larger Third World countries, who were able to borrow from private banks on the thriving Eurodollar market. But everything depended on the Americans. The dollar's convertibility into gold fixed its value and the values of the many other currencies which were tied to it. This stability in world exchange rates provided a firm and predictable basis for international trade. That trade in its turn was stimulated by the willingness of the United States to finance it through a large overseas deficit, and to import freely.

This halcyon period ended in the seventies. The American deficit became a 'dollar overhang' – larger than the reserves which were supposed to back it. Convertibility became impossible to maintain, and protectionist measures to reduce the deficit itself became inevitable. In 1971, the dollar ceased to be convertible, and a 10 per cent import duty was introduced. The devaluation of the dollar which followed accelerated as the oil price hike in 1973 caused the American deficit to worsen. The dollar began to be consciously 'managed' in the interests of the US economy. The oil price rises also caused widespread balance of payments problems for the other industrialised countries, combining with American protectionism to reduce both international economic activity and export outlets for the Third World. Oil prices, the growing trade recession, and a deterioration in the terms of trade for commodities (see Figure 1.1), on which the countries of the South largely relied for their overseas earnings, exacerbated their plight. The larger among them were able to ride the recession by increasing their overseas loans (mainly from the surpluses of the oil-rich countries), but this expedient was not open to the smaller and poorer countries, whose situation therefore continued to deteriorate.

The subsequent recovery in world trade hardly benefited the Third World at all. By the early eighties they were paying more in interest and repayments on loans than they were receiving in new finance, and this situation has worsened since. Against a total net inflow of funds of $147 billion during the five years up to 1982, the following five years saw an outflow of $85 billion (World Bank, 1988, p. 29). Even the International Monetary Fund (IMF) accepts that since 1985 it has been receiving more from underdeveloped countries than it has lent to them. It predicts that this particular trend will be reversed, but it remains to be seen whether this will have any perceptible effect on the overall payments situation disclosed by Figure 1.1, especially for the poorest countries.

The global recovery itself was very short-lived. To combat inflation the industrialised world introduced tight monetarist policies, and also adopted various disguised forms of protection (World Bank, 1987, pp. 133ff). The contraction in export

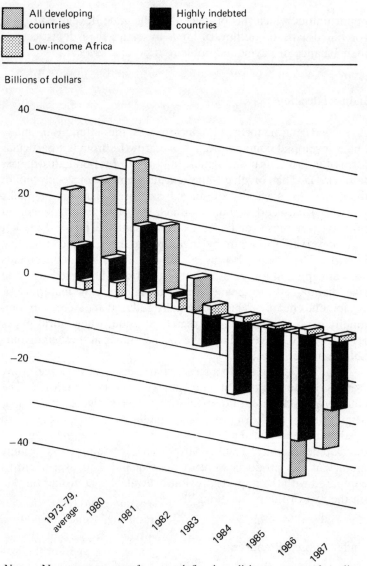

☐ All developing
  countries

☐ Low-income Africa

■ Highly indebted
  countries

Billions of dollars

Note: Net resource transfers are defined as disbursements of medium-
and long-term external loans minus interest and amortisation payments on
medium- and long-term external debt.

Source: World Bank (1988) *World Development Report* (New York:
Oxford University Press).

Figure 1.1 Net resource transfers to developing countries 1973 to 1987

opportunities which this produced for the underdeveloped world, combined with the outflow of funds to service their debts, caused their balance of payments problem to become critical.

Industrialisation

A second major focus of concern was the attempt in many underdeveloped countries to achieve growth through a particular form of industrialisation, namely import substitution industrialisation (ISI). This involved the encouragement of local 'infant industries' by a variety of special measures. The urban public services, roads and so on, on which they had to rely, received priority over those for the rest of the country. The local market was preserved for them by measures to keep out competitive imports. They were also given subsidies and other inducements such as capital at low rates of interest. Often a high exchange rate was maintained, to enable them to import raw materials or equipment cheaply. This incidentally reduced the value of commodity exports originating in the countryside, when world prices for them were converted into the local currency at these unfavourable exchange rates.

All of this amounted to a substantial transfer of resources away from agriculture and an already impoverished rural majority. The countryside stagnated. Powerful urban interests were established. Migration to the towns was stimulated on such a scale as to become a major social problem in itself. Meanwhile the industrial development which resulted from such cosseting was usually inefficient. Its products were of poor quality and overpriced as compared with the imports previously available – a further burden on the rest of the population.

Under-utilised Resources

There has been a long and learned debate as to what is meant by the term 'surplus labour' when applied to traditional forms of land tenure and cultivation ever since Lewis's seminal paper appeared in 1954 (Lewis, 1954; Singh, 1978, pp. 43–133). All members of a family or community group may have a right to employment and a share of the produce from such land. This means that the marginal product (that is the product of the last units of labour utilised) will be low. Some would say that it is actually zero.

Productivity might be improved by adopting better methods of husbandry. This does not have to be less labour-intensive, but if it is the labour thus released will be available for some other productive work, presumably in industry. Unfortunately industry as at present constituted is unable to employ the labour already on offer to it except in one or two countries; elsewhere large numbers of those who have migrated to the towns in search of industrial work remain unemployed. Mass unemployment is no longer unknown in the North either, but the waste of resources involved is on a different scale. In the South, labour resources are also wasted in another way; they are 'underdeveloped' because of deficiencies in education and training.

Natural resources are as underused as human resources. Development takes place in enclaves in urban or mining areas at the cost of neglecting the rest of the country. Inadequate water management leads to drought or flooding, often in succession. The environment is often despoiled, and the fertility of the soil neglected.

Competing Solutions

Most development economists contend that, if development is to take place in the Third World, it must follow the same path as that which led to success for, first, Britain, and then the other industrialised countries of the world during the nineteenth century. They differ about how this is to be achieved. Adherents to the neoclassical school argue for reliance on the free market and the price mechanism. This *laisser-faire* view is contested by the structuralists, who point to the many obstacles which stand in the way of growth in the circumstances of an underdeveloped country. Planned intervention is necessary if these obstacles are to be circumvented.

Opposition to economic orthodoxy in both of these forms comes from dependency theory, which rejects the view that underdeveloped countries can follow in the footsteps of the Northern countries. The nature of the economic relationship between the two is seen as creating underdevelopment. The activities of transnational corporations loom large in this kind of analysis. Most *dependistas* are neo-Marxists, but other Marxists take a more traditional Marxist view. They emphasise the positive virtues of capitalism in stimulating growth and democracy, and argue (as did Marx) that socialism can only be achieved after capitalism has run its course. With them, the wheel has come full circle. Like Karl Marx himself, the revolutionaries have made common cause with the neo-classicists, whose ideas will now be examined.

The Neo-Classical Answer

Neo-classical economics combines the early classical ideas of Adam Smith and David Ricardo with the later developments in marginal and equilibrium theory associated with names like Walras, Jevons and Menger. Although neo-classical theory was eclipsed for a period during the economic crisis of the 1930s and in the years of reconstruction after the Second World War, it is the mainstream tradition in economics, and is currently predominant among the governments of the powerful industrialised countries, and in the international agencies – the IMF, the World Bank (see World Bank, 1988) and the General Agreement on Tariffs and Trade (GATT).

Adam Smith wrote his *Wealth of Nations* as long ago as 1776, but his image of the way in which the self-seeking actions of a multitude of individuals are magically transmuted into a 'hidden hand' working for the common good is still central in neo-classical thinking. Essentially this states that the most efficient allocation of resources is achieved if individual consumers and entrepreneurs are free to choose for themselves between different objects of expenditure or investment after comparing the utility (to them) with the market prices of the various alternatives.

How is this to be applied to the problems of the underdeveloped country? Left to itself international trade would distribute itself in accordance with the law of comparative advantage; that is, countries would find themselves concentrating on those products in which their cost advantages were greatest. Protectionism, subsidies for infant industries, or false prices like the artificially low interest rates or artificially high exchange rates associated with ISI distort this process. They create uneconomic ventures which are unable to sustain themselves without support. Meanwhile worthier objects for investment languish, and the country's development suffers.

But before the market can be allowed free rein, remedial action has to be taken to put right the consequences of past mistakes. Consider the balance of payments deficit. This requires action to reduce imports but without protective restrictions on trade. Also industry (no longer propped up by subsidies and so on) has to become a competitive exporter, in place of its present ISI pre-occupation with the domestic market. The means for realising these objectives are well known. They are the kind of 'adjustment policies' usually imposed by the IMF before it is willing to provide temporary foreign exchange support for ailing economies, viz. deflation, and devaluation of the currency.

Deflation is to be achieved by cutting back on public services and other forms of government expenditure, and restricting credit by raising the rate of interest and tightening up direct controls over borrowing. The effect of such a programme would be to reduce economic activity, concentrating it in the most efficient under-takings. It would also increase unemployment. This would reduce the demand for imports, but also help to bring down wages, and with them industrial costs.

The other strategy, devaluation, by reducing the overseas purchasing power of the local currency would make imports more expensive. At the same time it would make local products cheaper for foreigners. This, combined with lower wages, and greater efficiency among the industrial survivors, would provide a stimulus to exports. The balance of payments problem would be on the way to solution.

The short-term social consequences of such programmes are bound to be painful. Lower wages and higher unemployment have already been mentioned. The rural population would suffer also. Deflation of the economy would reduce consumption in the countryside as well as in the towns.

Cuts in government expenditure would inevitably affect the social services, which might otherwise have been able to mitigate some of the more deleterious short-term effects. There would not be all that much room for manoeuvre. Priorities like the health services and water supply would have to be maintained. Education, as a slowly maturing investment, could not be cut back very drastically without long-term damage. Then there would be expenditure on the physical infrastructure. If, for instance, the roads and other forms of communication were allowed to decay, the anticipated economic recovery could be stifled at birth.

But according to neo-classical theory, the new, efficient exporting industries would eventually employ more labour, to attract which wages would have to rise. However, so long as there remained a reserve of poorly-rewarded surplus labour in agriculture, wages would still be lower than in the industrialised countries. This would enable local industry to preserve its comparative advantage in labour costs, at least for a time.

Agriculture in its turn would gain by the removal of the discrimination formerly practised against it under the ISI policy. It would also benefit from the 'external economies' generated by a thriving industrial sector, whose spirit of enterprise and innovation would spread to agriculture, helping to make the land more productive and therefore more rewarding to those working on it. The industrial population would have to be fed and, being better-paid it would provide farmers with a market for profitable luxury foods as well as the staples on which they had previously had to rely. Furthermore, as industry provided alternatives and better-paid forms of employment and reduced the labour surplus in the rural areas, the productivity of those remaining in agriculture would improve and this, combined with the competition for their services with industry, would raise their wages.

It is sometimes argued that, far from increasing employment, such a regime would reduce it. To be competitive industry would have to be capital-intensive. Machinery would be employed rather than people. Similarly with agriculture: the enhanced efficiency referred to above would be achieved through the amalgamation of small farms so as to achieve economies of scale, and it would then become profitable to invest in agricultural machinery. Even the modest tractor requires a certain size of holding to be worthwhile.

The neo-classical economists reject these strictures, and point to the experience of the 'baby tigers'. Both Taiwan and the Republic of Korea achieved industrial success by concentrating on products which utilised their comparative advantage in cheap and plentiful labour. Similarly with agriculture: land reforms were introduced in both countries, and farms remain small. Both eliminated their labour surplus, and as a result wages rose in both industry and agriculture (Reynolds, 1985, pp. 166–180).

Few would argue that such a scenario is likely to be realised in its entirety. It is an account of an 'ideal process', of trends. In real life, where many countries with widely divergent interests interact in world markets, and governments are subject to political and other pressures, there would be many departures from it, though at a price. This provides a starting-point for an important line of criticism: the 'theory of second best': '. . . if one of the Paretian optimum conditions cannot be fulfilled a second best optimum situation is achieved only by departing from all the other optimum conditions (Lipsey and Lancaster, 1956–7). In other words, half measures will not do. The elements of the adjustment process are interdependent; leave one out and it will not work. This opens up the possibility of planned intervention on a much wider scale.

The Structuralists

During the war with Hitler the resources of Britain were strained to breaking-point; comprehensive controls had to be established over the labour force, the supply and use of resources, and consumption. Such economic planning, in the very special circumstances of war, proved highly successful.

Some expected that there would be a return to *laisser-faire* at the end of the conflict. This was reflected in the philosophy of the Bretton Woods conference in 1944, and its creations, the IMF and the GATT; but the economic situation after the war made such an aim unattainable for the time being. Much of Europe's industry had been destroyed. Its foreign exchange reserves were exhausted. Everything was in short supply. To all intents and purposes, the countries of Europe on both sides were bankrupt. Government intervention was unavoidable.

Marshall Aid and overseas military expenditure by the United States helped to bridge to massive 'dollar gap'. Financed thus by the American overseas deficit, the economic revival of Europe and the subsequent boom of the fifties and sixties were ushered in, not by the unfettered operation of the market, but by state planning. Controls in Europe were now being abandoned, but in South

America, under the influence of the United Nations Economic Commission for Latin America (ECLA), they secured a new lease of life in the form of radical ISI programmes. The beginning of structuralism as an economic orientation is identified by some with these developments (Brett, 1985).

Although ISI by the South Americans has been much criticised there is no faulting them for seeking to achieve industrial development by an interventionist route of the sort which the Europeans had followed with such success. Taiwan and Korea are often referred to as examples of what can be achieved by free enterprise, but they put their development on course by widespread government planning and control. Even the subsequent economic liberalisation claimed for these two 'baby tigers' was limited; having started from such a high level of state intervention much intervention is still in place.

Japan's protectionist policies are well known, but industrial development was fostered by the Japanese government in many other ways. To give a single but very important example; the National Bank has always played a central role in the task of marshalling capital for enterprises with growth or export potential. Small wonder that the Japanese example was followed by other underdeveloped countries seeking to industrialise themselves. Economists of the structuralist school believe in the necessity for such intervention (Chenery, 1975). They point out that the neo-classical solution assumes a degree of flexibility in the economic system which just does not exist.

Some such elements in an economy may be quite intractable. There is, for instance the 'two-gap' problem (Chenery and Strout, 1966). The neo-classicists expect the raising of the rate of interest during the deflationary phase of the adjustment process to motivate an increase in savings and thus increase investment. But investment requires technology and equipment which cannot be produced at home, and cannot be imported by a country with an adverse balance of payments. Savings cannot therefore be effectively used in the process of industrialisation unless either loans or aid from abroad are available to fill the gap. An important factor in the success of both Taiwan and South Korea was the investment credits supplied to them by the United States in order to strengthen their anti-Communist regimes. (For a critique of the 'two-gap' model see Bruton, 1978, pp. 486–97.)

If adjustments, nevertheless, do occur, they often do so too slowly (Chenery, 1981, pp. 62–3). As a result they may be overtaken by events. They may also cause unduly prolonged social upheaval and suffering before the anticipated benefits of the new equilibrium come on stream. A case in point is the social fall-out from the unemployment, falling wages and social service cuts, which result from the use of deflation as an adjustment mechanism.

One way of conceptualising this inflexibility is to refer to it as a problem of substitution (Chenery and Raduchel, 1981). To satisfy the requirements of neo-classical theory both manufacturing and primary industry have (for example) to substitute an export orientation for one which relies on a protected domestic market. Consumers have to substitute domestic products for imports. Capital and labour have to be interchangeable one way or the other. Peasants have to substitute improved methods for traditional practice. The more disciplined orientation of the factory worker has to be substituted for that of the person who has spent all his life living in a village and working on the land. Merely to state the objectives in these terms brings out the extreme difficulty of achieving them. The 'elasticity of substitution', that is, the size of the incentive which is required in order to produce a given level of response, will vary according to the kind of change being sought, but is in principle capable of being empirically determined.

The importance attached to empirically derived facts as against deductive theory (though neither can exclude the other entirely) may be one way of distinguishing between the neo-classicists and the structuralists (Chenery, 1981, pp. 51–5). Some go further and suggest that the abstract nature of neo-classical theory divorces it from what is going on in the real world (Brett, 1985, p. 28). The point is illustrated by the unreality of the market prices which are so important to that theory. In all economies in the real world, but especially in the *dirigiste* Third World economy, prices are rarely free of extraneous influences. The subsidies which keep down the prices of industrial inputs provide important examples. The estimation of a 'shadow price' – the opportunity cost, in terms of what is foregone to make the purchase in question – is hedged about with difficulties.

Nothing illustrates better the difficulties faced by the neo-classicists in trying to obtain an approximation to opportunity cost than the social services (World Bank, 1988, p. 132). First of all they propose pricing a service on the basis of its marginal cost, the cost of the last unit of provision. This is the point at which a decision about an alternative use for the resources involved (that is, opportunity cost) would have to be made. But (in the absence of competition) there would have to be administrative safeguards to ensure that the marginal cost was not higher than it should be because of waste by the service providers. Also if there were increasing returns to scale the cost of the last or marginal unit would be lower than that of earlier units, and therefore a price based on it, would not enable total costs to be recovered. In such circumstances average cost might be used. But social services usually provide external economies (for example, the general benefit derived from health services) so a lower price than marginal cost would then be indicated. 'But how much lower? . . . it is almost impossible to estimate the price' (ibid.). In any case the poor could not afford the cost price, so some special provision would have to be made for them – entirely arbitrary it seems, and associated presumably with a stigmatising means test.

Exhibit 1.1   Structuralist empiricism

The empiricism of structuralist development planning shifts attention from broad generalisations to the numerous and interrelated factors operating in the situation of each individual country. Where such phenomena are realistically accessible to econometric analysis, complex equations are required. For example, in order to attempt a prediction of the consequences of various versions of the Pakistan national plan, it was necessary to develop a model incorporating sixteen 'parameters' (such as the cost of foreign capital, capital–output ratios, and allowable consumption growth rates), and also eleven 'variables' (such as GNP, gross investment, and traditional imports and exports) (Chenery and MacEwan, 1981).

Such a pattern of parameters and variables is unique to each country, but it is possible to proceed to groups of countries which have some such characteristics in common. More general formulations thus emerge from the ground up, rather than by inference from general principles. An example is the Kuznets hypothesis about the effect of growth on income distribution, referred to in the Introduction.

Modernisation

Whatever their other differences, both neo-classical and structuralist economists are in agreement that the interests of Third World countries require them to become 'modernised', adopting attitudes and patterns of social behaviour which are more like those of the peoples of the North. This would involve widespread changes in social norms, including changes in many of the traditional patterns of kinship support, and the related restrictions and obligations by which the economic freedom of inhabitants of non-industrialised countries is hindered – at least as it appears to Northern eyes.

These customary codes define what is or is not proper behaviour. They can be more controlling, and perhaps more oppressive than the laws of the industrialised countries, for they affect more aspects of behaviour, and are more prescriptive, saying what must be done as well as what is forbidden. They can also be more thoroughly enforced. In traditional societies, privacy is not an important value, and misbehaviour is therefore more observable and can be more easily controlled.

More specifically, customary rules regulate relationships between different individuals or families, and even between villages or tribes. They determine rights to land, and even the way it is to be cultivated. Individual property rights are subordinated to the rights of kinsfolk, especially those in need, like widows and orphans, the elderly or the disabled. This could be seen as a serious disincentive against hard work and saving. Kinship obligations and responsibilities in respect of communal land may hinder a man from moving from his village to places where, in a dynamic economy, labour would be more productive and opportunities would exist for him to better himself.

Conventional economic wisdom, whether structuralist or neo-classical, sees changes in these respects as a precondition for the economic transformation of the society. Capital and know-how may possibly become available but they still have to be effectively utilised, and this calls for a people with enterprising attitudes, and a society which rewards instead of punishing such attitudes. In such a climate, it is argued people would become ambitious. They would be more inclined to 'look forward', to plan for a more distant future than, say, the next sowing season. Such an orientation to the future would bring with it a greater appreciation of the value of education and training, and also encourage people to save, thus advancing the process of capital accumulation. Their traditional desire for interdependence with others, with its stifling effect on initiative, would be jettisoned, and they would become more individualistic and thrusting. And as they could now retain the rewards of effort for themselves, effort would be encouraged. There are unmistakeable echoes here of the theory developed by Max Weber in his classical study *The Protestant Ethic and the Spirit of Capitalism* (1962). According to Weber, it was the development of Calvinistic Protestantism which prepared the psychological climate within which capitalism could germinate and flourish. It is easy to see how congenial to a free enterprise economy would be the Calvinistic ethic of hard work and asceticism, and its doctrine of an elite who could demonstrate the priority of their claim for salvation by their achievements on earth.

Alternatively it has been argued that a change towards a Northern-style cash economy would bring about cultural changes in the direction of modernisation, which would appear to provide less support for the modernisation hypothesis than for the view of Marx, who argues that economic change comes first, bringing about attitudinal change as the population adjusts itself to the requirements of survival in a capitalist society. 'What else does the history of ideas prove than that intellectual production changes its character as material production is changed' (Marx and Engels, 1888, p. 68).

Some Marxist students of the Third World lay great stress in this connection upon the influence which city life has upon the burgeoning urban millions (Roberts, 1982, pp. 369–70). The cities are the centres of capitalist and Northern influence and can make a powerful demand for change. Meanwhile the migrants are free from the traditional pressures of the village which might otherwise have prevented them from complying. Eventually, of course, the commercialisation of agriculture would mean that the new attitudes would then also spread to the countryside.

The basic assumption of the modernisation hypothesis is that economic development in the Third World must follow the same course as that taken in the North. As will be seen, dependency theorists argue that this is prevented by the very nature of the economic relationships between the two, a relationship which eventuates in underdevelopment, not development. In such circumstances, 'modernised' attitudes operate more as ideologies supportive of the exploitative *status quo* than as a dynamic for independent growth.

Nor are individualistic impulses necessary to stimulate effort. Experience in the very different circumstances of the North (for example in the USSR, where, shortly after the revolution, attempts to eliminate pay differentials, had to be given up in favour of the euphemistically-named New Economic Policy) is no criterion. In the Third World the family and the community have always, in the past, provided enough motivation, often in the most adverse circumstances. That very materialistic attitudes are not incompatible with such loyalties is shown by the vigour displayed by the extended family in such rapidly developing countries as Hong Kong and Singapore. So perhaps the attitudinal aspects of modernisation, far from being a prerequisite for growth, are not necessary at all.

Dependency Theory

The assumption that development always follows the same course is called into question by many present-day theorists, both Marxist and non-Marxist (Roxborough, 1979). They point to the exploitative nature of the relationship between (in the current jargon) the 'centre' and the 'periphery'. They see this relationship, not as making for the development of countries on the 'periphery', but as maintaining them in a state of underdevelopment as the counterpart to, and a precondition for, the continued affluence of the 'centre'.

First of all, the terms of trade between the centre and the periphery is unfavourable to the latter, that is to say, their minerals or agricultural products are exchanged with the manufactured products of the developed nations at an unfavourable rate (see Figure 1.2). Obviously this situation is likely to vary according to the supply of or demand for Third World commodities at any particular time. Harvest failures may improve the price paid for them, though if it is the Third World harvest which has failed the improved terms of trade may not compensate for the fall in the quantity available for sale. Developments in the North may extend

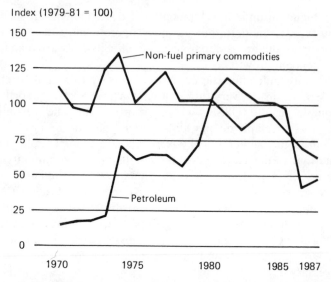

Note: Real prices are annual average nominal prices in dollars, deflated by the annual change in the manufacturing unit value index (MUV), a measure of the price of industrial country exports to developing countries.
Source: World Bank (1988), *World Development Report* (New York: Oxford University Press).

Figure 1.2   Real commodity prices, 1970–87

the demand and at least temporarily raise their value. Sometimes also, where a commodity is essential to the industrialised countries and producers can constitute themselves into something approaching a monopoly, they can force the price up. This is what happened in the case of oil.

Such outcomes are rare. Indeed the terms of trade in general seem likely to become more and more adverse to the underdeveloped world as the North develops alternatives. Shifts away from the consumption of a commodity occur. This is what has happened in the case of cane sugar, a staple export for various countries in the Caribbean and Asia since settlers from Europe introduced it in colonial times. European countries have begun to expand their cultivation of beet with catastrophic effects upon the world price of sugar. So the general trend in the terms of Third World trade is downwards (World Bank, 1982, p. 26, 1983, p. 12). The World Bank puts it like this: 'The weakness of the low-income countries' primary export prices reflects both their concentration in commodities for which demand is expanding slowly, and the inability of countries heavily dependent on one or two exports to vary their output-mix as relative prices change' (World Bank, 1981, p. 22). In exchange for its own devalued primary products, the South will be importing some consumer goods, but will also need from abroad oil and other supplies, as well as the means for the modernisation of its industry and agriculture (World Bank, 1982, p. 26). All of this makes for cheap commodities for the consumers of the North, while making it very difficult for the people of the Third World to maintain, much less improve their own standard of living. What is already, in a poor country, an adverse balance of payments will go even further into the red.

With overseas development aid not expanding as it should (Weiss, 1982, p. 35; World Bank, 1983, p. 34; UNCTAD, 1985), the gap will have to be filled by borrowing, bringing with it an increase in the burden of interest. Even borrowing is no escape for the poorest countries, as they can offer to lenders little in the way of security for their loans. The inability of a number of heavy borrowers (even among oil producers) in the Third World to meet their interest repayment obligations has led to something of a crisis among Northern banks, and caused them to be even more cautious (World Bank, 1983, pp. 32–3; World Bank, 1986, pp. 52ff).

Overseas venture capital is a possible alternative. As a form of direct investment it is much favoured by orthodox economists of all schools (Little, 1982). After all, Third World countries still possess the mineral resources and low-wage labour which made them attractive as colonies in the first place. Large corporations in Europe and America, and increasingly in Japan, will be eager to take advantage of the opportunities which these resources offer. If a country protects its domestic market from outside competition, this will be a further incentive.

Transnational Corporations

Because of their importance in the economies of Third World countries and their role in increasing economic dependency in those countries, it is worth giving a little more attention to these transnational corporations (Dunning, 1981; Brett, 1985, pp. 80–102; Kumar, 1980). They are often known as multinational corporations because they operate in more than one country, but the term 'transnational' corporations (TNC) may better indicate the nature of a company which is truly international, rather than one able to claim a multiplicity of nationalities. This does not mean that they have no nationality at all. No one who has observed their operations, and the support they can elicit from what are effectively their 'home governments', can accept this.

Nor is this support surprising when it is realised that, in the United States for example, as much as 97 per cent of all exports could be attributed to transnationals (Economist Intelligence Unit, 1981). Fortunately 'rootlessness' is not a necessary implication of the usage preferred here, which does at least call attention to their lack of commitment to any of the other countries in which they operate. Meanwhile their sheer size ensures that they can dominate the economies of the poorer countries in which they are established, and intimidate their governments:

> Today, for instance, the four largest transnational corporations together have an annual turnover greater than the total GNP of the whole continent of Africa. The top thirty-four companies, with turnovers over 10 billion dollars per year, outdistance the GNPs of some seventy countries normally ranked in the 'world economic hierarchy'. Together these companies have a global production in excess of the total product of some eighty poor countries in which over half of the world population live. (Hoogvelt, 1983, p. 57)

Their power does not merely reside in size, overwhelming though this is. It derives also from the fact that they already have plants in various countries, and that many other countries would welcome their interest. A transnational can therefore react to any lack of consideration on the part of a particular government by switching a proposed increase in investment, or even the whole of its operation, to a country which is more sympathetic. It goes without saying that it would do so anyway if this substantially increased the return on its investments, and trading and tax concessions in the gift of governments are often decisive here.

Private overseas investment of this kind has been increasing as other flows have begun to peter out. The financial benefit from this seems sometimes to have been exaggerated; more and more of the funds required are being obtained from local savers. With the repatriation of profits there may even be a net outflow. When the reinvestment of profits does take place, it is restricted to the sectors or regions in which the company is currently profitably engaged. This produces the sadly familiar phenomenon of a dual economy, in which advancement in certain industries and localities is purchased by squalor and neglect everywhere else. Such a parasitic relationship between the developing enclave and the rest of a country has very properly been described as 'internal colonialism' (Casanova, 1964).

Enclave development like this is not restricted to direct investment in productive assets, but includes infrastructural investment also. The transnational concerned may be willing to build roads to serve its factory or plantation, or to connect this with a port, a large domestic market or its source of raw materials, but will rarely be prepared to construct roads elsewhere in the country, no matter how badly they are needed.

The exception to this is seen where a company decided to build such roads as a goodwill gesture, with the idea of improving its image in the country – something which has been more common since Third World countries escaped from colonialism and acquired governments of their own who were beginning to see the nationalisation of foreign-owned undertakings as a possible option. But even a government, if it comes to believe that the presence and health of the foreign undertaking really is a precondition for progress, will be willing to concentrate its own infrastructural programme on the company's needs. Much rural neglect has resulted from such a policy.

It is not surprising that people move from the impoverished countryside to the enclave: the town or mining area which seems to offer better prospects. They do this in larger numbers than could ever be justified by the opportunities for employment, or the ability of the environmental or social services to cope. Thus emerges the overblown urban area, the 'primate city' (Mabogunje, 1980, pp. 166, 199), with its problems of hygiene and health, water supply, housing, personal relationships and public order. These in their turn force the government to devote much of its limited social welfare budget to the town, further impoverishing the countryside.

It has been seen that the net inflow of capital which results from the establishment of a TNC may not be large, and could actually become negative; and that the political and social price paid for it could be high. What about the further argument by development economists that it should provide a 'growth-pole' for employment: begin a chain reaction of development, stimulating employment by the local firms which supply it with its various inputs? The net increase in jobs (if any) is probably small. They create directly

> 'very small amounts of employment (one economist estimated that all the MNCs in the Third World employed only about four and a half million workers), monopolising scarce supplies of technically trained personnel, requiring large outflows of foreign exchange to cover the costs of the capital intensive equipment.' (Brett, 1985, p. 96)

The chain reaction effect on employment is usually equally limited. TNCs have advantages in competing with small local producers, and to the extent that they eliminate these they substitute their own modes of production, usually capital-intensive, for the more traditional labour-intensive methods of their competitors. Little compensation for this is provided by the new industries which are supposed to emerge to service and supply them. The TNCs import not only equipment but also components from their own subsidiaries back home, or from suppliers there with whom they have mutually profitable arrangements. This is strongly supported by feelings in the metropolitan country that any investment abroad by its companies should stimulate domestic business and employment.

More recently TNCs have modified these policies. They have been encouraged by industrial advances in certain low-wage Third World economies, notably the 'baby tigers', either to establish their own subsidiaries for manufacturing components in those countries, or to buy supplies from indigenous producers. This is an example of 'to them that hath shall be given'. It has not helped the most underdeveloped countries.

Spreading their activities over more countries in this way, a characteristically transnational mode of operation, has another advantage. It enables the corporations to exploit the device of 'transfer pricing'. By overcharging for equipment, materials and even skilled personnel and know-how imported from one country to another, they can inflate the share of their profits attributable to their overseas undertakings, and evade exchange controls intended to prevent the export of profits. Concealing part of their local gains in this way (Lall, 1980, pp. 91ff; Plaschaert, 1979) also helps them with any 'image' problem (and possible political repercussions) consequent on public awareness of the real extent of their profits. This strengthens any argument they might present for further concessions from the government. They are also able to declare their profits in the countries where tax advantages are greatest.

Some countries have sought their salvation through tourism and, whether this industry is dominated by transnationals (as is often the case) or not, there are similar factors at work to reduce the claimed employment spin-offs. There is a widespread belief, whether justified or not, that foreign visitors will not eat local foods or trust locally-made equipment. As a result such items are imported, and tourists find their familiar domestic environments painstakingly reproduced for them, diluting the foreignness for which presumably most of them had come. More important, local farmers and manufacturers gain no external economies from the expansion in tourism. In countries with a tourist industry of significant size there could be a valuable market from this source, especially for farmers and other food suppliers.

The claim is often made that, apart from providing jobs, TNCs help to improve the quality of labour, by training staff who eventually filter off into other employment. This could be an important external economy; trained managers in particular are in short supply. But Gershenberg (1987) found that only where a company is in a joint venture with government is there a significant contribution to management training.

Foreign firms often commenced their operations in Third World countries when those countries were colonies. It was obviously an advantage to the former imperial power to be able to continue these profitable activities after independence, but, in line with orthodox economic thinking, it was taken for granted that it would also be advantageous to the ex-colony itself. What results instead is the continuation of the economic exploitation which colonial dependence made possible, long after the political dependence of empire has been brought to an end. Orthodox development economics could be seen as an ideology to give legitimacy to this by apparently justifying its value to the dependent country, and thus obscuring the dependent underdevelopment to which it actually leads.

Such a process – involving as it does the export of much-needed capital in the form of repatriated profits, the rigid restriction of direct investment to the chosen enclave, with the consequent creation of serious problems of urbanisation, the distortion of government infrastructural investment, and even of social policy, and the absence of the externalities which might have contributed to a wider process of development – is not going to give much impetus to the economic growth of the Third World country concerned. Bearing in mind the rural neglect and inequalities which the dual economy generates, and the maintenance of the low-wage economy on which this kind of foreign investment thrives, it does little either, for wider aspects of development.

Cultural Dependence

The *dependistas* also reject many of the changes in personal and social attitudes brought about by dependent underdevelopment. Much of what is called the modernisation of attitudes is seen by them as a form of cultural imperialism.

To a people who have been convinced that Northern-style development really is on the way, the consumer patterns of the North will appear to be attractive and accessible, and these trends will be further stimulated by advertising and the media. This is development economics made intelligible for the man in the street (and it *is* town dwellers who are the main target). To those who aspire to these transplanted and usually inappropriate consumerist norms, the relationship with international capital which produces them is amply vindicated. They extend even into social policy, leading often, as will be seen, to the adoption of many ill-advised approaches to Third World social problems.

This 'false consciousness' is supported by the effect which underdevelopment has on the power structure within a country. Various elites – senior politicians and officials, import–export traders, and the employees of foreign companies and so on – all have a vested interest in preserving a dependency which is so profitable to them, and also in resisting social welfare policies which threaten the privileges which it has bestowed on them. They may not be the traitorous *compradors* sometimes alleged, but it is not difficult for them to convince themselves that such collaboration is in the country's interest as well as their own.

Classical Marxism

Many dependency theorists have been Marxists, but the most influential recent attack upon the position of the *dependistas* has come from a Marxist, Bill Warren (1973,1980). Warren has returned to the views of Marx himself, which bear a remarkable resemblance to those of the neo-classicists (Roxborough, 1979, p. 38). Any surprise at this should be tempered by the reflection that Marx and the neo-classicists both shared a common intellectual parentage, in the shape of the early nineteenth-century English economists of the classical school. Marx argued that, as capital expands beyond the scope for profitable utilisation at home, it seeks such outlets abroad. In so doing it inaugurates a capitalist era in the overseas country, whose economy then begins to evolve along the same lines as that of the home country. Marx himself writes:

> The bourgeoisie, by the rapid improvement of all instruments of production, by the immensely facilitated means of communication, draws all, even the most barbarian nations, into civilisation ... It compels all nations, on pain of extinction, to adopt the bourgeois mode of production; it compels them to introduce what it calls civilisation into their midst, i.e. to become bourgeois themselves. In one word, it creates a world after its own image. (Marx and Engels, 1888, p. 53)

Warren believes that this process should be fostered as an essential interim stage on the road to a socialist society. Foreign investment should be assisted towards profitability, capital equipment and technical advances from abroad should be welcomed, and the restrictions on mobility and enterprise by cultural traditions be removed.

Exhibit 1.2   A Marxist case for capitalism

Dependency theory, according to Warren, painted too gloomy a picture of the relative bargaining strengths of the under-developed and developed countries. The latter needed the food and minerals of the former. As evidence of this he offered the somewhat exceptional case of the oil-producers. Nor were the industrialised countries as united as was often suggested. They could be played off against each other.

The problem was not one of dependence, but of internal obstacles to 'independent industrialisation' within the under-developed countries themselves.

In particular he denies that capitalism in the Third World has led to a stagnant per capita GNP, increasing inequality and unemployment, and a decline in the quality of life. These are very contentious claims. They run counter to statistics presented elsewhere in this book. Some of them also contradict generally accepted research results (to be cited later) not all of which emanate from scholars of the dependency school.

Perhaps as debatable as any is his argument that the emergence of parliamentary democracy, an important aspect of development certainly, is a spin-off from capitalism. Consider, for instance, the regimes of South East Asia, much vaunted for their capitalistic success.

At least Warren, unlike some Marxists, does not attempt to argue that a socialist objective justifies the means even if they involve intolerable privation for the mass of the people. He accepts that his advocacy of a speedy transition to capitalism must be judged at least partly by its 'fruits'. And he accepts that his ideas apply only to industrialisation, not to agriculture.

Is a Synthesis Possible?

Many underdeveloped countries are questioning the necessity of economic dependence and indeed recognising the hindrance to development which it represents. On the other hand the reality is that they do need capital and technical know-how from overseas, and have to face a change in some of the traditional attitudes which are inimical to progress. Must it all be done 'cold turkey', as the neo-classical economists and Warren, from their different points of view, both contend? Or is it possible to pursue a middle course, planning for structural change over a period of time but so as to take account of and neutralise the deleterious consequences of dependence?

The first step must be for a country to regain control over its own economy. Some governments see the nationalisation of foreign undertakings as the way of achieving this (Little, 1982, p. 257), and are prepared to sacrifice the latters' potential for capital investment. They would also have to brave the hostility of the government of the countries in which these companies are based, with the attendant danger of development aid being withdrawn. There is also the power which such companies and governments have to obstruct access to markets and to alternative sources of investment through banks and international agencies.

This is becoming less of a high-risk strategy than it used to be. There have been signs, for some years, of willingness on the part of some TNCs to negotiate terms for nationalisation. They are showing a shrewd preference for relying for their future profits on secured loans and the supply of technology and management to nationalised enterprises, rather than on running their own productive undertakings with all the economic and political risks entailed (World Bank, 1979, p. 34). Other underdeveloped countries are more cautious, contenting themselves with insisting that the corporation re-registers itself under local law, and transfers a substantial proportion of its shares, perhaps as much as 51 per cent, to the government. This ensures some degree of control over its activities, and some participation in the proceeds.

A third solution is to insist on the sale of a prescribed proportion of the corporation's share capital to the country's own nationals. In Malaysia this has been taken further with a requirement for sale to a favoured group within its population, the so-called *bumiputras*, or ethnic Malays.

If none of these expedients is adopted, it remains essential that the foreign interests concerned should be brought within the scope of a national plan for development. Such a plan would moderate the present obsession with industrialisation in order to make fuller use of the human and natural resources of the rural areas. Foreign corporations might be required to reinvest part of their profits in the underdeveloped parts of the economy, perhaps as a condition for being allowed to repatriate the rest. This is less likely to lead to attempts at evasion than is complete prohibition.

Much will depend on the readiness of the industrialised countries to bring about an international economic order which is conducive to development among their poorer neighbours. At the present time the atmosphere is not favourable to this. The adverse balance of payments of Third World countries, and their consequent lack of buying power abroad, is one of the most serious obstacles to their development. Nevertheless commercial banks, fearful of defaults, are fighting shy of further lending; and official development assistance from the governments of the developed countries has fallen to less than half of the 0·7 per cent of gross domestic product which the United Nations set as a target.

Lending by the World Bank, like that of the IMF, has shrunk, and is now often conditional on the acceptance of policies which set back the clock socially. IMF Special Drawing Rights (SDRs) are not conditional in this way, but they are very limited. And the developed countries, which control the IMF, have not been willing to link SDRs to aid instead of to the fixed IMF quotas, in order to ensure that they go where they are most needed. There is also the vexed question of access to overseas markets at a time of widespread if disguised protectionism in North America, the European Community and Japan. Unemployment in these countries makes it unlikely that they will abandon these policies in the foreseeable future.

An improvement in the terms of trade is very important here, especially as between the agricultural and other primary products of the South on the one hand, and the equipment and raw materials which they require for industrialisation on the other. At the moment protectionist policies shield European and North American farmers from competition in spite of the lip-service paid to ideas about free trade. If Third World producers can gain access to these markets at all, it is only at very low prices.

The Stabex programme of the EC is one way of trying to maintain their returns from such exports; it provides the countries included in the scheme with compensation when prices fall below a certain level. Unfortunately not all the countries who need this kind of support are included, and the list of commodities supported is very restricted. The alternative of a Common Fund, to maintain 'buffer stocks' of commodities to keep up prices, was put forward by UNCTAD, the United Nations Conference on Trade and Development (Williams, 1987, pp. 34ff). But UNCTAD, as the only one of the major international agencies not controlled by the rich countries, cuts little ice. The proposal has been subjected to much destructive criticism (Little, 1982, pp. 336–42) and little progress has been made, which seems to indicate hypocrisy in view of the use made of buffer stocks for its own purposes by the EC for example (beef and butter mountains, milk and wine lakes and the rest).

What will be developed in this book is a form of structuralism: a programme of active, planned intervention aimed at achieving development in its broadest sense. Such intervention would recognise that welfare was more than the social services, being radically affected by economic growth and the direction which such growth took; and that growth in its turn was influenced for good or ill by welfare policy. But structuralism in its orthodox form would not be enough. Evidence of the exploitation of underdeveloped countries because of the way in which they are integrated into the global economy has already been presented, and will continue to manifest itself in the chapters which follow. So structuralism has to be seen in the context of dependency.

This may seem too pragmatic for some tastes, but if theoretical purity has to be put into the balance against the realities of the real world, there can be no doubt as to the outcome. The problem is one of Third World poverty, and nothing should be allowed to stand in the way of finding a solution to that.

2

Poverty

According to the World Bank there were a thousand million people in absolute poverty in 1980; the situation cannot have improved since then. Ninety per cent of them lived in the rural areas. Half of them were small farmers, and about a quarter landless labourers (World Bank, 1982, p. 78). Such poverty is not merely a question of insufficient income; it spills over into squalid housing and living conditions, malnutrition, high infantile and adult death rates, poor general health and substandard education – the latter including, of course, a high illiteracy rate. These other aspects of poverty will be examined in later chapters.

Absolute and Relative Poverty

In the discussion of Third World poverty, it is 'absolute' poverty, though very difficult to measure (Cutler, 1984; Scott, 1981; Mencher, 1967; Griffin and Khan, 1982, pp. 236–41) which is usually referred to. This implies that there is a definable level below which the human organism cannot survive: below which starvation and exposure to the elements will eventually kill.

This definition was used in Rowntree's earliest studies of poverty at the turn of the century (Rowntree, 1901), but he eventually came to recognise the significance of 'conventional necessaries' in the standard of life of almost everybody (Rowntree, 1918, p. 129). It is arguable that what people actually value is not simply their bodily existence, but also their existence as socially significant persons. This is what accounts for the fact that a poor family in Africa or Asia will deprive themselves still further to meet ritual obligations to pay for a lavish funeral, to meet kinship obligations, or to find bride-wealth or a dowry to enable a child to acquire a spouse in accordance with custom.

In consequence poverty in recent years has been increasingly defined in relative terms, based on differences in life-style (Townsend, 1979; Mencher, 1967). Relative deprivation exists when a person cannot afford the minimum required for social (as distinct from merely physical) survival, in the circles to which he/she normally looks for approval and acceptance. The danger is that this could become a justification for the preservation of inequalities – between wealthy elites and the deprived masses in the Third World, and between the underdeveloped countries and the affluent North.

The concept can have moral validity therefore only in setting minimum standards – ensuring that people are at least as well treated as those with whom they habitually compare themselves. Beyond this, why should the livelihood of the people of the Third World be fixed at a level which is permanently inferior to that in developed countries, simply because they have been used to being in that position? Or if it comes to that, why should the poor of any country be prevented from catching up with their better-off compatriots for such a reason?

Nevertheless the relative concept probably has special relevance in the Third World context, where there are so many customary obligations for the sake of which people are willing to make painful sacrifices. This may seem irrational to Northerners who do not share their values, but they have their own forms of obligatory social expenditure.

Kinds of Poverty

Poverty centres mainly on certain groups: the elderly with no children to support them; the chronically sick or disabled; bereaved dependants; the landless or near-landless; the armies of unwanted children in the cities; and the urban unemployed. Poverty may emerge at certain stages in the life cycle. For persons on the margins of subsistence, responsibility for dependent children means descent below the poverty line, but when children begin to contribute to the family's livelihood, the margin may be surmounted again – only to be crossed for the second time when the main breadwinner becomes too old to work, or is displaced by the private appropriation of land or by labour-saving innovations. This is a way of looking at relative poverty which will become more and more applicable to the Third World as the extended family retreats before the advance of modernisation (Goode, 1968), throwing nuclear family groupings more and more onto their own resources for survival.

In his concept of the 'poverty ratchet', Chambers (1985, pp. 114–31) has called attention to another aspect of this dynamic element in impoverishment. Poverty ratchets 'are like movements down past a cog which are difficult or impossible to reverse, making poor people permanently poorer'. Examples are the meeting of costly customary obligations; disasters like sickness, the death of an ox or a mule, or a natural cataclysm; or economic changes or exploitation forcing the sale of land, the break-up of a family and so on. These may all be poverty ratchets, but their origins are very different. Some call for financial support at the critical time. Others are part of the price paid for underdevelopment.

Then there is unemployment: a particularly difficult idea to apply in the circumstances of many underdeveloped countries, especially in Africa. This is because much of their population will be involved in subsistence farming on a customary landholding, and not in paid work at all. They are not employed in the normal sense of the word – but neither are they unemployed. They may seek seasonal agricultural employment outside their own villages, say in the tea plantations, where the maximum demand for labour happens to fall at a different time from their own harvesting and ploughing seasons. It could hardly be argued that they were only employed when they were working away from home, just because a cash wage was involved.

Some migrants to the towns, or to mining areas like the Copperbelt in Zambia or the South African gold and diamond mines, will also be seeking only seasonal employment. Others will want more permanence. If they cannot find work and are landless, they will be identified unambiguously among the unemployed. If they still have land to return to and choose voluntarily to stay out of work in the city or mining enclave (perhaps in the hope that something will turn up), the situation is probably no different from that of the

European who chooses to remain out of work rather than take a job which is considered disagreeable or too low in pay, status or level of skill.

But what of those who return to the family holding and resume work on the land pending further opportunities in the city? Though failing to secure paid employment, can such persons properly be described as unemployed? Much depends upon how they perceive themselves. If they have made such a change in their own conceptions of themselves that they see themselves as urban wage-earners who cannot get jobs, but whom necessity has driven back to the land, then it is right that government policies for stimulating employment and for supporting the unemployed should make provision for them.

To define unemployment in this way as depending on a 'state of mind' may seem dangerously uncertain, but it is not dissimilar from the problem in the North of defining unemployment among married women. There also, a distinction must be drawn between the woman who stays at home voluntarily and the woman who stays at home only because she cannot get a job. Not that the concept of 'voluntary unemployment' is all that firm either (Standing, 1981).

Against this 'self-report' method of ascertaining the level of unemployment, it might also be argued that it presents a poor country, still short of capital, know-how and markets, with the impossible task of finding waged employment for all who choose to want it even if an alternative exists for them on the land.

But it is a state of mind which has to be contended with, and a state of mind can change if people come to believe that, through a plan for regional development, opportunities will be as good in the country as in the town. Underdevelopment and the dual economy are the real villains of the piece. A massive unsatisfied demand for urban waged employment may force a government to face up to these basic problems.

Poverty and Inequality

It is central to the free market philosophy that all should enter the competitive arena on an equal basis. Privileges derived from birth, wealth, political influence and so on could prevent goods and services from being allocated strictly in accordance with their relative utilities, causing that allocation to be less efficient than it should be. However in the real world imperfect markets are the rule rather than the exception, and according to the theory of the second best (see Chapter 1) the existence of any such imperfections casts doubt on the viability of the market solution as a whole.

Poverty is a very powerful market imperfection indeed. Opportunities for the poor are anything but equal, causing their poverty to become self-perpetuating. Thus a poor country's lack of 'clout' hampers its efforts to improve its position in the world economy. This is demonstrated by the inability of UNCTAD, the voice of the underdeveloped world, to influence the policies of the rich countries who control the IMF and the World Bank.

Inequality of opportunity within countries matches that which exists between them. Wealth is concentrated in the hands of a minority – a feudal elite perhaps, bureaucrats or politicians, indigenous capitalists or the beneficiaries of overseas capital. This means that they also control the state. They will not voluntarily use their power to remove barriers to advancement among the 'have nots' when this would threaten their own privileged position.

Side by side with the political powerlessness of the poor is their lack of the personal assets which health, a good diet, and above all education can give. In this connection, Oscar Lewis has described what he calls the 'culture of poverty' (Lewis, 1967). This refers to the all-embracing nature of poverty, but also shows how it engenders attitudes of hopelessness and apathy. The process of child-rearing within families then causes such attitudes to be transmitted between generations. As a result the same families are very likely to constitute the poor, generation after generation.

There can be no doubt about the handicap which personal attitudes such as these represent. They are reflected in the preference for 'living for the present' rather than in planning for the future – so-called 'short-run hedonism', which has been noted as a central characteristic of the life-style of many deprived people, such as formerly enslaved groups in the West Indies (Jones, 1981, p. 57) or lower working-class groups in the developed countries in the North (Jones, 1965, pp. 12ff). In a hostile world such an absence of ambition and of a programme for realising it will mean that they stay where they are, among the poorest sections of the community.

A manifestation of short-run hedonism with particular implications for life chances, is unwillingness to invest time and effort in getting an education. The educational advantages of the middle classes are probably the chief single reason why they have such a monopoly of good jobs and social power. At the same time it must be remembered that attitudes such as these (which Lewis is right to see as constituting a 'culture' transmitted like other cultures through the normal processes of socialisation) are not evidence of some form of original sin or congenital incapacity on the part of the families concerned. They are the cultural consequences of prolonged deprivation, and will remain as long as such economic and social injustices continue. In such circumstances apathy is a realistic response to the circumstances of one's life.

Certain conservative politicians such as Sir Keith Joseph (1972) have failed to understand this. They have acknowledged the existence of what they call 'the cycle of deprivation', but have mistakenly seen the problem as solely one of changing the attitudes of the poor, as though they were somehow the authors of their own misfortune. Without a change in the structure of opportunities available to them, they will (quite reasonably) fail to change their attitudes.

Poverty and Development

Such inequality in life chances may be socially unjust, but remedying it would not by itself solve the problem of poverty. Countries which are in the fortunate position of having much wealth to share out are in a tiny minority in the Third World. On the other hand economic growth cannot provide a solution either, unless it is accompanied by some commitment to a wider distribution of its benefits. The case of Brazil and its north-east has already been mentioned. The World Bank gives another example; '. . . the proportion of the population below the poverty line in 1975 was more than twice as high in Colombia as in South Korea even though the average incomes of the two countries were close' (World Bank, 1980a, p. 37).

Further relevant figures are provided by the World Development Report of the World Bank. At the time of the last survey the poorest 20 per cent of households in the desperately poor country of Bangladesh received only 6·6 per cent of total household incomes; but the same 20 per cent in two of the successful 'baby tigers' for which figures are available received even less, viz. Hong Kong 5·4 per cent, and Korea 5·7 per cent (World Bank, 1988, pp. 272–3). What we are talking about, therefore, how underdeveloped nations may combine social justice with an improvement in their economic position in the world. *Laissez-faire* will not achieve this. It requires structural planning directed towards growth, but with most attention to those sectors of the economy where expansion will help to improve the position of the poor. In many countries this will mean agricultural and rural development and investment in welfare.

The trade-off against growth which is expected where structuralist planning incorporates elements to reduce poverty (Ahluwalia and Carter, 1981, p. 486) need not occur; indeed growth should actually be enhanced. An improvement in present low levels of welfare provision, for example, constitutes a productive investment in 'human capital', quite apart from raising of morale and motivation among the mass of the people as a result of a more just distribution of social rewards. Growth and social justice must therefore always be examined in relation to one another, as will be the case throughout this book.

In the meantime people are in need. In the past this need has been largely met by traditional means within the kinship group or the local community. Where this is no longer sufficient, the only alternative is some form of state relief.

State Provision

State relief payments, if they exist at all, are very small; they are mainly a relic of a colonial poor law system, providing aid in kind rather than in cash, and sometimes involving, like the nineteenth-century British workhouse, some kind of grim residential requirement. There may not actually be workhouses any more, but old people's homes, children's homes and the like often reveal their origins in their gaunt aspect, and the rudimentary provision which they make. This kind of relief, incidentally, is self-defeating for a poor country, as (like all forms of residential service) it is very expensive – as compared with, for example, monetary payments to support the efforts of the family or kin-group.

A publication of the United States Department of Health, Education and Welfare (1981) claimed that there were at the time of writing, 130 countries with social security schemes which included some insurance elements. Many of these, however, cover only a small part of the population (Midgley, 1984, p. 174). And in many of the poorer countries (and even some relatively rich ones like Singapore) they are merely provident schemes in which people in employment pay regular sums in order to obtain a lump sum payment on retirement. These sums are in no way an adequate substitute for a retirement pension.

Few make provision for the unemployed; apart from countries in Latin America, Midgley mentions only Cyprus and Egypt (ibid, pp. 136–7). The very poor are usually excluded, and anyway the pensions are often too small to live on. So-called 'survivor' payments, made to the widows or children of employees who have died before retirement, are merely an extension of such a scheme. Very few of them provide medical benefits – not even for the worker himself, much less his dependants. Typical of this approach are the smaller island nations of the English-speaking Caribbean, viz. Dominica, Montserrat, St Kitts–Nevis, St Lucia and St Vincent (Jenkins, 1981).

Among the larger and rather better-off countries of the region (such as Jamaica, Trinidad and Barbados), short-term sickness and maternity benefits and workmen's compensation have been added. There are still no medical benefits, except sometimes for injuries at work as part of the industrial compensation scheme – and of course no unemployment insurance. And it is worth noting that, even in these countries, only a minority of the population is covered – less than one-third in Barbados, less than one-fifth in Jamaica, and less than one-thirteenth in oil-rich Trinidad and Tobago (ibid., p. 635)!

The French encouraged social insurance in their former African colonies in the 1940s and 1950s, beginning with child benefit and later including retirement, 'survivors' and invalidity (not always sickness) benefits (Midgley, 1984, pp. 120–1). Anglophone Africa tends to rely more on provident funds similar to that of Singapore. In some of these countries (for example, Kenya and Swaziland) the only provision made is for retirement, invalidity and 'survivors' benefit (ibid., pp. 142–3).

Exhibit 2.1   Social security in South-East Asia

Hong king, apart from providing subsidies to private charities, relies entirely on means-tested relief. Singapore supplements minimal non-contributory relief by the device already mentioned – the Central Provident Fund. This is a form of compulsory saving, according to income, mainly to provide a lump sum on retirement and very short-term benefits for sickness, maternity or redundancy. Taiwan (Chan, 1984; Kaim-Caudle, 1983) and Malaysia (Chin, 1984, pp. 33ff) have more full-fledged social insurance schemes, to which both employers and workers contribute.

Malaysia finances not only certain medical services, but also a lump sum for maintenance in disability or old age, or to meet funeral expenses – likely to be considerable in a Chinese country. The Malaysian scheme covers only two contingencies, viz. disability due to industrial injury, or invalidity which prevents gainful employment. There is no retirement pension. In respect of industrial injury there is medical treatment by panel doctors or in government hospitals, though not for dependants.

The better-off countries of South-East Asia are in a position to do more, but in spite of a certain amount of variation among them, a common theme of frugality is to be discerned (Chan, 1984). They represent a gradient of diminishing dependence on means-tested, non-contributory forms of relief (see box). In all the countries mentioned there is some apprehension about possible disincentives. Consequently the only support for those not covered by social insurance (which in most countries includes the unemployed) is either that given by charitable organisations, or the exiguous benefits provided by a deterrent, means-tested relief system. Of the latter, in the countries which he studied, Chan writes (Chan, 1984, p. 416):

The Social Assistance Schemes in Hong Kong, Singapore and Taiwan are provided on a very residual basis whereby only those vulnerable people who have no close kin to protect them will be cared for by the government. In the meantime cash allowance has been kept at the level far below subsistence requirements with the purpose of discouraging or deterring people from relying on the state.

Assistance even of this grudging kind is usually not available to the rural population, or to the able-bodied, whether in town or country (ibid., p. 171).

Equity

In spite of much pro-family rhetoric, none of the programmes reviewed provide either benefits specifically for dependants, or supplements for those with family responsibilities. Where short-term benefits, say for sickness or redundancy, are income-related, the amount of the benefit for a family would be larger only if the wage had been.

But longer-term benefits, notably pensions based on premiums paid over many years, would not have the advantage of even this hypothetical increase. Past wages would have been lower, and perhaps relate to a time when the individual had no family. Subsequently there would have been inflation as well as a rising general standard of living. Benefits which ignored these changes would obviously be inequitable, and lead to real hardship in cases where family responsibilities were considerable.

As contributory schemes are confined to employees, they also unfairly discriminate against the self-employed poor in agriculture, fishing and so on. This limitation also represents a substantial urban bias: most waged employment is found in the towns. For these reasons, any subsidy to the schemes out of taxation must mean a transfer of resources from the poor to the better-off. The injustice of such a situation is exacerbated by the fact that civil servants and the army, in most countries, receive benefits which are either entirely non-contributory or provided on very advantageous terms.

On the other hand, these programmes do all involve differentiation in both contributions and benefits according to income. This is of course one way of giving expression to a definition of poverty which is couched in relative terms. But it is also inegalitarian in its effect, though in so being it is not inconsistent with the overall self-help tenor of the schemes.

Exhibit 2.2   Social insurance and social justice

There are various possibilities available. The most advantageous terms of all are usually given to civil servants, the army and
the police, who pay very low contributions or none at all. This is a
price for national (or governmental?) convenience and security
which is exacted, according to the degree of regressiveness in
the tax system, largely from the poor. The other possible patterns
form a gradient of increasing regressiveness, or inequity:

(a)   income-related contributions with flat-rate benefits,
      which bring about the greatest degree of redistribution
      from rich to poor;
(b)   income-related contributions with income-related bene-
      fits, which achieve no redistribution at all.
(c)   flat-rate contributions (which involve the poor in paying a
      larger *proportion* of their incomes than the rich, and are
      therefore regressive) combined with flat-rate benefits. This
      is the predominant British system;
(d)   what would be the most blatantly unjust of all: flat-rate
      contributions and income-related benefits. This, which
      would bring about a transfer from the poor to the rich, could
      only be made to work in an overtly exploitative dictatorship.

A special case is represented by Islamic countries where the
religious duty of alms-giving is represented by the voluntary tax of
the *Zakha*, and the obligation, known as *Alwakfs*, to bequeath, at
death, part of one's possessions for charitable purposes. The
religious texts define the purposes for which these funds may be
used in very broad terms. These include not only making provision
for the needy, but also for 'those whose hearts it is necessary to
conciliate'. This could include many political purposes remote
from social welfare in any sense.

Incentives

Political ideologies resulting from the dependent role of the Third
World in the global economy remain an obstacle to progress. We

have already noted the attachment of politicians in 'middle-income' countries to the 'Victorian value' of self-dependence: this in spite of what they must know about the lack of real opportunities, even in their more affluent countries, for achieving this. But this attitude is not confined to the better-off countries. Leaders of some of their poorest contemporaries will also argue with every bit as much fervour that providing poor people with state support will deter them from seeking a livelihood in the informal sector.

Such views gain respectability from current neo-classical ideas, and the support given to these by the international agencies. The World Bank, for instance, suggests that social security may reduce savings because it makes them less necessary, and may also persuade people to retire early on pension. Some argue that even social insurance benefits could make the individual less willing to work for a living (Standing, 1981, pp. 573ff)! This in spite of the much-vaunted self-help character of such schemes – and the fact that few make any provision for unemployment apart from that due to sickness or old age. There is perhaps more to be said for the view that the per capita payments which an employer might have to make to such schemes increase the marginal cost of labour to him, and so could provide a disincentive to his taking on as many workers, and thus result in an increase in unemployment.

As an alternative to what they see as 'hand-outs' many governments make proposals for stimulating domestic industries, such as basket-making or the making of mementos for tourists. Desirable in themselves, they will hardly absorb the growing army of the unemployed. In any case they will need expanding markets if their effect is not to be even more marginal. Which brings us back to the underdevelopment trap.

Financial Aspects

Reference has already been made to the potential of insurance and provident schemes for the mobilisation of capital which can then be used for development (Parthasarati, 1978; Mouton, 1975). This is well recognised to have occurred in Singapore, where the public housing programme has been largely financed from the National Provident Fund. The danger is always that (as in Malaysia) it will be a consequence of contributions which are too high, benefits which are too low, or of the government's having paid either no interest or too low a rate of interest on its borrowings from the insurance fund. Whichever may be the case, the fund is not then being run on a strict actuarial basis.

One can only agree with an expert, St. Rose, cited by Jenkins (1981, p. 637) who (referring to the Caribbean) agreed that governments certainly 'should earmark funds deriving from social security contributions for capital development projects, but only those projects "which are directly productive and self-liquidating"'. In other words, the money has to be capable of becoming available for the social insurance purposes for which it is being collected, and it must also be yielding profits which enable benefits to match inflation. One might add that the investments should also be profitable enough to enable beneficiaries to share to some extent in any increase in the general standard of living. Otherwise their poverty, in the very important relative sense, will have increased.

A way of dealing with any shortfall in these respects is by what the International Labour Office (Jenkins 1981, p. 637) calls the 'partial funding method', in which there is a government contribution which varies to meet the exigencies of inflation and rising expectations. This is adopted in various Caribbean schemes. British experience suggests that, over a period of years, the share met out of general taxes will then become the major element, and the actuarial principle almost inoperative. In the light of the discussion below, about the nature of welfare rights (Walton, 1975), this may not matter very much.

Welfare Rights

A possible argument in favour of such a scheme is that people may be more willing to pay up if they believe that their contributions are directly related to their welfare benefits, even if that is not really the case. However, a decision to mislead the people is hardly a good foundation for either good government or a sound taxation policy. The contributions become a form of taxation, and the benefits are paid for directly out of current revenue.

This makes no longer tenable the view that these benefits are different from so-called non-contributory benefits because they are 'paid for'. It used to be argued on such grounds that social insurance benefits were due to the beneficiary 'as of right'. Nowadays many people would argue that all social benefits were 'paid for', through a lifetime of social contribution, and that all should therefore be received 'as of right'.

This is the basis for the modern concept of welfare rights. For example, because of rising expectations in the population at large, and the operation of the principle of relativity discussed earlier in this chapter, the retirement pensioner eventually comes to receive more than has been provided through the insurance fund. This is not because of the generosity of the non-retired sections of the community. Their affluence, by reference to which the income of pensioners has been fixed, is based in part on the capital created by the tax payments, savings and labour of the latter and their contemporaries in the past. It is the good fortune of the present generation of employed people that they are present to benefit when the fruits of those efforts come to hand. That the founders of the feast should also benefit would seem no more than their due.

Welfare rights, therefore, should not depend in any way on contributions paid. Nor, though 'uncovenanted' (in a term often used at one time to refer to non-contributory benefits), should they, being 'rights', rest on the discretion of any official, but be unambiguously defined by the law and enforceable in the courts. This is a way of looking at help for people in trouble which should be very congenial in parts of the world where traditions about mutual rights and obligations are still honoured. Such a view of welfare rights kicks a main moral prop from beneath the idea of social insurance, by arguing that paying out money in contributions is not all that important as compared with what you do for the community. At the same time it does present the wider society with the problem of deciding who has the greatest need of any help that can be afforded.

This is less of a problem for an extended family or a village, who have all the inside information they require, than it is for bureaucrats from the capital. The latter will almost certainly try to resolve their difficulties by the usual reflex response of borrowing ideas from the North, and will then come up with some kind of stigmatising and not very practical means test (see Chapter 6).

On the fairly safe assumption that a radical innovation, like delegating the decision to those with local knowledge, will not be adopted, there might be something to be said for borrowing, and properly 'indigenising', the idea of the negative income tax (Dilnot *et al.*, 1984). All, rich and poor, would give an account of their financial position. This would not avoid the practical problems associated with a means test, but it would not carry with it the stigma and the often censorious attitudes associated with such inquisitions. The outcome would be that the rich could then be assessed for tax, and the poor (strictly in accordance with the regulations) for benefits.

There is obviously scope for a more egalitarian approach if only ideologies were more favourable to this. A more equal distribution of such wealth as there is, through the agency of a country's taxation and social security systems, would allow better care to be taken of its neediest citizens. But in very poor Third World countries redistribution would make little inroad on the problem of poverty – though it might have important symbolic value. Unless, therefore, international aid agencies are prepared to accept the legitimacy of using their funds to provide interim support for the poor in these countries, instead of insisting that aid must be invested in growth of a more obvious kind (as does even the World Bank now) the suffering of the poor will continue.

Meanwhile their situation has been much worsened by the exclusivist policies adopted by Northern governments over recent years. Racist immigration legislation has dammed what had been a steady trickle out of the poor countries. Now most of these would-be emigrants have to stay put. The result of having to share a static or slow-growing GNP among so many more mouths has exacerbated what was already a crisis of survival, let alone of unemployment.

Summary

Poverty is usually defined in absolute terms: lack of the bare means of subsistence. However, persons who are not in absolute poverty may nevertheless be in relative poverty if they cannot meet certain forms of expenditure expected of them by their peers. In a traditional society there are many such obligations, which people will meet at whatever cost. Because the concept of relative poverty is based on expectations in the individual's social context, it does have inegalitarian implications.

However poverty may be defined, certain groups are more exposed to it than others. For less vulnerable, but still marginal groups, poverty is connected with stages in the life cycle, or with those vicissitudes of life which have been called 'poverty ratchets'. For still others it results from unemployment. Unemployment presents its own problems of definition because of the existence of alternatives to wage employment, in the form of work on a traditional landholding. One solution is to accept the individuals' own definition of their status. They are unemployed if they see themselves essentially as potential wage-earners looking for jobs.

Linked to poverty is inequality of opportunity, resulting from lack of political power and of the personal assets and attitudes which make for success. This combination of adverse factors amounts to a 'culture of poverty', perpetuated from one generation to another, and ensuring that the children of the poor remain the poor.

Growth by itself will not eliminate poverty unless it is accompanied by a commitment to social justice. This involves steering economic development in directions which will improve the position of the poor, accompanied by some redistribution through the social services. This could be a productive investment in human capital.

Meanwhile direct state provision for the poor is very limited. The less impoverished countries have some social insurance which may provide pensions or lump-sum payments for the elderly, or benefits for the sick or those incapacitated by industrial injury. These are paid for by contributions linked to employment, and shared in varying proportions between the employee, employer and the state. Such payments may be either progressive or regressive in their incidence on employees. The insurance fund thus built up may then be used for development purposes; for example, in Singapore it is used to finance the building of public housing. It is obviously important that any such investment should yield a return large enough to pay the benefits.

Social insurance schemes appeal to neo-classicists, and to Third World governments with a similar value orientation, on the grounds that they cover their own costs if they are actuarially sound, and that being 'paid-for' and received 'as of right' they do not sap the independence of recipients. Against the latter argument is posed that for welfare rights: that people have already paid for their welfare benefits through their past contributions to the common store of capital. Social insurance schemes also have two other disadvantages. One is their limited scope; in no case, for example, do they include employment benefits. Secondly, they are biased in favour of those in waged employment, which also means in favour of the urban areas. For the rural majority all that is available, apart from private charity, is a grudging public relief system based on a means test, and available for some only in an institution.

3

The Rural Majority

A viable strategy for achieving the twin aims of economic growth and social justice would, as we have seen, (Ahluwalia and Carter, 1981, p. 486) be one in which the economy was stimulated most in those of its segments which provided most benefit to the poor. This would have to mean, for many countries, concentrating on the revival of agriculture and the rural areas. For, as the World Bank statistics quoted in Chapter 2 show, this is where most of the poor are to be found.

Agriculture also has great growth potential. Past neglect means that it offers more scope for improvement than other sectors of the economy. And because of its basic nature it can generate external economies of great importance to the other sectors. Thus, given a fair market for its exports, it can earn the foreign exchange needed to buy the equipment and know-how which industrialisation requires. Also the factory workers have to be fed, and this must depend on agriculture being even more productive. Taiwan is only one example of the benefit which a fledgling industrialisation can gain from the existence of a thriving agricultural sector (Reynolds, 1985, pp. 171–2).

The Industrial Bias

Adopting such a strategy would involve rejecting much conventional wisdom in the Third World. Impressed by the wealth of the industrialised North, many countries have seen industrial development as the solution to their problems, and followed the Latin American example in choosing ISI as the way of achieving it. This has weighted the scales against their farmers.

53

High tariffs, introduced to preserve local 'infant' industries against foreign competition, have caused the prices of the products of those industries to rise, and their quality to decline. Urban unionisation enables workers in the towns to obtain a share of the higher prices, but not the farmer or farm-worker. They have to try to pay these prices from their existing low incomes.

At the same time the national currency is maintained at an artificially high value in order to reduce the cost of the raw materials and equipment needed for industrialisation. As a result the financial return for agricultural exports, when changed back into an over-valued local currency, is low. This is quite apart from the possible loss of overseas markets through retaliatory action by overseas countries who are offended by such industrial protection measures (Baer, 1965).

It is this discrimination against agriculture and the rural areas which prompted Ruttan (1984, p. 397) to assert that 'improvements in the domestic terms of trade represent a more powerful instrument than any of the more direct consumption interventions in shifting the distribution of income and consumption in favour of the poor'. Where attention has been directed to rural development, it has been, until recently, with the aim of increasing the output of cash crops, perverting the 'green revolution' into an industrial revolution in agriculture. More will be said about this later in the chapter. It would obviously be congenial to some neo-classicists, with their belief in the importance of export-led growth, but it has not been to the advantage of the rural poor.

In spite of the precedence thus given to the cities, the population of the underdeveloped world is still largely a rural one. Two-thirds of the population of Third World countries were living in rural areas in 1980. Although urban populations are expected to more than double over the last two decades of this millennium, it is anticipated that the number of people living in the countryside will continue to grow at a substantial rate – by almost 25 per cent over the twenty years – as against an absolute decline in the rural populations of the North. At the end of the period they will still constitute much the largest part of the population of the Third World, and no less than nine-tenths of the rural population of the world as a whole. Without underrating the amount of deprivation among the unemployed and slum-dwellers of the cities, there is general agreement that there is more in the countryside, if only

Table 3.1. Rural and urban populations, Estimates for 1980, 1985 and 2000 (in millions), more and less developed regions (United Nations, 1985b, pp. 186–8)

	Rural			Urban		
	1980	*1985*	*2000*	*1980*	*1985*	*2000*
More developed regions	334	324	284	802	849	992
Less developed regions	2343	2505	2892	974	1164	1959
World population	2677	2829	3175	1776	2013	2952

because of the joint effects of neglect and the larger population. The concentration of attention on industrialisation and the cities is therefore largely beside the point as far as the mass of the people are concerned.

China and Tanzania have taken the lead in reversing this trend. Instead of siphoning off funds from agriculture, the Chinese ensure that industry's surpluses are reinvested in the land. Indeed it is expected to make a contribution to the prosperity of the rural areas by devoting part of its own resources to the production of cheaper and more efficient farm machinery and the supply of fertilisers, insecticides and so on (Aziz, 1980, pp. 97–8).

There is now an increasing willingness, in other countries also, to examine the basic needs of the rural majority – for shelter, health, education and social care, and above all (with recurrent famines in mind) for food. But it is not only a question of rural poverty. To allow the agricultural sector of the economy to remain derelict or even to regress, when it feeds the population, employs most of them and provides the greater part of the domestic market, is not a credible way to try to advance economic growth.

Living Conditions

Housing, like so many other things, is seen as mainly an urban question, and it is true that the mass flight from the countryside has led to large numbers of people in the towns living under grossly unsatisfactory conditions. However, traditional rural dwellings, constructed of mud or bush material, are not exactly ideal homes either. According to a UN Report (admittedly in 1960) less than 1 per cent of rural dwellings in Indonesia were permanent structures, with 26 per cent in the Philippines and 8 per cent in Malaysia. According to a survey in India (in 1953–4) 85 per cent of rural habitations had earth floors, 83 per cent had mud walls, and 70 per cent had roofs of straw, weeds or similar substances (Mabogunje, Hardoy and Misra, 1978, p. 33). There is no reason to believe that the position has changed much since then.

The great advantage of rural dwellings is that they often have space around them, and can be readily extended to meet the needs of a growing family, or occasional exigencies resulting from traditional obligations. But they usually lack good sanitation, and water supplies are often suspect. In the 1953–4 Indian survey already mentioned, 95 per cent were found to have no sanitation, and over 55 per cent no piped water. Among a majority even of Latin American countries, less than 10 per cent of rural dwellings had piped water (ibid., p. 32). In most African countries the situation is almost certainly worse. (See also Hardoy and Satterthwaite, 1981, pp. 244–5, noting their scepticism about governmental statements on these matters.)

The older members of the community may not be able to carry out the constant repairs which such dwellings require if they are not to deteriorate, letting in rain and wind. And if they lack kin their difficulties may remain unnoticed for a critical period. These are lacks which health and social work aides (if they exist) can ensure are made good.

But something more than palliatives is required. There is every reason why as much thought should be given to rural housing as to that in the towns. The first need is to design 'low-cost' housing for rural living, using readily available local materials, such as timber and stone, and so constructed that they can be built by self-help teams, and fairly easily maintained by their occupiers. The possible need for extension should be borne in mind. In Guyana, where a traditional rural house is built on 'stilts', the covered space beneath the house is used at first for a variety of domestic and recreational purposes. When the number of children multiplies, or other dependants join the household, there is this space to enclose in order to provide the extra accommodation required. There must be many other ways of achieving the same ends.

New construction of this kind would perhaps make it possible to improve the local infrastructure at the same time. The 'site and services' approach (see Chapter 4) is based more on urban than rural needs, but much could be done with the aid of local labour to clear roads, improve and protect wells, and ensure the availability of properly located earth closets. Self-help organised as part of a community development programme has a part to play in this. However China has shown that, as paid work, it can be timed so as to relieve both chronic rural unemployment and the seasonal underemployment characteristic of agriculture (Aziz, 1980, pp. 51–2). And in the process it would make important infrastructural contributions to agricultural productivity.

Such facilities are easier to provide, of course, if settlements are 'nucleated' rather than 'dispersed' (Mabogunje, 1980, p. 109). Much the same is true of schools, medical services and personal social services. If children have to travel some distance over rough country in order to attend school, possibly making an adult escort unavoidable, this will be a further 'cost' of schooling, to add to the many other disincentives for poor families.

The clinics or other places housing local primary health workers must also be readily accessible if they are to carry out the educational and preventive function which is probably their main role. Health and social workers will be handicapped in their work with families if too much of their time is absorbed in travelling. It will also be argued later that many of these services involve work with communities, or at least extended family groupings. Isolated homesteads would make such work very difficult, if not impossible.

Tanzania, with its emphasis on rural development, has made the most thoroughgoing attempt at nucleation (Nyerere, 1968; Hyden, 1980, pp. 125ff). Its *ujaama* villages had two aims: to enable basic services to be provided for the rural population; and to foster rural socialism, by facilitating a more collective and egalitarian pattern of agriculture and rural life. The 'villagisation' aspect reached its peak in the 1970s (not without some coercion and social and administrative stress) (Kahama *et al.*, 1986), but the *ujaama* (or socialist) aspect is still largely to be realised (Nyerere, 1977; Hyden, 1980).

Examples of the distress and upheaval which reorganisation of this kind can cause if it is done insensitively and with too little consultation are to be found in the attempts to settle nomads in some countries of the Sahel; and in the plans of the government of Guyana to eject a number of Amerindian communities from their villages and hunting-grounds in order to make way for a massive hydroelectric project. One of the few benefits of the economic crisis precipitated by the oil price increases (a crisis which has hit Guyana with special force) is that the capital has not been obtainable to carry out the latter project. Similar developments in Brazil, however, are receiving support from Northern financial institutions.

Persuading people to move into nucleated settlements, even if this means better housing and amenities, may be particularly difficult if the move is seen to be part of a wholesale reorganisation of land use. This is certainly going to be required in many countries, but it is not going to be successful in achieving its objectives if it is exploitative (or even if it seems to be to those who lose by it). Where, as in Guyana, ethnic groups are spatially separated, anything done on one group's living-space can look to them like 'internal colonialism'. And to an ethnically partisan government geographical segregation does offer opportunities for this.

The Large Estates

In Latin America it is the great family estates, the *latifundia*, which are the main obstacle to social progress in the rural areas (Gilbert, 1977, pp. 149ff). Indeed the influence of some of these families, through their investments in industry, is felt as much in the cities as it is in the countryside. They make or destroy governments, and many a military take-over can only be understood in the light of their activities, often in partnership with American TNCs. So there are many reasons why the breaking up of the *latifundia* would contribute to social development.

In the rural areas, however, these families are, effectively, the government. They employ, either directly or indirectly, most of the people who live on their land and, as monopoly employers, can virtually fix the level of wages as they like. Needless to say that level is invariably low. In some cases tiny plots, the so-called *minifundia*, are let to tenants, usually on oppressive rate-cropping terms, under which the peasant pays over a proportion of his crop to the landowner, and perhaps also does a certain amount of work for him. Even if no work for his *padron* is required of the *minifundista*, what is left to him from his land is never enough to allow him to escape from paid employment on the estate.

Whatever the formal constitutional arrangements may be, this economic dominance means that the *padron*'s word, over the vast area of land which he owns, is law. Personal liberty, freedom to marry, and even life and limb, may be at his disposal. He may run his own courts and impose his own penal measures. Local officials and even police chiefs know better than to object. The *latifundia* are the heart of a despotic social system which keeps the majority of those within its boundaries in a state of subjection and poverty. They are not even economically successful (Griffin, 1981, pp. 185ff). Their sheer size and non-intensive methods of cultivation, the backward-looking, feudal atmosphere in which they operate, the low morale of their workforce, and their monopolistic position, all make for low unit returns to the large amount of land in use. Yet any attempt to break them up and redistribute the land has to contend with powerful social, political and (with some exceptions, notably Peru) military forces, not all of which may be within the country. Small wonder that the history of land reform in Central and South America has been so chequered (Gilbert, 1977 pp. 149ff).

Side by side with these feudal estates are others run on commercial lines, usually by TNCs based abroad. Although they are much more efficient, they pay the same low wages and maintain the same bad working conditions. They also exercise, because of their wealth and the backing of their metropolitan governments, no less in the way of political influence. Their political role is in some respects more objectionable than that of the local landed oligarchy, for it puts much of the country's social and economic policy at the disposal of foreigners, who have even less interest in its balanced development than home-grown potentates. Among the more notorious of these are the United Fruit Company of America, Fyffes, and Tate & Lyle.

What is surprising is that some socialist countries (Cuba is an example) have also retained and even increased the number of large units, after taking those which already exist into public ownership. Bookers, the TNC which once owned most of Guyana's vital sugar industry, having made a shrewd calculation of their long-term interest, had taken the initiative in allocating land to peasants for the smallholder cultivation of cane, intending gradually to confine their own activities to processing it and marketing the finished product. With the nationalisation of

Bookers, the new owners, the self-proclaimed socialist government of Guyana, reversed this trend.

Many factors are influential in these decisions, including, for
example, the complications caused for national planning where
there are a large number of small independent producers. More
will have to be said about this in later chapters. No doubt some
socialist governments also are swayed by Marx's belief that
peasants are socially reactionary (Marx, 1852). The opposition to
collectivisation by the kulaks in the USSR, and by their later
counterparts in Cuba, has given credence to this belief. Similar
problems were encountered by China, en route to its commune
system (Aziz, 1980, pp. 11–14).

However an important further aim is shared by socialist governments and capitalists alike: to achieve the economies of scale
which have been so decisive in the shaping of manufacturing
industry. This aim is probably misguided. As will be seen, it is not
true that larger farms are necessarily more productive.

Monocultures

Large commercial estates arise in many parts of the world (for
example, tea plantations in Sri Lanka, sugar plantations in Guyana
or Cuba, or rubber estates in Malaysia) though in recent years
some of them have been wholly or partly taken over by the
government. But where the TNCs have maintained their grip they
are continuing the kind of exploitation which made colonies
valuable in the nineteenth century, when they were the source of
cheap food and raw materials for the expanding cities and the
factories of the 'home' country.

Although the interest is now in a world market, there is the
same profit as in colonial times to be made out of a 'monoculture' –
the concentration on a single, or very few commodities, for the
production of which the Third World country in question has
advantages of climate and soil, as well as a cheap, docile and
experienced labour force. The outcome then, as now, has been the
creation of a kind of specialised agricultural enclave in an otherwise undeveloped country.

It is depressing that this agrarian counterpart to the industrial
pattern of dependent underdevelopment in the cities and mining

areas should still continue in spite of the dissolution of empires. As late as 1971, after generations of independence, many Latin American countries were still locked into patterns of specialisation which were not favourable to their development. At that time 63 per cent of Colombian exports were coffee, 72 per cent of Chilean exports were copper, and no less than 91 per cent of exports from Venezuela were oil products (Gilbert, 1977, p. 21).

Malaysia originally became attractive to foreign entrepreneurs because of its resources of tin, but under British rule rubber became the monoculture. Since independence there has been some diversification, but in 1976, rubber still constituted 23 per cent of all exports – more than twice as large a proportion as any other export. Four products alone (rubber, tin, petroleum and palm oil) made up 56 per cent of the total (Young *et al.*, 1980a, p. 27). Cocoa and groundnuts have a similar significance in West Africa, as do sugar-cane and bananas in the Caribbean, Central America and parts of Asia. Recent shifts in specialisation to commodities with a lower labour input, such as from rubber to oil palms in Malaysia, and from coffee to soybeans in Brazil, have even more dire implications for the rural poor.

Commodity exports like these are nevertheless of great importance for the balance of payments in many countries. It is true that the trend in the terms of trade for commodities is not very auspicious, but this only makes it even more vital that the economic return should accrue to the country which produces the exports rather than to a foreign TNC.

Land Reform

In tackling all these problems much importance is attached to the reform of land tenure, leading to sweeping changes in the structure of agriculture. These proposals are varied, and profess a variety of irreproachable objectives. Sometimes they seek to combine tiny holdings, and sometimes to break up great estates. In some cases the changes are intended to emancipate peasants or farmworkers, bound in a quasi-feudal relationship to great landowners.

Overlapping with this may be the objective of relieving rural poverty, by providing land for the landless or lifting some of the economic pressure from farmers with too little land to yield them a livelihood. Usually these purposes are combined with that of making agriculture more profitable, though in a way which will benefit those who live and work in the rural areas, and not, say, some overseas TNC. Enough may have been said to make it clear that although land reform has important economic implications, its implications for social policy may be even greater.

The number of different meanings given to land reform is not the result of confusion or disagreement (though plenty of room must be left for the latter in view of the importance and complexity of the issues under discussion). It merely reflects the varied nature of the social conditions found in rural areas, not only in different countries, but sometimes within the boundaries of a single country.

Because of the misuse of wealth or political power, or the inefficiency or greed of some of those who take part, the objectives claimed for these schemes are often not attained. In Mexico, those to whom communal *ejido* land has been allocated for cultivation have connived at its invasion by squatters in order to secure government compensation (see Chapter 4). In countries like Bolivia and Mexico a local political boss, or *cacique*, has sometimes emerged as a kind of *padron*, in place of the great landowner. He has it in his power to bestow privileges in land tenure, or access to credit or agricultural inputs in exchange for political loyalty or even cash payments (Esman, 1978, p. 16). 'The Latin American *cacique* system and its role as patron and exploiter of the rural poor has functional equivalents in all areas of the world' (ibid., pp. 16–17).

Above all the combined hostility of the great families and the international 'agribusinesses' has been sufficient to deter governments from effective action (Feder, 1970, pp. 173ff). Even foreign governments have become involved, if more discreetly. More than one military regime in South America has owed its existence to what was seen as a political threat to American plantation interests. As a result, the redistribution of land among small cultivators has barely begun. For example, it had been on the agenda in Latin America for a very long time, but apart from limited progress in Bolivia and Mexico little has been achieved (Gilbert, 1977, pp. 149ff).

The Land Shortage

Meanwhile many families have to survive on holdings which are too small to provide a living for them. Aziz (1980, p. 137) suggests two hectares as the minimum for affording the necessary inputs. Nevertheless in South Korea one-third of all farms are only about two-fifths of a hectare, and the average barely one hectare in size (Reynolds, 1985, p. 177). The average size of holdings in India is only 2.3 hectares, half being below one hectare (Mehta, 1984, p. 38). Little (1982, p. 173), considers that the explanation is often to be found in off-farm earnings. In Taiwan, for instance, half of the earnings of those with half a hectare or less come from such employment. There will be little opportunity for these in the more underdeveloped countries.

An important factor in reducing the size of farms in parts of Africa, and in Asia and Latin America, is the pressure upon the land of rapidly increasing populations (Bairoch, 1973, p. 15). Where all members of a clan of kin-group have a traditional right of access to land, an increase in population leads to the continuous sharing and subdivision of what may already be very small holdings. Thus 55 out of the 81 'developing countries' listed by Aziz (1980, pp. 150–2) had less than half a hectare per agricultural person to distribute, and only nine (six of them in Africa) had more than two hectares.

Land reform can do something to alleviate this situation, but, as Esman has shown, does less for the landless. It is more likely to upgrade small farmers into what Esman calls 'middle farmers', who then constitute as dominant and exploitative an influence in the countryside as did the large landowners whom they had displaced (Esman, 1978, p. 41).

One answer to these problems is to extend the area under cultivation, through the occupation of previously virgin territory. This was the pattern of European colonisation in the 'new' countries of America and the Antipodes in the past, and the 'expanding frontier' is now once more being advocated as a way of meeting the insatiable need for land. New roads, like the Pan-American Highway in South America, penetrating previously uninhabited areas, provide a stimulus to settlement, especially if they are related to new urban developments. The construction of Brasilia in the jungle, as a new national capital for Brazil, was perhaps the most dramatic example of this.

There is a price to be paid for all this, of course. Many ecologists are concerned about the global effects on the environment (notably on the atmosphere and the climate) resulting from the

ravaging of rain-forest areas, of which the jungles of South
America are the most important. The pressure of population in
India and Nepal, leading to deforestation on the slopes of the
Himalayas, has been blamed for the catastrophic nature of the
floods in Bangladesh in recent years. In regions like sub-Saharan
Africa the livelihood of pastoralists and other nomads may be
threatened by the encroachment of settled agriculture on their
traditional grazing areas. Overcropping may lead to the spread of
desert areas (see Figure 3.1).

The amount of good land is obviously going to be limited but, as
in Mexico, irrigation may enable previously arid areas to be
occupied and brought under cultivation. But here also caution is
required. If the water used for this purpose is withdrawn from
domestic or industrial use, it may be at some human or economic
cost (Arnon, 1981, p. 31). There is also the possible salination of
the soil through the drawing up of heavily mineralised, subter-
ranean water. Another risk is of an increase in water-borne
disease, for still water can be the breeding-ground of malarial
mosquitoes as well as other disease vectors.

There is also the high cost of many such schemes. The slowing-
up of the Mexican government's programme of irrigation because

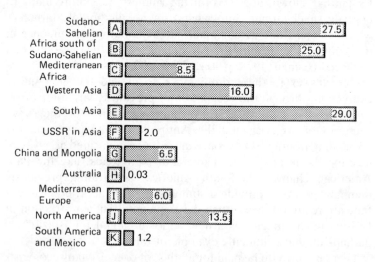

Source: United Nations, *State of World Population 1988.*

Figure 3.1   Rural population affected by severe desertification (millions)

of cost, points to the economic constraints which can limit not only irrigation, but land improvement generally. These difficulties should not be exaggerated, however. In many countries there still seems to be scope for further colonisation, and irrigation will often play a part in making it possible.

The human problems implicit in mass resettlement must not be underestimated. Guyanese experience is very instructive in this regard. Although the government has made periodic attempts to colonise the country's jungle hinterland, the population still crowds onto a narrow coastal strip. The reasons in this case are partly historical – an aversion to working on the land, on the part of urbanised blacks, which dates back to their enslavement on the sugar plantations.

But even where such a reason is absent, tribal or other traditions may make the link between an individual and his home, and particularly land which has always been worked by his family, a very close one. In countries where traditions are less strong or on the wane, opposition may be less, especially if the government can provide electricity, housing and so on as an incentive to those who might otherwise be unwilling to sacrifice the 'fleshpots' of the settled areas.

The other solution is to make the land more productive. Land reform can help in this, if it places otherwise under-utilised land in the hands of small cultivators who must make the best use of every square inch. An example of its potential is to be found in Taiwan – but before that country embarked on its equally successful ISI policy (Fei *et al.*, 1980). If, nevertheless, farms are too small to be economic, farmers might be encouraged to combine with others on a co-operative or village basis. Ways could be found of achieving this without arousing the opposition which might be evoked if the actual ownership of land was threatened. As Mehta's account of rural co-operatives in India shows, such feelings can be very important. Action may also be required to prevent domination of the co-operatives by the large farmers (Mehta, 1984, pp. 90–1).

Co-operative organisation could also facilitate the purchase of fertilisers and insecticides and the use of expensive equipment where this was helpful. It could also make the process of marketing more cost-effective. Joint research and training, directed towards locally consumed rather than exported crops, is also a possibility. Perhaps most important of all, mutual credit unions have provided the most effective alternative to rapacious money-lenders as sources of capital or of loans at times of stringency (ibid., pp. 92ff).

The 'corporate villages', which have replaced the largely traditional but now ineffective *panchayat* in parts of India, are one model which seems to have been successful. They perform varying functions, including the maintenance of schools, roads and wells; the control of grazing, fishing and irrigation; and the organisation of bulk grain sales (Wade, 1988; World Bank, 1988, p.152). But if co-operatives are to be successful, experience shows that more training will be needed by those who are to run them.

Co-operation with neighbours, say at harvest time, is taken for granted in traditional agriculture, for example among women, who are the main subsistence cultivators in many African countries (Rogers, 1980, pp. 106–7). What is being proposed here goes much further than informal mutual aid of this kind, but at least it would not be as unfamiliar and unwelcome a concept as it tends to be in the more individualistic societies of the North.

The 'Green Revolution'

The so-called 'green revolution' (Arnon, 1981, pp. 284ff) has improved agricultural productivity, but mainly by the adoption of new farming methods: the use of hardier and more prolific seed varieties, and the replacement of the traditional methods of husbandry by more scientific approaches. In particular the nurture of the land itself has come in for attention. Only if methods of cultivation are thus improved, it is argued, can the redistribution of land through a policy of land reform be expected to increase productivity.

Much is made of the unwillingness of peasant farmers to modernise their farming methods, and some commentators such as Hyden (1980) see this as a major obstacle to development. To Third World peasants, he says, farming is more than a production process; it is part of a network of social and emotional obligations, the 'economy of affection'. The price incentive has only a limited appeal to them: 'They work to live not live to work.'

This view of the peasant, as what Hutton and Cohen call 'obstacle man' (Hutton and Cohen, 1975), has lost ground in recent years. His decisions as often very rational in the light of the material and social problems confronting him and his family. For example, the penalty for a failed experiment could be disastrous to the family of a marginal farmer. Even in strictly agricultural terms, his local knowledge may mean that his practice is wiser than that pressed on him by an outside expert (Chambers, 1985, pp. 75ff).

Broadly speaking, two traditional methods are in use. One is the intensive cultivation of a family holding, using a good deal of labour, especially where there is a land shortage, as in countries like Tanzania, Bangladesh and India. The other method, where land is less scarce, uses shifting cultivation, in which an area of land is cleared by the drastic process known as 'slash and burn'. The rich, weed-free tilth, further enriched by wood-ash, is then cropped, with little further cultivation. Even the tree stumps may be left *in situ*. After several seasons the fertility of the clearing begins to decline. It is then abandoned to the encroaching bush, and another plot is cleared.

The sweeping condemnation of shifting cultivation or 'bush fallow' as an inefficient use of land ('land robbery', according to the Dutch colonists in Indonesia) is on the retreat nowadays in the face of empirical evidence (Clark and Haswell, p. 1971). Attention has shifted instead to ways of improving the techniques used. Multiple cropping, but of complementary rather than competing species, utilises nutrients and light and water more effectively. The increase in the density of vegetation also smothers weeds. Cutting more and burning less avoids excessive soil disturbance. Mulches constituted from weeds and crop residues, and even chemical fertilisers and insecticides, could be used (Greenland, 1975).

The aim in the case of the other, more intensive form of cultivation, is to bring about a 'green revolution' by the use of new seeds, the adoption of a proper crop rotation, the use of pesticides and fertilisers, and more efficient ploughing and weeding. There has also been some emphasis on the use of modern equipment culminating in the tractor being seen 'as a symbol of modern agriculture in some parts of Africa'. This is recognised as damaging to weeding (Lele, 1975, pp. 33–5). More important is the bias in favour of large holdings, and its adverse effect on employment. It is said to have displaced the equivalent of 2·5 million workers in the decade up to the 1970s (Abercrombie, 1972, pp. 315–34).

There are many difficulties confronting small farmers in their attempts even to survive, let alone improve their practice. They have always been fair game for the moneylender, on whom they have had to rely to tide them over when their crops are destroyed by drought or pests, or when prices are low. To such financial problems are now added the need for capital to buy the new seeds and fertilisers, to introduce irrigation in order to be able to control the supply of water in the way required by the new crop varieties, and perhaps, as has often been the case in India, to try to keep up with their neighbours by acquiring a tractor.

Elliott (1975) has pointed to another adverse effect. Many subsistence farmers could cope perfectly well so long as they were producing by traditional methods for their own families or a small local market, but found the new agriculture with its rigid requirements as to water supply, fertilisers and methods of husbandry quite beyond them. Not only was the new approach so much at variance with the natural rhythms and customary lore which had governed their activities previously, but it often required a degree of sophistication or even formal education which they did not possess. Nor, as we have seen, was it always an advance on traditional practice.

The scales have been weighted still further against small farmers by the emphasis given by the 'green revolution' to 'cash crops' with a ready overseas market, rather than to the cultivation of manioc, millet, maize, and other foodstuffs consumed by the local population (World Bank, 1982, pp. 67–8; Chambers, 1985, pp. 76–7; Hereford, n.d.). For example, too little research has been conducted to discover better varieties of these staples, or more efficient ways of cultivating them, as compared with such grains as wheat, or non-food exports such as rubber, tea or palm oil. A start has been made with rice, and to a lesser extent with maize (World Bank, 1982, pp. 67–8), but a general shift towards a consumption rather than an export orientation still has to take place (ibid., pp. 57ff): this in spite of the fact that subsistence farming is still predominant in many countries. It constituted 75 per cent of all agriculture in Tanzania in 1968 (an actual increase over the previous nine years), amounting to 30 per cent of the country's total GDP (Hyden, 1980).

Small Farms or Large?

Where, in spite of the difficulties referred to above, the new methods can be applied by small farmers, they are as successful as on larger farms. As Berry and Cline (1979, p. 128) put it: 'Agricultural strategies focusing on small farms start with a major advantage: the demonstrated capacity to achieve high productivity of what is usually the scarcest resource, land (especially in Asia), largely through the application of the abundant resource labour.' In other words, through intensive cultivation. And no doubt by virtue also of the industriousness of the peasant farmer as compared with the hired hand.

Similar conclusions have been reached by Cornia (1985) in a study of fifteen underdeveloped countries. All but three of them showed higher yields to small farms due to greater intensiveness of cultivation, justifying land redistribution so long as there was a labour surplus, especially if water and fertilisers were made available.

But larger farmers are in a better position to develop the new agriculture. They are not wedded to traditional methods and find it easier to obtain scarce inputs and cheap credit (Little, 1982, pp. 71–2). In the event that they still end up with lower marginal returns to land, they can use machinery to achieve higher labour productivity. And in a cash-crop economy they also have marketing advantages, especially in exporting their produce. Such factors give rise to a strong likelihood that holdings will increase in size, calling for even higher levels of management skill, as well as for capital, neither of which the small farmer can mobilise.

Consequently many small farmers are being dispossessed. Already in 1978, according to Esman, a majority of the rural households in Latin America were 'landless or near-landless', (see Figure 3.2). The proportions ranged from 53 per cent of rural households in India and 60 per cent in Mexico, to 85 per cent in Bolivia, Guatemala and Java (Esman, 1978, pp. 6–8). Even in Africa he estimates that 8–10 per cent were landless and another 31 per cent near-landless – proportions which are increasing rapidly (ibid., p. 9).

Mehta quotes similar comments about the effect of the 'green revolution' in the Punjab in India – often represented as an example of the success of the new methods (Mehta, 1984, p. 88):

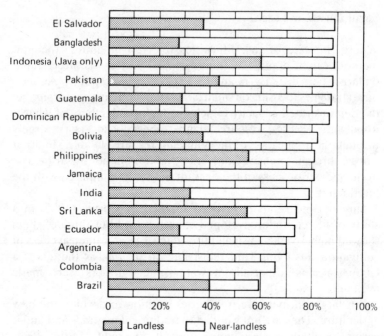

Source: Milton J. Esman *et al.*, (1978) *The Landless and Near Landless in Developing Countries* (Ithaca, N.Y.: Cornell University, Center for International Studies).

Figure 3.2   Percentage of landless and near-landless rural labour force

'Benefiting by the early adoption of the new technology, the larger farmers have started an expansion (in spite of land ceilings) which is driving the poor farmers into the landless category, and is increasing the degree of polarization in the society.'

The long runs of the large farm make the use of machinery instead of labour particularly profitable. As a result there will be few opportunities for alternative employment even as waged labourers for those so dispossessed.

A form of economic development which results in the creation of a new destitute class of landless and often unemployed peasants is hardly a satisfactory solution to the problem of poverty, but the damage extends much further than that. A common landholding is often the main support and cement of a family or kinship group. This group in its turn provides its members with the security of a cultural background, and the society with an agency which social-ises people into conformity, and provides sanctions against de-viance. It also maintains a traditional welfare system which helps its own widows, orphans, elderly and disabled, and others in need, with food, shelter and emotional support.

The destruction of the traditional landholding pattern may be the beginning of the end for this social system, causing the burden of social control and welfare which it formerly carried to fall more and more on the state. A vicious circle is set in train which generates social problems in both town and country, while render-ing impotent the communal institutions which provide a safety net for social casualties.

Such damaging consequences notwithstanding, the 'green revolution' is very profitable to the agribusiness multinationals, who supply the products it utilises. They therefore have a stake in maintaining its momentum, irrespective of its value for the de-velopment of the Third World countries concerned (Dahlberg, 1979).

Communications and Markets

Side by side with other measures to help small farmers must go an improvement in the local commercial infrastructure through better communication and marketing arrangements. Better roads are a vital part of this, but another aspect is planning for the growth of local towns as marketing centres (Epstein, 1982). A factor inhibit-ing the growth of these has been the existence of large plantations, largely self-sufficient and with their own distribution facilities to ports and other export outlets.

Such small towns would be able to develop a symbiotic relation-ship with the surrounding agricultural area. Thus they could provide distribution centres and markets for the products of the farms, and also offer employment in this and in the making and repairing of farm equipment and the provision of supplies and amenities for rural dwellers. The more highly-mechanised indust-rial activities would presumably be left to the larger towns, while traditional crafts, or some development of these along the lines of what has come to be called 'intermediate' or 'alternative' techno-logy, would be able to use the plentiful local labour instead of scarce capital and know-how. An improvement in the economic position of the rural population should stimulate the demand for such local products. This is a very positive form of 'trickle-down'.

Hunger and Food Aid

The case for the 'green revolution' is often made on the grounds that it is necessary if the world, and particularly the Third World, is to feed its rapidly growing population. Ever since Malthus terrified British radicals in 1798 with his axiom that, while land is limited, human passions, and therefore population growth, are not, the possibility of world starvation has never seemed far away. Without voluntary restraint on reproduction, Malthus saw the cutting-back of population through war and disease as the only alternative to famine. He could not anticipate the increase in food supplies from the agrarian reforms in Europe, and the opening-up of the vast wheatfields and prairies of North America.

Malthus nothwithstanding, it is easy to believe that even the recent unparalleled rate of increase in world population (see Chapter 12), still has not caused a global food shortage. Vast food surpluses are currently being produced in Europe and North America (Lappé and Collins, 1979). The only problem, it seems, is one of distribution. The food is there, but in the wrong places. Such a judgement would be superficial (Oram *et al.*, 1979, pp. 25–6). Such imported food (except for relief aid) has to be paid for, but the countries of the Sahel, the Horn of Africa and of Asia, where famines are most likely to occur, are all countries with an adverse balance of payments. The North might be urged to provide the food free or at nominal cost, but are reluctant to do this in case it 'spoiled the market'. After all the reason for keeping buffer stocks like these is to stabilise and maintain prices. Nor would the provision of food in this way solve the long-term problem.

Secondly it may be the wrong kind of food. A surplus of wheat in North America, for example, is of little assistance to countries whose diet is based on tropical cereals, or on root crops like manioc. It is very difficult to change long-standing dietary habits like these. And if they were changed it would present problems for the future, in those countries where natural conditions such as

Exhibit 3.1   Famine and food aid

According to the 1980 World Development Report of the World Bank:

> The famines in Ethiopia in 1973–4 and Bangladesh in 1974 were not caused by a fall in the average amount of food available per person. Rather, droughts caused local declines in farm incomes, so that people in affected areas could not afford to buy food from the unaffected areas. (World Bank, 1980b, p. 61)

What Patrick Marnham calls 'an imaginary mass famine' among Sahelian nomads in 1973 is illuminating in this regard:

> The relief agencies responded ... by treating the situation as one of simple food shortage, and shipping in 250,000 tons of grain. This they did despite the fact that adequate grain supplied *from within the Sahelian countries* were known to be available throughout the crisis. (Marnham, 1979, pp. 7–8)

Marnham (supported by Lappé and Collins, 1979, pp. 282ff) goes on to suggest that the real motive for the mass importation of food during such emergencies was not the relief of famine but the opening up of an outlet for surplus foreign grain. Whether this is the case or not, such imports are bound to play havoc with the local grain market (Nelson, 1981b pp. 31ff), reducing the demand for home-grown grain (and its price), and thus creating severe hardships for native farmers. It would be surprising if they were not then also discouraged from trying to meet future local food needs.

Maxwell and Singer (1979, pp. 230–3) argue that appropriate government policies can prevent such an outcome, but the chances of such policies being adopted are not great. Indeed Third World governments may utilise food aid as a way of putting off changes in land tenure and investment in agriculture, even though (quite apart from issues of social justice) such reforms may be required to increase the amount of home-grown food available. Some hard-pressed administrations even use the aid to bolster up their budgets or improve their balance of payments. As a result they become more dependent than ever on the North.

climate usually prevent them from producing such foods for themselves.

But some insist that, even an area within the Third World which is struck by famine or natural disaster, there may be no real food shortage. The only problem may be the maldistribution of such food as there is; facilities for moving it are inadequate, and poverty in the hungry areas prevent their inhabitants from affording the food even if they could gain access to it.

'Food for work schemes' are attempts to link food aid more directly with development (Cathie, 1982, pp. 69ff; Maxwell and Singer, 1978). Some northern food for which there is no commercial market is provided either to governments for resale, to meet part of the cost of clearing land, building roads, sinking wells, irrigation and so on or direct to the workers employed on development projects. Few of these schemes have been without problems. There is an inbuilt conflict between the government's desire to maximise its return from the food, and the requirement that it shall be sold cheaply so as to reach the poor who need it most. In the event, most of the benefit goes to the rich.

Nor are projects in which labour is paid by 'food for work' all that successful. Food by itself is not such a strong motivation, except at times of acute shortage, and the imported food often does more harm to food producers than it does good to those receiving it. Such schemes may also have unanticipated and unwanted consequences unless they are very discriminating. A case in point is that of the Indian pastoralists, already overgrazing their land, who were encouraged by 'food for work' subsidies to further expand the size of their herds (Cathie, 1982, pp. 74–5).

The great justification for food aid, except at times of famine, would be if it went to the poorest sections of the community, and therefore had the effects both of reducing inequalities and of operating as an investment in human capital (Schuh, 1981). In practice, such selective direction of benefit has proved difficult to achieve. It is very expensive (Nelson, 1981a, p. 5) and often benefits urban rather than rural dwellers (Nelson, 1981b, pp. 40–1).

It would be unwise to assume that there is no overall shortage of appropriate foodstuffs: that any problem can be dealt with either by emergency relief or redistribution between deficit and surplus regions. Figure 3.3 shows the large areas in which the produce of the land is insufficient to feed its population. According to the

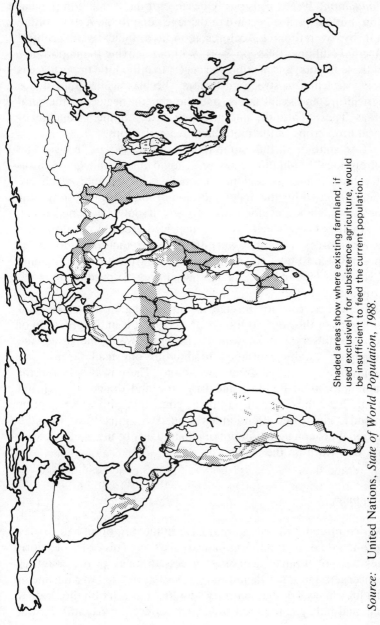

Shaded areas show where existing farmland, if used exclusively for subsistence agriculture, would be insufficient to feed the current population.

Source: United Nations, *State of World Population, 1988.*

Figure 3.3 Unproductive land

United Nations Population Fund report, *The State of World Population, 1988*, this is partly because of the increase in population, but partly also because of damage done to the fertility of the soil by overcropping, deforestation and faulty water control (United Nations, 1988, pp. 8–9). Without denying the importance of these factors, it is possible to suggest that too little importance is being attached to structural factors: the bias against subsistence agriculture and small farms, and the general neglect of the rural areas. There is also the shift already noted from the production of local food crops to the more lucrative cash crops.

If, in spite of all this, some food shortages can be shown to be purely local, it should be borne in mind that an adequate infrastructure and gross regional inequalities of income, which are jointly blamed for the maldistribution of food, are part of what is meant by underdevelopment. They will only be remedied by regional policies which help the deprived areas to develop their own resources. Then they will either produce their own food or be in a position to take any advantages to be gained from a regional division of labour by exchanging what they do produce for food grown elsewhere.

There is a role for foreign aid in helping to solve the food problems of the South (Oram *et al.*, 1979). It is in the provision of seed, fertilisers and know-how directed towards increasing the supply of locally consumed food crops on small farms – an 'appropriate' form of 'green revolution'. There is also a need for capital for road building and irrigation and drainage. Such aid would have the virtue also of being consistent with wider reforms aimed at giving due attention to the needs of agriculture within the national economy, and improving the quality of life for those who live and work on the land.

Summary

Agriculture and the rural areas have in the past often had to play second fiddle to attempts at industrialisation. This order of priorities has not brought economic success to many of the countries concerned, but it has damaged rural society and led to a decline in the life chances of that majority who live and work on the land. A regional policy is required which will reduce poverty in the rural areas, and slow up the flight to the towns. Such an attack on the dual economy, releasing the productive potential of the country-side, would also pay off in economic growth.

At the same time the programme should be such as to encourage larger crops of locally consumed food, to provide a safeguard against malnutrition or the occurrence of famine. Except in emergencies, this is a more worthwhile object for foreign aid than food imports, 'food for work' schemes and so on. It can be achieved only by a policy which takes proper account of local needs and attitudes and makes proper use of indigenous institutions.

A number of measures have been discussed, such as land reform to break up large holdings where they exist – notably the great *latifundia* of South America and the oppressive social system which they sustain. The colonisation of virgin areas may also be possible in some land-rich countries. Such steps should be associated with a determined effort to ensure that the very poor, the 'landless or near-landless', benefit from these.

Any increase in the number of small farmers which results need not cause a decline in efficiency, though it will call for the organisation of co-operatives between them – possibly for production, and certainly for many other common purposes, such as marketing, bulk purchases of inputs, and credit. The 'green revolution' has not on the whole benefited the small producer, but he could benefit from help in introducing improvements in his practice which are more appropriate to his circumstances. He is not as resistant to new methods as is sometimes suggested. When he does reject the advice offered to him, it is often for good reasons not especially apparent to outsiders.

Such a policy for the rural areas, which should also include improvements in the housing and amenities available to those who live there, may slow up both the decay in the extended family system and the rush to the towns. This would give a much needed breathing-space, but it is unlikely to halt these trends entirely.

4

Third World Cities

Cities in the underdeveloped countries of the world are facing a crisis of growth, symbolised by the arrival on the scene of those enormous urban agglomerations which the United Nations has called 'mega-cities' (United Nations, 1982a, p. 154). The results of this galloping urbanisation have included unemployment and poverty, the lack of the basic services required for health and hygiene, and the emergence of slums, overcrowding and homelessness on a vast scale.

The solution has to be found partly in recognising that the mega- or 'primate' cities are a symptom of underdevelopment, to be attacked at that fundamental level. Meanwhile those committed to the urban way of life have the right to live under civilised conditions. Various approaches to the housing problem are examined below – the phenomenon of squatter settlements, prepared sites for self-built accommodation ('sites and services' schemes) and government provision of low-cost housing, including so-called 'core houses'.

As in all aspects of social policy, however, it is not simply a matter of finding practical solutions. There are political implications, and these cannot be ignored. For instance, the roots of the present urban crisis lie in the role which the cities of the South have come to play as they experience the explosive impact of Northern capitalism.

Evolution

Although urban centres existed in these countries long before they were colonised and eventually industrialised from the North, these

78

incursions did change their character, and dramatically increased their rate of growth. They continued in their historical role as centres of government and administration, but it was alien governments who were now established in them. And exports, which had been relatively unimportant during the pre-colonial period, became the main reason for colonising them – in order to secure raw materials and foodstuffs for the factories and cities of the Northern countries. Sometimes these commodities were already being produced in the colony; in other cases they were introduced by the settlers.

As a result cities began to fulfil new functions: they were established in mining areas, or became entrepôts for collecting together the new products, or ports through which they could be exported. Large-scale undertakings involved in this trade developed side by side with the indigenous craftsmen and small traders, and in their train came imports to satisfy the increasingly Northernised tastes of those whom they employed.

The role played by these cities in replacing local consumer preferences and attitudes with 'modernised' ones, has been explored by Redfield and Singer (1954). Such changes were bound to have a depressing effect on the traditional economy of a city. And because of the road and railway links with the interior of a country, which were established to supply the needs of the new commerce, these effects were often experienced over a wider area.

As the old economy declined, the new patterns of trade took charge of the cities' growth. Inevitably they developed in their amenities and size; and, where some limited industrialisation also took place in them, their rate of growth accelerated. In some cases, indeed, a city was virtually created from a very small settlement, or even virgin territory, especially in previously remote mining areas. A striking example of this kind of development was the establishment of the urban centre of Arawa in connection with the massive copper mines at Bougainville, in the North Solomon Islands off Papua New Guinea (Conyers, 1982, pp. 81ff). This gave rise to many social and environmental problems in what had previously been a rural backwater.

The expansion of these towns was not limited to that required for commercial or industrial purposes. They became a magnet for unsettled peoples from the countryside; and as colonialism began to inflict major changes on the rural areas, the trickle of migrants became a flood. An early example of this was seen in the West Indies, especially Guyana, where slaves from Africa had been settled for a long period on the plantations. When emancipation gave them their freedom, they not surprisingly shook the dust of the plantations from their feet and made for the urban centres. Later migrations of this kind, and much larger ones, followed and continue to follow from the neglect and poverty of the rural areas. In spite of consequent unemployment, and congestion and bad living conditions in the towns, their populations continue to rise.

Growth

The extent to which this rate of urbanisation exceeds that of the developed world is demonstrated by the Tables 4.1 and 4.2. Although the rate of increase is expected to decline, it is still likely to run at a very high rate. In accounting for these changes, the undoubted growth caused by migration seems to have been pushed into second place in recent years by urban rates of natural increase. Thus rural–urban transfer as a percentage of urban growth in underdeveloped countries was predicted as declining from 59.3 per cent to 42.2 per cent between 1950 and 1990, the decline being rather less in Asia than elsewhere (Mabogunje, 1980, pp. 176–7).

The many issues raised by this question of population growth

Table 4.1   Estimated Percentages of the population living in urban areas, more and less developed regions (United Nations, 1985b, p. 182)

	1970	1975	1980	1985	1990	2000
More developed regions	66·4	68·7	70·6	73·4	74·2	77·8
Less developed regions	25·2	27·1	29·4	31·7	34·4	40·4

Table 4.2   Percentage annual urban growth rates, more and less developed regions (United Nations, 1985b, p. 186)

	1970/5	1975/80	1980/5	1985/2000
More developed regions	1·6	1·3	1·1	1·0
Less developed regions	3·9	3·7	3·6	3·5

are discussed in Chapter 12. But it is worth noting that the contribution of migrants to this urban natural increase is greater than that of non-migrants, and that the direct effect of migration also remains considerable (United Nations, 1985b, pp. 200ff). The exodus from the countryside, taking into account both these direct and indirect effects, seems still to be the most significant factor overall.

Some commentators have suggested that urban growth, that is, the growth in the size of certain cities, may prove to be a more significant feature of Third World society than urbanisation, in the sense of the proportion of the population living in towns (Jones, 1966, p. 36). This calls attention to the *primate city* (Linsky, 1969; El Shakhs, 1972), that phenomenon of the Third World in which one or two urban centres vastly outstrip all the others in size, leaving a hiatus between them and the rest.

In 1950 there were only two cities, London and New York, with populations of over ten millions (United Nations, 1982a, p. 156). By 1980 there were seven, four of which were in the Third World. Of the 35 largest cities in the world (those with over four millions) in that year, 22 were in the Third World. By the year 2000, it is anticipated that there will be 22 cities with populations over ten million, of which 18 will be in the Third World. The largest city in the world is expected to be Mexico City, with a population of 26·3 millions, followed by Sao Paulo in Brazil with 24 (United Nations, 1985b, pp. 197–8).

This phenomenon of the primate city has been seen as one of the consequences of underdevelopment (El Shakhs, 1972), but as Mabogunje points out (1980, pp. 166–9) its foundations were laid 'quite early in the colonial period', when the imperial power would often choose the main port, the centre of the import and export trade of the colony, and therefore of its road system, to be the centre of government. It was only to be expected that commercial enterprises would be attracted by the same practical considerations, as well as by a wish to locate themselves within easy reach of the officials whose decisions could make or mar their prospects.

A certain amount of concentration was therefore bound to occur, but it would be exacerbated by the enclave development which followed. The assets gained by a city as a result would soon be formidable. There would be the port itself. From it, roads, and sometimes railways, would fan out into the mining and plantation areas. A commercial infrastructure would emerge, of banks and insurance houses, along with professional advisers such as lawyers, accountants and engineers. The tastes and attitudes of a growing labour force and consumer market would become increasingly well adapted to the requirements of Northern industry. Such a city would be irresistible to companies planning to establish themselves in a country.

This process would feed on itself. In accordance with the logic of enclave development, companies would use subsequent investment to support and expand their existing enterprises – which means that much of the investment would take place in and around the port where that enterprise had been established. It is this final stage which is peculiar to the underdeveloped country, turning a great city into a primate city with a power to attract immigrants from the countryside which its lesser sisters cannot hope to equal.

Modernisation

Most economists argue that the fact that some city-dwellers still acknowledge their traditional affiliations, and the obligations these bring with them, is an impediment to economic growth (Elliott, 1975, pp. 292–3). Structuralists would expect this, but neo-classical theory would insist that migrants from the country should eventually come to recognise that there is neither work nor living-space for them in the city. Instead they compound the problem of urban congestion by staying on because they are being supported by kinsfolk or fellow-villagers. Also the draining of goods and money back to the village, which custom enforces, provides a disincentive to effort and accumulation.

This is to take too narrow a view of the value of traditional practices such as these. As we have seen, these features of what Hyden (1980) calls 'the economy of affection' fulfil many functions which some may consider detrimental to growth, but which are important for development in its broadest sense.

The modernising role of the city is in any case very powerful. Bryan Roberts (1982, pp. 369–70) refers to what Redfield and Singer call its 'heterogeneic' role: 'that of introducing new ideas and styles of life into traditional society'. The city is the home of enclave growth, of industry, imports and exports, TNCs. It is the beach-head of the North, bringing with it the North's way of looking at the world, and indeed it sees such a perspective as a prerequisite for its own efficient operation. It is not therefore surprising that those employed in the city or seeking employment there try to adapt to such demands. Against such economic pressures the ethnic subculture is bound to suffer, albeit gradually (Jones, 1981).

For a time the migrant from the rural area honours his customary obligations – of compliance with traditional norms of behaviour, of loyalty to and support for his family back home, of hospitality to visitors and so on. As he becomes more permanently settled in the town, however, and comes to see his future as lying there rather than in the village of his youth, such obligations seem increasingly onerous, and may well be abandoned, together with his village contacts.

Changes of this kind can have a devastating effect on rural life, denuding the land of its younger workforce, impoverishing families, destroying the traditional mutual aid welfare system, and weakening the forms of social control which have maintained order and stability for so long. Unless these effects are anticipated and functional alternatives to the old institutions are provided, some degree of social disorganisation will follow. Some of these problems as they occur in countries of southern Asia have been outlined by The United Nations Educational, Scientific, and Cultural Organisation (UNESCO) (1984a), but they are probably even more severe in many countries of Africa.

Urban Social Problems

City growth in nineteenth-century Europe and North America generated appalling social problems, but the human consequences of such growth in the Third World have been even greater. This is partly because its urbanisation has been on so much larger a scale; it is in the primate or mega-cities that these problems exist in their most extreme form. But it is partly also because of the presence in the background of underdevelopment.

This is illustrated by the way in which the privations of the countryside and the problems of the city are linked together. It is not a zero-sum situation, in which the losses of one are the gains of the other. All are losers. Thus migration to the town makes for decline in the countryside and weakens traditional social institutions, at the same time as it causes unmanageable congestion and squalor in the town itself. It brings into the urban centres a larger population than can be employed there, so that urban poverty is widespread, but rural poverty is not thereby relieved. The departure from the villages of the younger and more vigorous means a decline in the viability of family agricultural holdings, as well as even less likelihood that a 'green revolution' will be successfully brought about within the traditional landholding system.

The urban congestion already referred to adds the pressure of a concentrated population to the influence of the enclave developers, and ensures that social and infrastructural expenditure by the government also centres on the town. As a result the pressing needs of the countryside – land reform, agricultural improvement of an appropriate kind, the provision of development capital, and the expansion of local industry and markets – are neglected.

There is no doubt that the problems of urban unemployment and poverty would be greatly eased if there were programmes of rural development which offered better prospects to those who were tempted to leave. In part, however, these problems are an outcome of underdevelopment in the town itself. Enclave development involves investment on a very narrow base, with little spill-over into the urban economy in general. Subsidiary industries are few because of the policy of importing the supplies required; and the repatriation of profits starves the country of capital. Some government action to ensure a more broadly-based and balanced industrialisation is required if conditions of life in the towns are to improve.

Neo-classical theory suggests that such industrialisation could be on such a scale as to occupy the existing unemployed labour force in the towns and in addition absorb some of the surplus labour in the countryside (Little, 1982, pp. 86ff). Baer and Hervé (1978, pp. 89–90), pointing to experience to the contrary in Latin America and Asia, give little support to this optimistic view. Industrialisation could nevertheless offer modest expectations if governments took control of their own industrial future.

Housing Problems

The most obtrusive expression of urban deprivation is the 'squatter settlements' which encircle the great cities of most underdeveloped countries. The hills around Caracas, the capital of Venezuela (a middle-income country, rich by the standards of most Third World countries) come to life with the lights of these settlements every night after dark. The shacks of West Kingston in Jamaica, and the *cuevas barriada* in Lima (Turner, 1967) are but two more of the many forms which these settlements take in many countries of the Third World – in Africa, Asia, Latin America, and the islands of the Pacific and the Caribbean. Eye-catching though they may be, they do not in themselves represent the only urgent urban problems confronting underdeveloped countries.

Attention should also be given to the inner-city slums and the health risks and privations to which the poor who inhabit them are exposed. Although some of them have a vital community life, others are properly described, in Stokes's phrase, as 'slums of despair' (Stokes, 1962). Remedying their miserable housing conditions and lack of civilised environmental health services and amenities should be priorities for government action.

It has been estimated that only 59 per cent of town-dwellers in the majority of Latin American countries are served by piped water, with another 17 per cent receiving water from standpipes. In many parts of Africa and Asia the situation is even worse. Thus in Libreville, in Gabon, only 25 per cent of households have piped water (Mabogunje, 1980, p. 191). The origin in polluted water supplies of gastric illness and water-borne infection, both of which are major health problems in underdeveloped countries, indicates the kind of threat which this situation poses. The close relationship between lack of adequate water supplies and urban death rates is well illustrated by data available from Brazil (Mabogunje, Hardoy and Misra, 1978, p. 55). This is quite apart from the need for pure water as an amenity, the lack of which must be seen as a sign of unacceptable poverty in the later part of the twentieth century.

Equally serious from the viewpoints of both health and amenity are the deficiencies of urban sewerage systems. United Nations figures for 'adequate excreta disposal' in the towns range from 18 per cent in Nepal, 32 per cent in the Philippines, 35 per cent in Brazil and 41 per cent in Nigeria, to an optimistic 100 per cent in

Bolivia and Jordan (Hardoy and Satterthwaite, 1981, p. 244). The extent to which sewage and water supplies intermingle is one of the major causes for concern. As for electricity, entirely unavailable in the country areas, it is by no means adequately provided in the poorer areas of the towns. A class-biased distribution is common to all these environmental services, and represents an important part of what urban poverty means. Life for the poor is that much grimmer and more sordid, and health and survival that much more at risk.

Not only are inner-city slums the last of the recognised areas of settlement to be provided with such environmental services as a pure water supply, sewerage and electricity, but the dwellings themselves are small, were shoddily built in the first place, and are only minimally maintained, and even then in a makeshift fashion. Thus holes in the roofs or the walls will be repaired with whatever cheap material is to hand – tarred paper, scrap metal, or even cardboard torn from boxes, often with the name of the product still visible. Landlords are rarely willing to do proper repairs, and such desperate expedients may be all that a poor family can afford. In a tropical country such a dwelling may be habitable during the dry season, but when the rains come....

Overcrowding

Ramshackle as they are, and offering minimal shelter from the elements, the slums are also often overcrowded. In Calcutta, 79 per cent of the families are crowded into a single room, some even sharing it with another family. 'In Madagascar half the population of Tanararive lived in one-room dwellings' (Mabogunje, Hardoy and Misra, 1978, pp. 32–6). All of this is possible because of the pressure of population in these overgrown conurbations. Landlords may subdivide not merely dwellings but also rooms in order to maximise their return in rent. An example is the way in which rooms in old Chinatown, even in a modern city like Singapore, were partitioned into cubicles providing just enough room for a single person to sleep (Kaye, 1974, pp. 191ff). Their demolition has been halted because of protests from sentimental conservationists.

There is also, of course, the size of the Third World family to take into account. This is not only an aspect of the 'natural increase' to which reference has already been made, but is the result in part of a family and kinship solidarity which keeps relatives together. The structure of African traditional housing as described by Schwerdtfeger (1982) reflects this. The same kinship solidarity also imposes obligations of hospitality on urban house-holders.

It must be accepted that the overcrowding which results from all these factors occurs in a different social and psychological climate from that arising in the North. It is therefore unlikely to lead to such strong feeling of deprivation, or such deleterious effects on social behaviour and mental health. Nevertheless it gives rise to serious health hazards, both for the slum-dwellers themselves and for the city at large. It is only fair to add that these adverse consequences are not admitted by all observers (Odongo, 1979, pp. 31ff).

It is not good enough to say that these are indigenous conditions, and therefore to be tolerated. There are even those who would attempt to justify not merely the overcrowded family house but Third World slums in general, on the grounds that the conception of the slum is Northern and therefore inappropriate to an underdeveloped country (Drakakis-Smith, 1979, pp. 25–6). But the urban slum is not an indigenous form; it is a pathological outcome of rampant urban growth.

In the rural area, a crowded house will have breathing-space around it, and there is usually land for extensions to be added or for residents to overflow into during the day. In the city slum, in contrast, such planning regulations as exist are often ignored with impunity, so that conditions which even the city authorities themselves have decided should not be tolerated tend to persist. Houses in these areas will have been built too close together in order to maximise the use of the site, and higgledy-piggledy. Already overcrowded, their proximity to one another greatly increases the danger of fire or epidemic disease, quite apart from the effect of such congestion on the daily lives of those who have to put up with it.

Zoning regulations are of course framed so as to protect the quality of life and therefore the property values in more salubrious areas, but the slum usually continues to suffer from the amenity-destroying presence of (ironically enough) both dereliction and industrial development. The cynical excuse, though not often openly expressed, is that there is very little amenity to destroy in the slum.

Low-cost Housing

Third World slum problems are not, in most cases, going to be solved by the expedient of providing government financial aid for the upgrading of unsatisfactory dwellings. Many of them are beyond repair, and if similar populations are to be housed in a civilised fashion on the same areas, will have to be replaced by buildings more suitable for multiple occupation. The sites themselves also need to be tidied up and replanned and the supply of water and electricity and the disposal of sewage improved.

Slum clearance, accompanied by extensive government rehousing programmes, falls foul of the poverty of the countries with the greatest need, and the reluctance of both the international agencies and donor governments to provide aid for social expenditure rather than for what they see as 'productive investment'. There are also the rapidly growing populations of these cities, so that the destruction of shelters, however poor, would make many people homeless. This would cause any extensive policy of slum clearance to become a political powder keg for any government rash enough to undertake it.

It has been tried on a small scale by some of the 'middle-income countries', but the subsidised 'low-cost housing' with which these governments have replaced them, where they are for sale, are not accessible even to many of those who are in regular employment because of the lack of the necessary down payment. Building societies or their equivalents are rare, and even where they exist, incomes for the majority are too low and job security too precarious to enable them to obtain loans for this kind of home ownership.

Where government 'low-cost housing' is available for letting, rents are invariably still too high to be within the reach of the average family. In such circumstances state subsidies for low-cost housing are an example of the poor subsidising the well-off. Anyway, as Marris points out, the cost of providing enough low-cost housing, in the face of the enormous demand, greatly exceeds the resources available to the poorer countries for such a purpose

(Marris, 1981, p. 76). This demand is continuously fed by rising national populations, as well as by migration to the cities.

There are exceptions, notably in Singapore, where a large population crowded onto a small island could have produced an ecological catastrophe. Fortunately dramatic economic growth, and compulsory saving in the form of the National Provident Fund, made it possible for the government to provide satisfactory rentable housing, most of it high-rise. Many sizes and types of apartment are available, and allocation takes account of need (especially family size) as well as income.

In most countries, of course there will also be private-sector housing, available to the better-off in both the working and middle classes. While for the former it may not be much different in both style and price from government 'low-cost' housing, for the latter it can be very opulent indeed. Some of the most extreme contrasts to be seen are between the housing conditions of, on the one hand, government ministers and senior civil servants, the senior executives and expatriate staff of TNCs operating in the country, and foreign diplomatic staff and, on the other hand, of the inhabitants of the slums.

Squatter Settlements

Many of those who endure unsatisfactory housing may decide to take matters into their own hands, and establish themselves elsewhere. This is the origin of the so-called squatter settlements. This is not a small issue (Huque, 1982, pp. 19–24; Dwyer, 1974, p. 205). As Dwyer points out, 'Spontaneous settlement has become a major urban form throughout the Third World during the last thirty years; and in the future it will undoubtedly grow further in relative importance.' The frequent use of terms like 'shanty town' to refer to the settlements is an indication of the disfavour in which they are held by many foreign commentators. Those indigenous governments which have been most influenced by Northern ideas also tend to see these spontaneous irruptions as untidy re-creations of the inner-city slums on the outskirts of the city. Juppenlatz, writing in 1970 with the authority of a former United Nations official, saw them as 'a malady . . . a plague', and condemned 'their excessive squalor, filth and poverty'. For good measure, he

---

Exhibit 4.1   Growth of settlements

According to Dwyer (1974, p. 205):

In 1961, 320,000 or 23% of Manila's population were living in *barong-barongs* or spontaneous settlements; Djakarta had 750,000 people, or 25% of its population in such settlements in the same year; there were 580,000 spontaneous settlers in Hong Kong (17% of total population) in 1964 and such persons comprised 200,000 of Delhi's population, or 13% of the total the same year. Already one-third of the population of Mexico City lives in such *colonias proletarias*, nearly one-half of Ankara's population in *gececondu* and one-fifth of the population of Caracas in *ranchos*. And undoubtedly this situation will soon become worse.

---

described them as the source of human depravity, deprivation, illiteracy, epidemics and sickness.

That a general reappraisal is now being undertaken of this wholly negative picture of the squatter settlement is largely owing to the writings of J. F. C. Turner (1967–82). By 1976, the self-help trend which the settlements embodied had received the imprimatur of a United Nations Conference on Human Settlements (the Habitat Conference), held in Vancouver in that year (United Nations, 1976). It is now becoming clear that such a community is not always the first, underprivileged port of call for rural migrants to the city. Sometimes it is, but more commonly it consists of people who have previously lived in the inner-city slums, and see the move as a change for the better.

Thus Nelson reports that, often, squatters have lived in the city for some years beforehand, or even been born there (Nelson, 1979, p. 102). According to figures quoted by Turner, (1969, p. 521) only 5 per cent of a squatter settlement of 60 000 in Lima, Peru, in 1960, were recent arrivals from the countryside. In Huque's 1982 study of four settlements in Dacca in Bangladesh, 368 out of 450 heads of households (82 per cent) had lived in the city for over ten years (Huque, 1982, p. 91). Others may have joined their kinsfolk when the settlements were observed to have become more settled and permanent.

In this connection, Turner has developed his interesting distinction between 'bridgeheaders' and 'consolidators' (Turner, 1968a). The former are the new arrivals from the countryside, having few resources and an urgent need for jobs. They seek inexpensive dwellings in the inner city – either in the established slum areas, or in a centrally located squatter site if such exists. The 'consolidators' have established themselves a little more, and value the amenities of a site further out. There is a price to be paid for such 'upward mobility', of course, in their being less available for employment, and also in travel costs from home to workplace.

Some settlements are created by an act of spontaneous self-assertion on the part of deprived families, but not all see their origins in such a favourable light (Huque, 1982; Ward, 1984, p. 148). Ward points out that some are instigated by individuals with ulterior motives: politicians seeking popularity, or speculators aiming to make money from illegal land divisions. The land may not even belong to the speculator. From his experience in Mexico, Ward (ibid.) described cases of settlements on *ejido* land. These are communal holdings distributed under land reform programmes, over which the peasants have user-rights only. Urban growth has made the land much more valuable as building sites than for agriculture, and it becomes profitable to the *ejidatarios* to allow invasion and then claim compensation from the government for their loss. The settlers then have to pay the government (Gilbert and Ward, 1985, p. 90).

Speculators involved in illegal subdivisions are also able to avoid the expense of providing the basic services required on more legitimate sites. The settlers move in without such services, and then demand them from the government. But the sites are still in breach of planning laws and tenure is uncertain, giving the authorities ample excuse for clearing them if it becomes politically advantageous to do so (ibid.).

Sometimes, however, squatting does begin with a popular invasion of a tract of what may be government land, or privately-owned marginal land, usually though not always on the perimeter of the city. As long as the sites themselves have little commercial value (they are often on waste land – a rubbish dump, marshland, or a mountainside as in Caracas) the squatters need not at first fear disturbance. When the government does attempt to remove them it is often because they have settled on a site to which urban growth has given development potential. Then the illegality and the environmental and health drawbacks of the squatter settlement begin all at once to loom large. If suburban, the site may be one which has now become attractive to rich people, seeking a semi-rural location for their luxurious dwellings. It is ironical that the poor and the rich may in this way be locked in competition for the same *lebensraum*. When this is the case, the outcome is only too predictable.

If the authorities do give them some kind of *de facto* recognition (ibid., pp. 72–4), perhaps by numbering the dwellings, or providing some rudimentary services, it is usually for reasons of political expediency. Gilbert and Ward (ibid., p. 172) distinguish between recognition based on what they call 'technical rationality', concerned with effectiveness and cost, and that based on 'political rationality', which aims to 'legitimize the state'. But the latter provides a very insecure kind of tenure. The basic illegality of a settlement is always available to the government as a means for an end if the political situation changes.

Once they do acquire tenure the residents of settlements find that, in a situation of land scarcity, they are the proprietors of valuable real estate, which they can they sublet or sell on a rising market (ibid., p. 69). But, in the face of this rise in land prices, the number who must rent because they cannot afford to buy increases (Amis, 1984). Those who rent in the settlements are probably the poorest of the squatters (Gilbert and Ward, 1985, pp. 121–7), which demonstrates the inequities in access to land, which invasions or illegal subdivisions do little ultimately to remedy. This is particularly blatant in some places where the letting of accommodation on such illegal sites has become a highly organised commercial activity. In Nairobi, for instance, landlords with as many as twenty units to let are not uncommon, and while some are sympathetic to those who cannot pay their rent, others evict the defaulters immediately (Amis, 1984). Those who rent are often the younger families, a factor which introduces a generational element into the hierarchy of deprivation.

Government action to ensure the allocation of sites on the basis of social priorities might meet the requirements of social justice better than the current hand-to-mouth approach through the legitimation of invasions and illegal subdivisions, but state regulation and planning of these developments does have its own problems, as will be seen.

Initially the settlement will be a sordid and unhealthy place. Dwellings will be leaky and overcrowded, and constructed of cheap materials which are bound to deteriorate rapidly, making them, as time goes on, even less suitable for human habitation. Of course there will be no services – water supply, sewerage, refuse disposal or electricity. The lack of any planning of the site will make it inaccessible and inconvenient, and life there stifling and full of conflict (Dwyer, 1975, pp. 2–6).

This state of affairs is sometimes not very long-lived (Ward, 1982). Inhabitants begin to organise themselves, or to utilise the organisation which already exists among them. For, as we have seen, squatting is not always a spontaneous act. There are cases on record in Latin America where much advanced planning has been undertaken, including the building up of carefully vetted lists of participants. Even if no form of co-operative organisation exists before the occupation takes place, it usually begins to emerge shortly thereafter.

An initial need for the squatters is to protect themselves from any attempt by the authorities to eject them. As with all communities, it soon becomes necessary also to regulate relationships between themselves. Somehow they have to learn to live together. Until the settlement has been officially recognised (and taxes begin to be paid) they can hardly expect this duty to be undertaken by the police and other civil authorities. Castells (1977, pp. 365ff) gives a vivid account of such developments in squatter settlements in Chile in the early 1970s.

Some squatter communities, however, are able to go very much further, and build up their own rudimentary social services, for which the city, even if it comes to accept their legitimacy, usually remains very unwilling to find money. These services include the enforcement of certain basic rules of social hygiene, the disposal of human and domestic waste, the supply of water and electricity, and sometimes even the provision of education. Meanwhile the dwellings themselves are improved and made more permanent. Drakakis-Smith cites areas around Ankara in Turkey as good examples of such developments (1979, p. 25).

These improvements do not take place in all squatter townships, and Dwyer at least considers such a course of events to be atypical (Dwyer, 1975, pp. 204–7). Huque (1982), on the basis of his study of four locations in Bangladesh, forecasts that standards in the settlements are more likely to deteriorate than to improve. On squatters in Semarang in Indonesia, whom the government stigmatise as 'non-citizens', Budihardjo writes (1985, p. 147), 'Due to their poverty and the existing problems of housing, education and backwardness in many aspects of life, the non-citizen people are in great need of outside help before they can begin to help themselves.'

Many settlements certainly do remain centres of poverty, disease and deprivation, lacking all facilities, and offering a constant invitation to 'modernising' governments to pull them down. If they are to be seen as a permanent feature of the urban scene in the Third World, it is necessary to find out what distinguishes those which do 'improve' from the rest.

Poverty, as Budihardjo indicates, is the most disabling factor. Beyond this, three factors seem to be important. The first is whether the squatters see themselves as permanent urban residents, or merely as visitors, who intend to return to their villages after what they hope will be a lucrative but limited stay in the town. Many of the Latin American settlements seem to be of the former kind, and those of sub-Saharan Africa (aided by government hostility) seem to be of the latter (Lea, 1979, p. 53).

The second requirement, if squatters are to invest their time and limited resources in improving conditions in the settlements, is that they must feel secure in the possession of their homes. If they have settled on sites which are privately owned, this will not happen unless the state is prepared to buy the land, or to make laws to require reluctant owners to sell. If ownership is traditional, as with land belonging to a family, a village or a tribe, there are different, but possibly even more complicated problems to be solved.

Nevertheless people will not want to make much of an effort to improve their living conditions if they feel that one day a private landlord, or the state, may snatch their home away from them. Both will have an additional incentive to do this if the site of a settlement has become valuable through improvements introduced by the squatters – for example the draining of swamps, the enhancement of the area's appearance or reputation, or the generation of business activity within it. This is of course only a further manifestation of the economic truth that landowners, unless they are prevented, will inherit the 'betterment' value of land in towns, although this is a social product, and properly belongs to those who created it. Land tenure is clearly as important for urban development as it has been seen to be for development in the rural areas.

A further factor, which applies to state policy in the provision of low-cost housing, and 'sites and services' schemes (see below) as well as to squatter settlements, is the standard of housing which the government feels should be enforced. In setting such standards, governments are often over-influenced by the example of the North, insisting on a level of provision which neither the residents nor the country can afford (Mabogunje, Hardoy and Misra, 1978).

There is increasingly, as a result of the work of Turner (1968b), a recognition that the adoption of an 'appropriate technology' in the field of housing will be required if progress in providing shelter for the urban population is to be made. Such a technology will be based more on the local life-style, and on indigenous ideas about building materials, space requirements and amenities (especially as influenced by the needs of the extended family) than on the not very relevant experience of the developed world (Dakhil, Ural and Tewfik, 1978: Kirke, 1985).

To emphasise the vitality which some of these communities show, writers like Turner (1969, p. 508) prefer to call them 'autonomous' rather than 'squatter' settlements – with all the implications of illegality which the latter term carries. It remains true that they are illegal, at least initially, and that their future will become assured only when they cease to be autonomous, that is, are recognised by the government, which then provides them with both security of tenure and services. For although squatters do often display great determination in providing services for themselves, as many an illicit line from the electrical mains cable shows, these are often dangerous makeshifts, and do nothing to integrate the squatters with the surrounding community.

Many governments have now undertaken settlement upgrading campaigns to aid and encourage improvement of the sites (Martin, 1983). But these, and other forms of implicit recognition by the state often bring with them regulation and the enforcement of standards as well as taxes and expensive services. These may blunt some of the buccaneering motivation which has led to the establishment of the settlements, and may even price them out of the reach of some people. In the end the prospect for the homeless may be worsened. The extra cost of official upgrading schemes is bound to have a particularly savage effect on the very poor among them. Nevertheless, properly used, there is a valuable dynamic to be drawn on here by governments aiming at the improvement of settlements, as projects in Zambia (Jere, 1984) and elsewhere (Shah, 1984) clearly show.

Sites and Services

Governments find the untidiness of these settlements an embarrassment, and object to the way in which their 'autonomy' frequently allows the residents to avoid paying their share of state and municipal taxes. Out of such considerations has emerged the now popular alternative of the 'site and services' scheme (Payne, 1984; Rodell, 1983), in which illegal squatting is to be replaced by the controlled occupation of government sites which have been prepared in advance. Attempts to eliminate the settlements without providing an alternative usually meant that they were almost immediately established elsewhere, but many governments have begun to develop 'sites and services' policies as that alternative.

These will not replace the squatter settlements unless they can meet certain requirements. The first is that enough sites can be prepared to meet the need – which the cost makes an improbable supposition. The cost to the potential squatter is also important. Will it be low enough to be afforded by poor people, and to compete with tax-free and sometimes rent-free squatting? This will depend in part on whether the government makes unrealistic demands as to the level of services to be provided and the standards of houses to be erected on the site.

People in underdeveloped countries have many kinship and similar communal sources from which they can obtain labour and traditional building materials, but most of the work in sites and services schemes is still done by hired labour (Rodell, 1983, pp. 30–1). The schemes would offer more scope for the poor if the self-help potentials inherent in the extended family were released and stimulated. Settlers could then build within their own budgets and to their own requirements. It is one of the advantages of uncontrolled building in the settlements, according to Turner (1968b) and also United Nations (1976), that settlers can match their dwellings to their own budgets and needs in this way.

Instead, up to half of the more expensively serviced plots in Zambia were still empty by the time that all the plots with more basic provision had been taken up. The relative failure of Tanzania's policy of insisting on expensive 'core' houses points in the same direction (Rodell, 1983, pp. 33–4). This is quite apart from what residents may feel to be the inappropriateness of an imposed 'core-house' design (ibid., p. 30).

Mutizwa-Mangiza (1985, pp. 93) estimates that, among the poor of Harare, Zimbabwe, '42 per cent cannot afford any of the available housing options; 36 per cent can afford a serviced site without any core and 7 per cent a 'wet core' (that is with WC and shower only). Of the remainder, five per cent can afford a one-room core; 2 per cent can afford a two-room core; 1 per cent can afford a three-room core; and only 7 per cent can afford a four-room core, the minimum specified by government policy.' The further government requirement that the four-room core must be completed within eighteen months administers the final *coup de grâce* to any suggestion that the scheme provides a solution to the shelter problems of low-income families.

In contrast, Malawi, where families are allowed a high level of autonomy, is one of the few countries to house as much as 10 per cent of its population in these projects (ibid., p. 38). It is experiences such as these which have led Guhr (1983, p. 102) to argue for the elimination of controls, so that 'low income house-builders can in public sector projects embark upon house production on similar conditions to those prevailing in unplanned settlements'.

There is clearly a tension between the requirements of organic and spontaneous growth (on which any improvement in the Third World problem of homelessness must depend) and the need for rational planning in the urban areas. Plans are required not only for efficient site development, but also to relate this properly to off-site provision, such as transport and jobs, as well as sewerage, refuse disposal and water supply. Kirke (1985, p. 37) describes a master plan in Cairo to supply treated water for domestic use at the rate of 50 litres per capita daily, even though half of the domestic housing stock was not equipped with outlets to utilise more than a tiny fraction of this.

Ward (1984, p. 152) argues that the real costs of providing

shelter will escalate anyway, with the general lowering of living standards in a Third World country and the inevitable increases in land prices which population pressure brings about. It is not surprising in these circumstances that many even of those who acquire sites leave them unused for long periods of time. Ward (ibid.) speaks of 50 per cent of plots in some Mexican projects still being unoccupied after a year and a half. An incidental disadvantage of such piecemeal development is the lack for a long time of any sense of community on an estate (ibid.).

Cross-subsidisation between better- and worse-off households, perhaps through a differential pricing system for sites, would do something to equalise the burden of land costs. Another proposal is to subsidise the poorer families by appropriating for their benefit the 'betterment' in land and property values which their occupation of the site brings to an area (Dix, 1985, p. 5). Zimbabwe has also attempted to control escalating construction costs by encouraging local authorities to establish 'housing brigades', which are then given a monopoly in the construction of low-income housing. Another aim of this, incidentally, is to provide more stable employment for building workers than that made available by the private construction industry (Mutizwa-Mangiza, 1985, pp. 86–7).

In general, housing subsidies are frowned on by the professional planners (Dix, 1985, pp. 5–6), on the grounds that they reduce the householder's sense of responsibility. Some even object to the government's meeting all the costs of off-site infrastructure (Tym, 1985, p. 31), but this view seems to be animated more by Northern individualistic ideas about motivation and incentives than by the traditional collective values of the Third World. Direct state subsidies may, however, limit a government's ability to expand its shelter programme, which is why cross-subsidisation may be preferable as a way of reducing the burden on the poor.

Employment

The main obstacle to improving conditions of life for the low-income residents of the settlements and the slums, as well as of the 'sites and services' projects, is the lack of work opportunities, and the *Habitat Report* (United Nations, 1976) emphasised the importance of planning for employment as well as shelter. Jobs in the formal sector are few. Where they do exist they are often in the central area, remote from either sites or settlements, with transport which is both inadequate and expensive.

The Informal Sector

In the absence of conventional waged employment, some occupants of the slums or the settlements seek a living in the informal economy, for example as street traders, or workers at home or in other informal workshops. Standing (1981, p. 568) points out, however, that it is anything but a 'free entry or "sponge" sector'. Where it does not consist of 'illegitimate activities or begging and "informal" employment relief, it often has highly structured labour and product markets with considerable costs of entry, while average incomes are liable to be very low'. It is often of considerable size. A study in a Uruguayan city (Portes *et al*, 1986) found that it absorbed a quarter of the city's labour force. It also contained marked class differences: many informal workers were not self-employed but worked either for other, better-off informal workers, or for people who were themselves employees in the formal sector. This study also reported average pay which was about half that of other workers, women receiving even less.

Modernising governments, embarrassed by the visibility and untidiness of some of these occupations, may try to restrict their development or, where this is not possible, to regulate them, perhaps gathering them together in 'market-places'. On the other hand, and although they are often exploitative, they are seen by some acute observers as valuable growing-points for the economy, providing incomes and services for the poor, as well as an avenue of upward mobility for the more enterprising (Marris and Somerset, 1971).

Informal occupations are often rooted in the slum or squatter areas of a city, and their fate is then tied up with slum clearance or redevelopment programmes. Unfortunately the regulatory activity of the state in restricting or even prohibiting informal employment in housing project areas often makes the work situation worse than it need be (Marris, 1981, p. 77).

Elite Housing

No picture of the Third World in complete without some reference to occupational housing. In the North, the 'tied cottage' particularly in agriculture, has been seen in the past as a mark of servitude, binding the worker to his employer no matter how bad his pay or his conditions of work, because he dare not risk losing his home. In the Third World this is also more likely to be true of the countryside in, say, sugar or tea plantations, than in the town.

In the city, in contrast, the accommodation provided by an employer is a mark of privilege. TNCs will provide their expatriate executives with cheap or even free accommodation which is usually superior to what they would be able to afford at home, and places them, in the Third World, among the rich. Senior civil servants, and of course politicians, are similarly located high in the local pecking order by their grateful governments. These examples of subsidies for the rich, transfers of wealth from poor to rich, are as unjustified as the housing subsidies for the middle class, represented by government-built and financed low-cost housing. The beneficiaries of this new version of the 'tied cottage' reside in pleasant suburbs or on cool hillsides, with the local upper classes – the professionals (especially lawyers), the import–export merchants who make money by satisfying the 'Northern' tastes of the local bourgeoisie, and the native executives and satellite businessmen, who draw large incomes through the operations of the TCNs.

The very richest are not alone of course in benefiting from underdevelopment and the poverty of many of their fellow citizens. Although TNCs employ much casual labour, the small numbers of skilled local workers whom they need to employ on a permanent basis can receive high incomes by Third World standards, as well as occupational welfare benefits such as housing, pensions and medical attention.

The United Nations declared 1987 to be International Year of Shelter for the Homeless. It is to be hoped that this has meant a recommitment of themselves by Third World governments to the provision of adequate housing for their people, but a recognition at the same time that this cannot be achieved if they follow the Northern model of urban planning on the basis of high technology, high capital costs, and high energy consumption; or, as in recent years, of relying on the operation of a free-market in housing. New patterns have to be found, more in keeping with the economic and social circumstances of the poor countries of the south. They will need help. The countries of the North should recognise that any aid for shelter provision would be a profitable investment in human capital.

Ghetto Life

The existence of slums, and the locations found for low-cost housing developments, squatter settlements and 'site and service' schemes, on the one hand, and the salubrious settings of private sector and upper-echelon occupational developments on the other, mean that these cities reflect the kind of residential segregation by class (Gilbert and Ward, 1985, pp. 62–5) which has shaped city development in the North also.

This is what establishes not only an underprivileged ghetto environment for the urban poor, but also enables a local culture of poverty, in the sense in which this term has been used by Oscar Lewis (1967), to emerge. It is not uncommon for such areas to display high rates of family breakdown, crime and delinquency, mental illness and illiteracy, as well, of course, as unemployment and poverty.

They also often possess qualities to which Lewis devoted less attention. These include a neighbourliness and understanding of (and also a lively curiosity about) each other's problems, as well as a willingness to help, so far as their poverty permits, which is lacking in areas occupied by the better-heeled.

In recent years there has been more interest in the idea of mixing social classes within a housing area, especially in 'sites and services' projects. If this proved practicable without raising rents for poor families, or causing them to be squeezed out by 'gentrification', it would have a dramatic effect on the quality of the environment. Bourgeois residents would not put up with the bad conditions found in ghetto areas, and would have the political know-how and muscle to do something about them. It might also enable cost-sharing for amenities to take place, to the advantage of the poor (Crooke, 1983, p. 175). Reference has already been made to the possibility of even more radical cross-subsidisation in the purchase of sites.

Exhibit 4.2   Squatting as exploitation

Roberts (1982, p. 379) writes:

> Part of the reason for industrial investment in the developing world is the relative cheapness of labor there in comparison with the advanced capitalist world. The urban environment is not, however, conducive to cheap labor. Costs of housing, of transport, of utilities, and of the total reliance on the market for food and clothing push up the costs of subsistence and thus the minimum wage that workers need to survive. The cheapness of urban labor in developing societies thus depends, as Portes has pointed out, on the availability of products and services that are produced with a minimum cash outlay, outside the formal capitalist system, on the basis of largely unpaid personal labour. Squatter settlements are a form of mutual aid in which people obtain land at minimal cost and build housing themselves, often from materials begged or scavenged. Squatting and self-construction is thus an integral part of a pattern of capitalist development based on wages that are so low that they are insufficient to pay the costs of regular housing.

If social mixing also increases social cohesion, those (like Fanon, 1980) who see these areas as potential cradles of revolution would regret the change. In fact, neither expectation is very certain to be realised. The admixture of social classes often leads to conflict which exacerbates social divisions (Leeds, 1981, p. 57). On the other hand, far from constituting a radical force, these deprived populations are often highly conservative (Gilbert and Ward, 1985, p. 15).

The problem of urban poverty is concentrated in the city-centre slums, where the poor live their lives under conditions of hopelessness and degradation. Not only do they suffer privation and lack opportunities, but, infected as they are by the more dysfunctional features of the culture of poverty, they soon give up the struggle to find work and maintain standards. And given their circumstances, this is a realistic position to take up. Succour provided for individual families living in these ghettos will, by itself, solve few problems. The corrupting physical environment and dispiriting psychological climate can only be dealt with by broadly-based community development projects (see Chapter 10).

Some Marxists see the herding of the poor into the slums and the settlements of Third World cities as part of the process of capitalist exploitation through underdevelopment. This critique is particularly directed against the squatter settlements, and the arguments of Turner and his supporters that they should be legitimised and improved. Thus Ward (1982, pp. 89–90) says that the settlements 'allow a large, permanent, industrial reserve army of labour to be cheaply installed in the cities'. This is a line of argument which might also be marshalled against sites and services schemes, with their self-built homes or cheap 'core' houses. Roberts also sees the other problematic aspects of the city, such as the informal sector of employment, in the same light: as props to a form of capitalist exploitation which could not exist without them.

If the ghetto fulfils such a latent function in maintaining the existence of an exploitable underclass, it is not likely to be replaced by a mixed area crossing class lines. Whatever advantages there might be in such a development for the poor, there is little in it for the better-off. Given the structural role attributed to it, how could there be?

Housing the Poor

Does all this mean that the avoidable suffering caused by home-lessness and slum life has to be tolerated? No doubt in the long run the millennium will be achieved, but in the long run we shall also all be dead – including many of the would-be inhabitants of these areas, deprived in the short run of the means of shelter. We do not have to accept the pessimistic view that, unless the world can be changed, nothing can be achieved. In Voltaire's famous phrase, the best is often the enemy of the good.

The cost and availability of land is the main impediment to progress, which suggests that land reform may have a part to play in the towns as well as the villages. A radical policy for a government which could summon up enough political will (and some governments would not even want to do this could start with a policy aimed, like that in the rural areas, at making land available to those who need it. As part of such a programme, government sites would be opened up for housing purposes, and privately owned land, if it was not being used for a justifiable purpose, would be subject to compulsory purchase. The doctrine of the public creation of betterment in urban land would be applied in fixing the purchase price.

After installing the minimum of essential services, self-building would be encouraged as the only practicable route to mass housing in a poor country. So far as resources permitted, the government would supplement this by constructing a variety of core houses which were within the means of the poor, and simple low-cost accommodation for rent.

While granting tenure to the householder, there is a strong case for the ownership of the land to remain either with the state or some other public agency – perhaps a housing co-operative responsible for the development of the site. This would ensure that, when the property was sold, the windfall accruing from the shortage of land would return to the community and not help to create a new privileged class with a stake in that shortage.

Summary

Urbanisation is proceeding faster in the Third World than it did in the North, a particular feature of this being the growth of very large primate cities. This is attributed to the joint effects of the neglect of the rural areas and the associated enclave development in urban centres. Problems of congestion, unhygienic living conditions and inadequate housing are the results. The limited amount of development which has taken place in the towns is also insufficient to occupy all those who have been attracted to them, so that there is mass unemployment.

Many of those who would otherwise be unemployed have found a living in the informal sector of employment. Untidy and unpopular with modernising elites though such employment may be, there is an increasing tendency to value it as a growing point for a dynamic society. Nevertheless action is required to try to achieve a more broadly-based industrial and commercial economy in the city. This must go side by side with a revival of agriculture in the rural areas in order to stem and even perhaps reverse the flow of migrants into the towns.

The immediate priority, meanwhile, on grounds of health as well as quality of life, is to improve the social infrastructure of the cities, as well as to alleviate the shortage of acceptable housing. The inner-city slums call most urgently for attention, but attention is often also attracted to the squatter settlements found on the outskirts. Some of these are exploitative and remain squalid and unhealthy places to live. Others are more spontaneous in origin, and represent for the residents a move up from the slums. Given favourable conditions (of which secure tenure is one of the most important), they can be helped to raise the standards of shelter and services which they furnish.

Government 'low-cost' houses cannot be afforded in sufficient numbers to satisfy the need, and in any case are too expensive for most of those who require shelter. The alternative is for the government to provide 'sites and services', sometimes associated with 'core houses' of varying size and cost. The main objections to these schemes have been concerned with the cost of the basic provision, or the high standards of building which government regulations enforce. Also core houses, when included, have been criticised as inappropriate to the needs of those who are supposed to occupy them, or as over-elaborate and therefore too expensive.

It is doubtful whether 'sites and services' will compete successfully with the settlements unless they can offer similar opportunities for autonomous development. These would include the option of putting up the house oneself (possibly with the help of friends and kinsfolk), and building to a standard and pattern which suits your needs and your resources. There is an obvious dilemma for authorities who want to raise standards, though the dilemma is less acute if they do not insist on inappropriate Western standards.

The segregation of social classes in different residential areas tends to perpetuate differences in the amenities provided. More mixing of social classes, with differential charges for land and services according to ability to pay, is one way which has been proposed for improving the quality of life of the poorer residents. Some Marxists, however, see the poor 'ghettos' as a way of 'reproducing' labour at low cost, to the advantage of the capitalist.

5

Development and Health

The human and social costs of ill-health do not require elaboration: the physical and mental suffering, the death and bereavement, and the deleterious effects on social and family relationships, either as a direct result of illness or of the economic privation which it brings in its train. Its impact on development in its narrower, purely economic sense, is no less serious (Abel-Smith and Leiserson, 1978).

Reference has already been made to the importance attached by the World Bank, on economic as well as social grounds, to what it calls 'human capital'. Weisbrod *et al.* (1973, p. 25) distinguish between the direct and indirect increments to output which result from improved health. The direct gains include less absenteeism from work or school, greater physical and mental productivity, and longer working lives. Indirect gains are seen mainly as a reduction in the costs of caring for the sick.

Weisbrod seems to have had in the forefront of his mind the more tangible consequences of a country's state of health, but one should not underestimate the significance of less easily measured factors, notably the positive motivation which may be evoked in a country which looks after the health of its people – the sense of being a member of a caring community, in which they therefore feel they have a stake. This is potentially a cumulative process of improvement, for high communal morale in itself seems to increase resistance to disease.

A policy for health is thus not only essential for social welfare, but also as part of any realistic plan for economic development.

It is therefore disturbing to discover (Morley *et al.*, 1983, p. ix) that public expenditure on health in the South averages US$11 per capita as compared with US$320 in the North. This suggests that the emphasis placed by the World Bank on cost-benefit analysis (World Bank, 1988) misses the main point. The underdeveloped countries just cannot afford to invest adequately in health, no matter how economically that investment is managed.

Mortality

It is against such a background that the health problems of underdeveloped countries, as reflected in their death rates and figures for life expectation have to be understood. Statistical data on these, as on so many other social phenomena in the Third World, are neither very complete nor very reliable. They are most dependable for the larger and more prosperous countries. In these countries they will also usually be the most favourable, for obvious reasons. The health situation in many of the poorer Third World countries can therefore be assumed to be worse than that presented in the Table 5.1.

Apart from the dramatic improvement in China and India, the main feature of these figures is the correlation between life expectancy and level of economic development. Even within the middle income group there persist substantial differences between lower- and upper-income countries. It has been estimated that about two-thirds of the variances in life expectancy at birth and in

Table 5.1 Life expectancy at birth (years), developed and less developed countries, 1965 and 1986 (World Bank, 1986, pp. 232–3; 1988, pp. 222–3)

	1965	1986
Low-income Economies	50	61
(excluding China & India)	44	52
(China & India)	52	64
Middle-income economies	52	63
(lower)	48	59
(upper)	58	67
High-income oil exporters	48	64
Soviet bloc	69	69
Industrial market economies	71	76

infant mortality are associated with income differences between the countries concerned (Cumper, 1983, pp. 27–8). But wealth is not the whole story, as is shown by a comparison of the high-income oil exporters with countries like Hungary, Poland and Yugoslavia. The latter have less than one-third of the GNP of the former but their life expectancy is some five years more. Social ideologies also play a part.

Further evidence for this view comes from the Indian state of Kerala. With a lower per capita income and higher population density than most of the rest of India, but with a greater commitment to social welfare, it has surpassed them in a whole range of social indices such as education, nutrition and the control of fertility. Not surprisingly this has been reflected in death and infantile mortality rates which are better than those of most of the other Indian states, including some of the richest and most powerful among them (Ratcliffe, 1983 pp. 64ff).

It should be remembered that these are not merely statistics. It must surely be intolerable that the average expectation of life for residents of the poorest Third World countries should be fifteen years less than that in the North. For most of the low-income countries (that is, all except China and India) this difference averages 24 years, and in some of the very poorest the situation is even worse. Thus life expectancy in Afghanistan (in 1982, the last year for which statistics are available) was only 36 years (World Bank, 1984, p. 262). Life expectancy in Sierra Leone in 1986 was 41 years, and in Guinea, 42 years (World Bank, 1988, p. 222). Eighteen out of the 37 poorest countries had life expectancies in the forties (ibid.).

Only very modest comfort may be taken from the improvement of eight years in average life-span in the low-income countries, excluding China and India, since 1965. It is a small enough gain in a period of more than twenty years, during which dramatic advances have been made in the fight against certain epidemic diseases prevalent in the tropics, particularly smallpox and malaria. And small as it is, it presents once again, as an average, an over-optimistic picture of the progress made in some countries. Uganda and Ethiopia, for example, appear to have gained only about three years in life expectancy between 1965 and 1986. The figures for Rwanda seem actually to have deteriorated by a year (World Bank, 1986, p. 232; 1988, p. 222). There has also been an ominous resurgence in malaria in recent years, partly as a result of the growing resistance of the mosquito to insecticides and the bacillus to vaccines.

An alternative measure to life expectancy is the mortality rate. Crude or overall death rates are misleading because of the large numbers of infant and child deaths in underdeveloped countries, which tend to swamp the average figures. Mortality rates in the younger age groups are presented in Table 5.2, which brings out the true enormity of the position. Infant mortality in the low-income countries (exclusive of China and India) is still running at over twelve times that in the Northern capitalist countries. Even their rate of improvement has been less – though once again China and India have done better than the rest.

It is well known that women in Europe and America live longer than men, but this is not confined to developed countries. In almost all the countries of the Third World women are the more viable sex. Occasionally, at very high levels of mortality, a country's female death rate exceeds that for males, and in Asia it tends to do so in infancy and during the child-bearing ages. An official Indian government publication (United Nations, 1982a, pp. 124–5) puts this down to a preference for male offspring, who therefore receive more care and attention. This brings out the importance to be attached to indigenous cultural practices in formulating a health policy in an underdeveloped country. In this

Table 5.2   Infant and child death rates (per 1000) in developed and less developed countries, 1965 and 1985 (World Bank, 1986, pp. 232–3)

	Infant (age 0–1)		Child mortality (age 1–4)	
	1965	1985	1965	1985
Low-income economies	127	72	19	9
(excluding China & India)	150	112	27	19
(China & India)	116	58	16	6
Middle-income economies	104	68	17	8
(lower)	132	82	22	11
(upper)	84	52	11	4
High-income oil exporters	115	61	33	5
Industrial market economies	23	9	1	NK
Others	33	32	3	4

NK = Not known

connection, the low status of women in many Third World cultures, leading sometimes to overwork and poor feeding, can exist, it seems, side by side with what is in general a longer life-span than that of males.

Disease Patterns

In spite of the regional variations outlined above, there are striking differences between the diseases prevalent in the South *per se*, and those of the countries of the North (see Table 5.3). This table does not include malnutrition, although there is no doubt about its significance as a debilitator, but it does bring out the relatively great significance of the group of infectious and parasitic diseases. It also indicates the scale of the Third World health problem as a whole, as compared with that of the industrialised countries. These differences are attributable in part to climatic conditions, partly to an underdeveloped infrastructure, but also simply to poverty and undernourishment.

Table 5.3 Number of deaths in major categories of cause by WHO region (thousands) (World Health Organisation, 1987, p. 72)

	Developing Countries	%	Developed Countries	%
Infectious & parasitic diseases*	16 020	40	810	8
Neoplasms	2 200	5	2 050	19
Circulatory and certain degenerative diseases†	7 620	19	5 710	54
Perinatal conditions	3 080	8	170	2
Injury and poisoning	1 980	5	690	6
Others and unknown	9 240	23	1 240	12

*Including diarrhoeal diseases, influenza, pneumonia, emphysema and asthma.
†Including diabetes mellitus, stomach and duodenal ulcer, chronic liver disease and cirrhosis, nephritis, nephrotic syndrome and nephrosis.

Prominent among the causes of death or sickness, then, are malnutrition, malaria and other infections carried by vectors of hosts, and diarrhoea. And side by side with the ancient curse of leprosy has appeared the newly identified menace of AIDS. The diseases of children are a cause for particular concern.

Malnutrition

This is the most important of all killers and debilitators. The World Health Organisation (WHO) (1987, p. 223) estimates that 430 million, or 10 per cent of the world's population, are affected, most of them, of course, in the underdeveloped countries. About 12 per cent of Third World children suffer from acute malnutrition and 39 per cent from chronic malnutrition. Another 41 per cent are underweight for their age (WHO, 1987, p. 90). The proportions now are probably very much higher in Africa, as a result of the ravages wrought by recent drought, crop failure and war.

In the more extreme form of malnutrition, kwashiorkor, the body may eventually be unable to digest food, even if it can be provided. About ten million children under the age of five are estimated to be suffering from this condition (WHO, 1987, p. 88). Kwashiorkor occurs mainly in Africa, around the age of two, when weaning at last takes place, By this time the mother's supply of breast milk has fallen off, and the porridge onto which the child is transferred has (in common with the diet of adults in these poor communities) little nutritive value (Whitehead, 1977, p. 59).

As well as deaths directly due to malnutrition, which contribute significantly to infant mortality, it resembles malaria in weakening resistance to other diseases, and thus adding to the death and sickness rates in this way also. When the results of a number of Latin American studies were combined, malnutrition was found to be a contributory cause of death, among infants under five, in 47 per cent of all diseases, reaching about 60 per cent in infective and parasitic conditions such as diarrhoea and measles (Sanders, 1985, p. 22).

Diarrhoeal Conditions

Stomach infections resulting from either polluted food or water supplies are also widespread, causing both illness and death. According to the WHO: 'it has been estimated that in 1975, there were about 500 million episodes of diarrhoea in children under 5 years of age in Asia, Africa and Latin America. These episodes, coupled with – for example – poor nutritional status, malaria, or lack of immunisation, resulted in at least 5 million deaths' (WHO, 1980, p. 88).

Among these conditions the number of countries reporting cholera for the first time has been reduced by nearly two-thirds since the mid-1970s, but 'it has become endemic in a larger number of countries, especially in Africa' (WHO, 1987, p. 76). Vaccines exist, but they are by no means infallible, and progress in immunisation is slow (WHO, 1980, p. 88). A reduction in diarrhoeal illness generally must depend on better sanitary arrangements and purer water supplies in the affected countries. Where these have been made available, the WHO notes that control is more effective. Progress in oral rehydration, by making up the fluid loss, has done much to reduce the number of deaths from all of the acute forms of the illness in recent years (WHO, 1987, p. 76; 1980, p. 88).

Vector-borne Disease

Apart from malnutrition and diarrhoea, the chief scourge of the tropics remains malaria. A calculation of the 'number of days of healthy life lost' through sickness and death shows, for example, that over 10 per cent of the total in Ghana was due to it (Morrow, 1983, pp. 283–4). At one time it looked as though, like smallpox, it was on the way out, largely as a result of the systematic spraying with insecticides of the pools and swamps in which the malaria-bearing mosquitoes bred. Quinine and its derivatives were also found to be effective in controlling the disease once it had been contracted.

The emergence of resistance among both mosquitoes and bacteria, in South America, Asia, and, more recently, Africa has changed all that, and trends are again upward. This was so in 9 out of 17 countries reviewed between 1979 and 1983, about half of the cases reported (2·6 million) coming from South-east Asia (WHO, 1987, p. 78). New prophylactics have suffered the same fate as the older ones based on quinine. The World Health Organisation has called for urgency in the search for preparations which can circumvent this resistance (WHO, 1983b, p. 79).

The mosquito can only communicate malaria if there are people in the community who already have it, but it is almost impossible to locate for treatment a large proportion of the cases of the disease because it is so widespread that people begin to take it for granted – as happened with smallpox in eighteenth-century Britain. Moreover distinguishing the fever due to malaria from other possible causes of fever is impossible without blood tests. As in previous successful campaigns, the priority must therefore be to kill the mosquitos by spraying their breeding areas.

Another major affliction is bilharzia (schistosomiasis): two hundred million are infected, and 5–600 million exposed to it in 71 countries (WHO, 1987, p. 78). It is the result of infestation by a parasitic flatworm carried by the snails which breed in tropical waters. Like malaria it does not always kill, but produces a lassitude which impairs the quality of life, as well as the sick person's contribution to society. New drugs are showing promise but real progress must depend on better control of water supplies. A discovery with cautionary implications for rural development is the breeding of the snails in irrigation ditches in some countries.

Filariasis (WHO,1980) is communicated by a parasitic worm carried by mosquitoes. Its near-relative, onchocerciasis ('river blindness') threatens perhaps as many as 300 million in Africa, Asia and the Pacific. Onchocerciasis is one of the most important causes of blindness in African countries, but its virtual elimination by a successful campaign against it in the Volta River basin offers real prospects of its conquest in other parts of the world also (WHO, 1987, p. 778).

There are other forms of infestation by parasitic worms with similar debilitating effects on what are still substantial numbers of people. Leishmaniasis, for instance, is carried by sandflies, and leads to boils and fevers. In all of these water-borne diseases the method of choice must be the insecticidal treatment of vector breeding-sites.

Sleeping sickness is the African form of a disease called trypano-somiasis. The former is endemic in West Africa, threatening about 35 million people a year (9000 cases annually according to the WHO's Sixth World Report: 1980, p. 87). The control of the tsetse fly, which carries the microbe, is hampered by the cost of insect-icides and the shortage of qualified manpower.

There is also an American form, found in the slums of Latin America. Destruction of the reduviid bugs, whose excreta carry American trypanosomiasis is, at present, the only practical policy for bringing the disease under control but, apart from the cost of such an approach, the bug is developing a resistance to existing insecticides. In the long run, improvement in the poor housing and sanitary conditions which encourage the bug must be the method of choice. Trypanosomiasis in both its forms is a much smaller problem than either malaria or bilharzia, for instance, but its localised nature gives it special significance in particular areas.

Leprosy and AIDS

Although leprosy is still found throughout the tropics and has developed resistance to the drugs used to treat it, experimentation on curative measures continues. Unfortunately many cases are discovered late, when much tissue damage has occurred, and the WHO (1980, pp. 91–2) rightly points to the need for better ascertainment. Treatment therefore being difficult, it is surprising that, as with tuberculosis, the WHO's report says nothing about the importance which as, an alternative, ought to be attached to better housing and more hygienic personal habits as a way of preventing the transmission of the disease. For leprosy is contagious only through fairly continuous personal contact. The WHO estimates that there were about 10.6 million cases at the time that its Seventh Report was published (1987, p. 76).

The world has lived with leprosy throughout history, but has now to come to terms with a new threat in the shape of AIDS. Although this is reaching epidemic proportions in parts of Africa, the main strategy of the developed countries, that is of focussing attention on vulnerable groups, mainly drug abusers and homosexuals, has little to contribute. A solution calls for an effective vaccine until such time as the causes of the disease have been discovered.

Blindness

Nothing better illustrates the price which has to be paid for poverty than blindness. The WHO estimate that at least two-thirds of this could be prevented or cured by the application of existing knowledge (WHO, 1987, p. 98). Cataract is the commonest cause, accounting for more than half of all cases. Occurring usually among the ageing in the developed countries, it affects mainly the young in the South. Among pre-school children blindness most often results from vitamin A deficiency (xeropthalmia) (WHO, 1987, pp. 86, 92). Both conditions could be readily and cheaply treated, but all too often this does not happen because of the poverty of the individuals or the countries involved. Even the most ardent protagonists of economic growth, in the World Bank and elsewhere, should be able to see that this is a form of human investment which would pay dividends.

At least in the case of 'river blindness' (oncherciasis) and also trachoma (another form of communicable blindness) some progress seems to have been made.

Childhood Diseases

Diarrhoeal infection mainly affects children, and is, with malnutrition and respiratory illnesses such as pneumonia, the main cause of child and infant mortality (Jelliffe, 1970, p. 13.1). More recently the United Nations Children's Fund (UNICEF) has begun to focus its attention on the unnecessary mortality among infants and young children caused by what it calls the 'big six': tuberculosis, diphtheria, tetanus, whooping cough, measles and poliomyelitis. These can be tackled by a single relatively inexpensive innoculation, and the aim was to immunise all children against them by 1990. It is clear now that this will not be realised. Some progress has been made, mainly in Latin America, but in other parts of the world, especially in Africa, it is still slow (WHO, 1987, pp. 39–40).

Diseases of 'Civilisation'

Meanwhile the diseases of the North, no respecters of national or climatic boundaries, have begun to penetrate into the tropical countries also. Runaway urbanisation with its accompaniment of unsatisfactory living conditions, together with poor nutrition, seems to have caused tuberculosis, at last under control in the developed countries, to emerge now as a very serious problem. About three and a half million people contract it and it kills more than half a million, mostly in the Third World, though even here rates of infection vary widely. In view of the efficacy of drugs in curing tuberculosis, the number of deaths reflects the inadequacy of treatment services in many countries.

As already mentioned, a world campaign is under way for the innoculation of children in order to reduce the ravages of the disease and the burden which widespread infection imposes on both individuals and countries. It is generally accepted that unsatisfactory living conditions can increase susceptibility to infection, but this fact receives no attention in the reference to this disease in the World Health Organisation's *Reports on the World Health Situation* (1980, 1987).

Another disease of the North which is now becoming a significant cause of death in the South is cancer. It is argued by the WHO that this is because deaths from some other potent killers are becoming less frequent (ibid., p. 104), but in the light of the research of the last decade it is difficult not to connect it with the increase in smoking in the Third World (United Nations, 1985b, p. 159). It is perhaps a further part of the price paid for the activities of transnationals: the current contraction of the market for cigarettes in the North has led the giant tobacco companies to seek new markets for their products in the South (Taylor, 1984). Major advertising campaigns and even bribery (ibid., pp. 263–7), have been used to increase their sales.

The resistance of the governments of some poor countries is weakened by their dependence on tobacco as a cash crop which provides them with employment for their peoples, tax revenue, and exports (ibid., pp. 242–60). The World Bank, and even the Food and Agriculture Organisation of the United Nations, collude with them in this, seeing these economic advantages as more important than the lethal impact of smoking on the populations of the countries concerned (ibid., pp. 242–5).

Cardio-vascular disease, a product of the stresses of 'civilisation', (and possibly of tobacco), is showing signs of following in the wake of cancer (WHO, 1987, p. 96).

Social Causes

The above brief and admittedly incomplete appraisal of the disease picture does at least bring out the role of socio-economic factors associated with poverty. Nutritional deficiencies, infestation by disease-carrying vectors and parasitic worms, lack of pure water and other insanitary living conditions – all play their part in producing the high levels of sickness and mortality. Cross-national comparisons made under the auspices of the World Bank (Cochrane *et al.*, 1980, p. 30) show that 'per capita income is highly correlated with life expectancy in all periods examined' (see also Table 5.1, above), yielding pride of place only to literacy.

Differences in death rates within a country, varying dramatically according to social class, the educational level of mothers, and rural or urban residence point in the same direction. Consider, for example, the figures for infant and child mortality in Tanzania given in Table 5.4. The correlation with social class is one found also in the developed countries (WHO, 1980, pp. 47–50). This only underlines the general point being made, but the very much higher general mortality levels give proportionately greater significance to such class differences in the Third World. The high rates among the agricultural self-employed give some inkling of the privations which the plight of the rural areas imposes on the families of peasant farmers.

The connection with the mother's educational level shown in Table 5.4 is not found in Sri Lanka or (as Table 5.5 shows) in Ghana, but Table 5.5 does suggest that they may be exceptions

Table 5.4   Child mortality according to characteristics of parents, Tanzania, 1973 (United Nations, 1982a, p. 177)

	Probable death rate per 1000 before age of:		
	1 year	*3 years*	*5 years*
Mother's education (years)			
0	113	126	151
1–4	106	107	131
5–8	83	59	74
9–13	41	29	28
Occupation of household head			
Professional	80	62	75
Clerical/sales	82	85	118
Other non-agricultural	101	100	135
Agricultural self-employed	114	128	150
Agricultural paid	94	118	165

Table 5.5   Proportion of children dying by age 2 years in various less developed countries, according to mother's level of education (United Nations, 1982a, p. 178)

	No education	Primary	Upper primary
Ethiopia	0·179	0·137	0·012
Gambia	0·275	0·194	0·118
Ghana	0·106	0·148	0·102
Sierra Leone	0·217	0·137	0·103
Zambia	0·174	0·164	0·093

which prove the rule. The conclusion of the World Bank review on the significance of literacy for general mortality has already been noted above. The same study, reporting on within-country differences in infant and child mortality, estimates that an additional year of schooling for mothers results in a reduction of nine per thousand in the expected mortality rate of children (Cochrane *et al.*, 1980, p. 52).

Higher death rates in rural as compared with urban areas have been found in many underdeveloped societies. The United Nations (1982a, pp. 177–181) give figures which show adverse rural/urban ratios of varying sizes for infant and child mortality in a range of countries from all parts of the underdeveloped world. The special hazards presented by the congested and unhygienic conditions in which many town-dwellers live (which do cause high rates both of mortality and sickness in some of the more deprived urban areas (Harpham *et al.*, 1985) seem to be outweighed overall by the poverty and lack of amenities in the country areas, and the concentration of social (including medical) services in the towns. Interestingly enough, Sri Lanka is again an exception.

Also to be taken into account, however, is the fact that the villages are the strongholds of traditional ideas, including ideas about diet, hygiene and the treatment of disease. Sometimes these ideas represent an accumulation of ancestral wisdom which serves the villagers well, but at other times they embody practices which, if they ever had any value, have long lost it. Sometimes they are positively harmful. Changing such deeply-rooted beliefs is an important role for health services in the Third World. It is worth noting in this connection that the mortality differential between educated and other mothers, already referred to, exists in the countryside as well as the town.

Exhibit **5.1 Mothers' education and child mortality rates**

How could the level of mothers' education affect child mortality? The beneficial effect of the mother's education may in part reflect the economically privileged position of educated mothers, education being as inequitably distributed as other elements in the standard of life. Lower socio-economic status implies a lower standard of life, including nutrition and housing conditions, and poorer amenities such as water supply and sewage and refuse removal. As already indicated, the more prosperous areas of a city are better provided with amenities than the slums or squatter settlements; and the impoverished rural areas are the worst served of all. The higher death rates of the children of the less educated could then be attributed to their poverty. There is also an association between the education of women and reduced fertility (see Chapters 7 and 12). One would expect large families, especially if they are also poor, to represent a special hazard for the health of children.

But also (or alternatively) education may incline a mother to be more receptive to modern ideas on child care. Literacy, in particular, would open up for her other than word-of-mouth sources of information on these matters, and thus weaken the influence of traditional ideas purveyed by neighbours, friends and older female relatives (Chambers, 1985, pp. 96–8).

Prevention or Cure?

In the North, the development of scientific medicine has placed a premium on the treatment rather than the prevention of disease. This bias is rapidly becoming untenable even in such rich countries. There seems to be no limit to the development of new surgical technologies (like transplants of various organs), or new ameliorative or treatment measures, often involving expensive equipment such as kidney machines.

As resources must be reserved at some point for other social purposes, the question is now being asked as to whether, for example, some of the money now spent on heart transplants would not save more lives if devoted to relieving family poverty, or to campaigns against smoking, obesity and other features known to be associated with high rates of mortality. Research suggests that the improved quality of sewage disposal services and of water supply has a more favourable impact on health, as measured by infant mortality rates, than the proportion of hospital beds. The latter may even have an adverse effect – presumably because of the consequent starving of the preventive services (Cumper, 1983, p. 36).

Such a debate is bound to arouse strong feelings, especially as the fate of the person awaiting an operation appeals more vividly to the imagination and the emotions than an abstract statistic, no matter how large. Nevertheless under conditions of relatively scarce resources (even in the North) such choices cannot be avoided any longer (see Figure 6.1, p. 137).

Many Third World countries have followed the lead of their richer contemporaries in over-valuing curative medicine. Such policies were often introduced by the rich countries in the course of a previous imperial relationship and were then continued after independence partly as a result of inertia. Carrying on in the same way was encouraged also by the prestige of the rich countries, as embodying all that was advanced and up-to-date. Governments, with an eye to their own and their countries' standing in the world, wanted shining new hospitals, and elaborately trained medical personnel, irrespective of whether or not this was the most appropriate way of solving their health problems.

Even countries like Tanzania and Cuba, with otherwise revolutionary ideologies, have succumbed to their seductive appeal. The dramatic improvements in the health of the people of Cuba has outstripped that of more affluent Latin American countries. But this is in spite of its remaining wedded to a hospital and doctor-based service which is inappropriate both to its needs and its economic circumstances (Werner, 1983 pp. 17ff).

The ubiquitous factor of economic neo-imperialism raises its head also. Transnational pharmaceutical companies (misnamed 'ethicals') are active in peddling their wares in the Third World (Abel-Smith, 1978, pp. 77ff; Muller, 1982; Medawar, 1979, 1983) and seem to have no qualms, even, about benefiting from the sale of pharmaceutical products which are banned in their countries of origin (Medawar, ibid.). These have included, among many others, anabolic steroids and various suspect analgesics, antibiotics and hormonal preparations. Shopkeepers are supplied with vitamin tablets which they sell indiscriminately, sometimes in random combinations, without much regard either for the needs of patients or for the possible interactions between components of a package. Quite apart from the danger which such practices represent to the peoples concerned, they often involve a prodigal waste of the meagre resources of the individuals and countries which buy them.

As a counter to this, the World Health Organisation has produced a 'short list' of essential drugs, which will probably be reduced still further. It has also been suggested that Third World countries could begin to produce drugs for themselves using local materials (Buckles, 1980) and 'appropriate technology' (Dunhill, 1980). Traditional practitioners, of course, do this, making effective use of local herbal remedies. India has gone further than most countries in developing a modern pharmaceutical industry of its own, but this has not been very successful, and attempts to control the prices of drugs have been frustrated, largely through the machinations of the transnationals who participate in it (Shepperdson, 1985, pp. 2.30–5).

Drugs are not the only commodities involved in this kind of exploitation, which also includes technology and training, buildings and plant, and many kinds of medical and non-medical equipment (Sanders, 1985, pp. 145–9). Technology and training often play a central role in all this, as they inculcate methods and establish relationships which ensure a good market in the future for the equipment and supplies manufactured by the country which provides the training. One of the less worthy objections raised against the British government's policy of increasing fees for higher education students from overseas was that it would not pay in the long run: that these market advantages would be lost if students from overseas were no longer trained in Britain.

There is also movement in the opposite direction. The recruitment by First World health services of many doctors and nurses trained at great expense by poor countries, and badly needed at home, is yet another form of exploitation. The personnel concerned are useful to the countries of the North because their training has been imbued with ideas which may be inappropriate to the needs of their own countries but are dominant in the medical practice of their hosts.

The profit to the rich countries from this outflow must not be underestimated. For the United States, according to Navarro (1982b, pp. 22–3), it was equivalent in 1971 to half the output of all the American medical schools. The annual loss to Latin America was estimated as equal to all American aid to that continent for the whole of the decade of the 1960s. Whether the traffic is one way or the other, it seems, it is the rich countries which benefit most from the relationship.

It is perhaps difficult to recognise all this as underdevelopment, but that is precisely what it is. It locks its victims into a pattern of development which is profitable to the metropolitan country, and which prevents real, that is appropriate development from taking place. In health policy, appropriate development would be largely preventive, and curative provision would take a radically different form from that of the North.

Summary

A comparison of life expectancy and mortality statistics between the countries of the North and the South, and between the richer and the poorer among the latter, brings out the association between health and economic growth. Growth leads to health, just as health does to growth – a reciprocal relationship like that postulated for other forms of human capital. More investment in health in the Third World is urgently needed for reasons of economics and of humanity.

There are also differences in life expectancy within countries according to social class, the education of the mother, and rural or urban residence. These differences raise important questions about social justice.

Malnutrition and diarrhoea, together with malaria, onchocerciasis and other vector-borne diseases are the main cause of illness. Inoculation has an important part to play in combating these; a campaign to immunise children against six target diseases is under way, but is behind schedule, especially in Africa. The treatment of vector breeding grounds with insecticides is also important.

Otherwise what is most needed is improvements in diet and in personal and environmental hygiene, including better sanitation and a pure water supply. Preventive action of this kind is the most cost-effective first step for the improvement of health in a Third World country.

There are strong interests ranged against such an orientation. Modernising politicians are attracted by the prestige which the possession of expensive new hospitals can give. Doctors, nurses and other health professionals prefer the curative approach based on hospitals with which their Northern-style training in scientific medicine has made them familiar. Because of this training a number of them are able to migrate to the industrialised countries for the better salaries and prospects available there, depleting the already inadequate resources of their home countries in the process. Transnational suppliers of equipment and pharmaceuticals also have a stake in a system with a curative rather than a preventive bias. All of this is recognisable as part of the ubiquitous condition of dependent underdevelopment.

6

Policies for Health

The term 'appropriate technology' is used for productive developments which are adapted to the special circumstances of underdeveloped countries. It is now generally accepted that, if the same criterion is to be applied to health policy, it will mean a shift to a mainly preventive service. Adopting a preventive policy will result in many countries having to retrace their steps, against resistance from those at home and abroad who have a vested interest in the *status quo*. These include the national hospitals which absorb the greater part of the countries' health budgets (over 50 per cent, for example, in both Bahrain and Djibuti (WHO, 1987, p. 35); and well-heeled health professionals who congregate in the big towns, providing little or no service for the remoter areas. As we have seen, commercial interests in the North also have a stake in holding back progress.

What has been said so far makes it clear how much scope there is for preventive activity in the broadest sense of the word 'prevention'. The alleviation of poverty and the improvement of educational standards (especially among women) are part of this, but they are discussed in other chapters. This chapter will focus on the roles of nutrition, public hygiene and primary health care. There will also be some discussion of 'appropriate technology' in the remedial services. Finally alternative methods of financing health care will be brought under review.

Nutrition

The connection between malnutrition and poverty is clear from the fact that it is in the poorest countries, those with a per capita

GNP of less than US$200, that it is most prevalent. These countries, which lie in a band across Asia and Central Africa, contain 1200 million people, of whom one-third to one-half suffer from malnutrition (WHO, 1987, p. 18).

This situation results partly from agricultural underdevelopment in countries with few natural resources and adverse conditions of soil and climate. In part it is also due to the inequitable distribution of the means of existence within the countries concerned. Even such poor countries have their affluent classes, who can afford not merely sufficient food, but expensive imported foods. Ignorance and despair among the poorest and the hungriest also means that it is they who will have the highest birth rates, and therefore the largest number of mouths to feed. Simply attempting to increase the overall productivity of agriculture will not be enough, therefore, unless this is accompanied by steps to ensure that what is produced reaches those who need it most.

One safeguard would be to ensure that the enhanced productivity is in locally consumed foods rather than in exportable cash crops (Lappé and Collins, 1979, pp. 23–4). The promotion of small agricultural holdings would also help, by increasing the amount of food which is produced for consumption by the farmer himself and his family. A study in Tanzania showed nutritional levels to be highest 'among families who had stayed outside the monetary economy and still clung to subsistence farming ... it was only when monetary income exceeded a certain level that nutritional status rose again' (Klouda, 1983, pp. 56–7). Beyond this, it will be necessary for a redistribution of purchasing power to take place.

This might be achieved by introducing Northern-style social security payments financed from taxation. A more basic approach requires structural planning for 'appropriate' forms of growth, steering more of its benefits in the direction of the most deprived (Ahluwalia and Carter, 1981, pp. 485ff). This would have to include land reform and a challenge to the existing pattern of enclave underdevelopment.

Such a programme would mean taking on landed interests, the transnationals and the local power structure. It would be opposed by some self-interested Northern countries and some of the international agencies on the grounds that it was interventionist, and therefore self-defeating. There is nevertheless widespread support in the Third World for more positive economic planning and more effective land reform measures, and transnationals which are faced by determined governments do seem at last to be beginning to face realities.

A smaller part of the problem results from dietary customs. One aspect of this is the preferential feeding of males, including male children. As a result, women and growing girls may receive only what is left over – often food which is not only less attractive but also less nourishing. The WHO (1987, p. 24) suggests that the limitation of traditional diets to one or two staple foods also results in a deficient diet. A slightly different problem is that foods of high nutritive value are sometimes taboo on religious grounds, or are considered to be unhealthy, especially for children or pregnant women. These include, for example, in Malaysian villages, the so-called 'heaty' foods, which it is believed should not be given to babies (Shamsiah, 1981). Sometimes the traditional methods of food preparation destroy some of the nutritive values in food. Many of these are dictated by long-established traditional beliefs, and their eradication calls for a prolonged campaign of persuasion, perhaps as part of a general programme of health education, to be discussed later.

But at least one faulty dietary practice has nothing to do with traditional values. This is the increasing unpopularity of breast-feeding in the towns – in contrast to the return to breast-feeding among mothers in the developed world. A WHO study showed that 33 per cent of urban upper-income mothers, and 15 per cent of urban poor mothers in the Philippines, do not breast-feed their babies and, of those who do, many wean their infants too early, that is, before the age of six months (WHO, 1980, p. 131).

The abandonment of breast-feeding seems to be less of a problem in the rural areas, though some concern is expressed about the failure to introduce adequate supplementary feeding at an early enough stage (Whitehead, 1976, pp. 59–60). Where it is occurring, however, it has to be understood in the light of the WHO's view that the 'single most effective measure for the prevention of malnutrition and protection against infection in infancy is breastfeeding' (WHO, 1980, p. 131; see also Winicoff and Brown, cited in Carrin, 1984, p. 8). Much of the responsibility for this change must be laid at the door of the transnational manufacturers of baby 'formulas', whose sales campaigns in the Third World have become notorious (Bader, 1980, pp. 249ff;

Medawar, 1979, pp. 100–9; Ebrahim, 1983, p. 17). Education in the value of breast-feeding may have to be accompanied by steps to curb the activities of these transnationals.

Public Hygiene

The provision of a pure water supply, and effective sewage and refuse disposal, must be given equal importance with nutrition in any preventive health programme. Indeed the two are related. Lack of a pure water supply makes the use of a formula instead of breast milk very hazardous. And diarrhoea, infections of the gut, and other water-borne ailments can have important effects on the ability to ingest food.

But water control has even greater significance for diet than the supply of water for drinking would imply, for it is required for food crops and stock, both of which may die off in a prolonged drought. During the rainy season, on the other hand, floods can cause widespread damage, as occurs almost annually in low-lying countries like Bangladesh.

So although the supply of pure piped water will, at a price, largely meet the requirements of the towns, drinking water, irrigation and drainage have to be planned together in the countryside. Solving these problems through pipework will be logistically and financially impracticable outside the towns, and becomes largely a question of finding and controlling natural supplies of water (rivers, lakes, wells, and the collection and storage of rain and surface water) and keeping drinking water used by humans separate from that for other uses. It is not uncommon for cattle to drink in the same river as is used for domestic and personal cleansing as well as for drinking.

Natural water supplies which are not carefully monitored are also a common source of disease. For example, they provide a breeding-place for malarial mosquitos or snails harbouring bilharzia flatworms. Solutions to some of these problems may often be quite simple: The storage of water for twenty-four hours kills the bilharzia larvae (Bradley, 1977, pp. 37ff). Other vectors are less easy to deal with.

The disposal of human and domestic waste poses similar questions about location. Latrines will sometimes be too near to the wells, or to a river used for drinking or for washing oneself or one's clothing, so that there is a danger of the water becoming polluted. Sometimes they are too near dwellings. A guide to Primary Health Care has been published by the WHO for the benefit of village health workers, emphasising these points and the importance of personal hygiene (WHO, 1977). But, once again, experience has shown that a prolonged campaign of community education will be needed if long-standing habits are to be broken.

For example, it is usually easier to secure help from members of the community in establishing a facility, sinking a well or building a dam, than it is to persuade them to maintain it in an efficient condition. Where the facility has been provided as part of an aid project rather than through the labour of villagers themselves, regular servicing of it is even more difficult to ensure. It is then common for wells to lose their covers or even become silted up, and for crumbling dam walls to remain unrepaired. The whole-hearted commitment of the village to a project is the only sure prophylactic against such an outcome.

Facilities for Treatment

The concentration so far on preventive services does not, of course, mean that there are no special considerations which apply equally to the curative aspect of health provision in poor countries. Only too often, governments have failed to understand these special requirements, trying instead to copy the kind of medical provision made in the rich North. They cannot afford to provide doctors, nurses, pharmacists and other expensive medical personnel, much less hospitals and costly equipment, on the scale of the North. In the end there is little or no provision in many parts of a country.

In spite of considerable variations between different countries in the Third World according to their relative affluence, there remains, as Tables 6.1 and 6.2 show, a yawning gap in provision between even the rich oil exporting countries and the developed world. A feature of Table 6.2 is the favourable picture presented by the ratios for the planned economies of Eastern Europe – though this is not reflected in recent mortality statistics. If the figures given in Table 6.2 are reliable, they nevertheless join other

Table 6.1 Hospital beds per 10 000 population, developed and developing countries (World Health Organisation, 1980, p. 198)*

	1960	1975
Developed countries	87	95
Developing countries	11	14
Least developed countries	7	8

*More recent figures, but for WHO region instead of level of development, indicate no improvement: S.E. Asia, 9.8; E. Mediterranean, 13·3; Africa, 19 (WHO, 1983a, p. 796). Similarly for Table 6.2 (see below).

Table 6.2 Population for each medical person, developed and developing countries (World Bank, 1986, pp. 234–5; 1988, pp. 278–9)

	Physicians		Nurses	
	1965	1981	1965	1981
Developing countries				
Low-income	8 570	6 050	4 920	3 890
Excluding China & India	26 620	17 670	7 250	7 130
China & India	4 230	2 550	4 450	2 920
Middle-income	9 830	4 940	3 290	1 400
Lower	17 340	7 880	4 780	1 760
Upper	2 310	1 380	1 690	900
High-income oil exporters	7 500	1 380	4 440	580
Industrialised countries	870	550	420	180
Planned economies	564	329	300	199

evidence already cited in suggesting that ideology (in spite of the convergency theorists) remains an important determinant of the extent of social provision.

The progress made in seventeen years by the poorer underdeveloped countries, excluding India and China, is not dramatic. Indeed each doctor has, on the average, over thirty times and each nurse nearly forty times as many people to provide for as in the North. Unfortunately these deficiencies are not balanced by a proportionally greater expansion of community medicine, which would be more relevant. Gwatkin, Wilcox and Wray have shown that an expenditure on primary health care of less than 2 per cent per capita income can bring about a reduction in infant and child mortality by one-half within five years (Cumper, 1983, p. 40). The main problem is how to provide effective primary health care, incorporating both preventive and curative measures, in countries with low GNPs, widely dispersed populations, and traditional beliefs and practices which are very resistant to change.

Primary Health Care

The WHO initiated the movement towards the development of a primary health care programme in the rural areas in 1975, and a study carried out by Djukanovic and Mach (1975) as a joint project for WHO and the United Nations Children's Fund underlined the lack of adequate health services in the villages. They advocated the appointment of primary health workers with broad backgrounds, and a commitment to community participation. Participation was obviously necessary if health education was to be relevant in local terms and effective in changing behaviour; but there was also the growing belief that people should have more say in something which affected them and their families so intimately (Newell, 1975; Morley *et al.*, 1983).

It is being increasingly recognised that such decentralisation should go along with more integration between the local health worker and those delivering other services, notably education, social work and community development. If the central administration were also devolved, say to the area or the district ('where suitable administrative and political organisations exist and which has comprehensive health service facilities') there would be scope for planning also to take place on an intersectoral basis (Vaughan *et al.*, 1984).

At the local level the necessary participation could be achieved through community health committees, but it would be important that they should be constituted in a way which took proper account of ideas about legitimate authority. For example, there would be little advantage in establishing an elected committee if it bypassed the headmen or elders to whom people really listened, and who would be in touch with local feeling. A case in point is reported in the 1980 World Development Report (World Bank, 1980b, p. 79):

> Among the Hausa in northern Nigeria, a program to eradicate sleeping sickness has been successfully sustained through strong leadership. Every year the villagers clear the undergrowth along the banks of rivers and streams. They do not fully understand the reasons, but they are willing to do what their traditional leaders ask.

The procedure does not have to be so authoritarian. Traditional leaders usually communicate more with villagers than this example suggests, which is a good thing. For, quite apart from the *right* of everybody to understand the reasons for decisions and to share in making them, people will only co-operate in a health programme intelligently and with conviction if they are thus involved. The ultimate aim after all is to establish habits consistent with health and hygiene as an accepted feature of daily life.

In 1977, the WHO published its Working Guide for primary health workers (WHO, 1977) giving detailed advice, in both words and pictures, about how to deal with local health problems ranging from childbirth and family welfare to village hygiene, and from the treatment of accidents or internal growths on the one hand to mental disorder on the other.

An International Conference on Primary Health Care at Alma Ata in the USSR, jointly sponsored by the World Health Organisation and UNICEF, followed in the following year. This has greatly influenced thinking about objectives, but progress on the ground has not even begun to match up to these aspirations (WHO, 1987, pp. 37–43). This is especially true of rural Africa, and of the poor even in the towns (ibid., p. 112). A working paper prepared for that conference by the directors of the two sponsoring bodies (WHO and UNICEF, 1978) and a subsequent report on health strategies by the year 2000 (WHO, 1979) raise most of the issues to which attention is currently being given. What follows is broadly in line with the ideas contained in these documents.

The key person in any scheme for primary health care in the Third World must be the community health worker (CHW). To enable the scattered populations of these extensive and still essentially rural countries to be served, substantial numbers of such workers will be needed. This rules out fully trained medical practitioners. Even if they could be afforded, most underdeveloped countries would not have the numbers of trained personnel required. (Few are as well supplied in this respect as Sri Lanka.)

In fact, as Djukanovic and Mach (1975) make clear (see also Lee, 1983a, pp. 107–9) doctors are not the best persons for the job that has to be done. It calls for social and communication skills which do not figure prominently in the training in modern scientific medicine. For, in addition to treating disease, the CHW will be responsible for health education – for encouraging better baby care in particular, and better nutrition and hygiene generally.

Newell (1975, p. 194) refers to the role of the primary health worker as that of providing 'total health care'. Recognising that patient demand is mainly for curative medicine, he urges that the worker must exploit this as a lead-in to educational and preventive work. As the nearest doctor or hospital may be several days' journey away, over a difficult terrain, the worker needs enough training to be able to cope with most of the medical and related social problems encountered in the village, but must also know enough to understand when further help is required. And that further help (presumably from a health centre or a hospital) must also be accessible, perhaps through some form of radio communication. In Guyana shortwave radio transmitters serve this purpose, and also that of enabling workers on remote postings to keep in touch and relieve their feelings of loneliness and isolation.

The CHW's background, training and duties will vary according to the customs and needs of different countries. Some may even have been employed already in one of the professions auxiliary to medicine, and have had some training in medical subjects. In Guyana, for instance, they tend to be either dispensers, many of whom would have had experience in the remote interior of the country, or nurses. But in most countries full-time highly qualified workers of this kind would have to provide a service for a group of villages, if not too large, or might even be assigned to area health centres.

More practical for poor countries are the less ambitious patterns described in a study for the International Hospital Federation (Skeet and Elliott, 1978; see also Abel-Smith, 1978, pp. 188–90). According to the WHO Guide (1977) referred to above, the worker will be 'a man or a woman who can read and write, and is selected by the local community authorities or with their agreement to deal with the health problems of individual people and the community'. Employment might be full- or part-time; there would be obvious gains in acceptability and local knowledge if health work was combined with the normal activities of a local farmer or housewife. Remuneration could be either in cash or kind, and be the responsibility of the local community. There should be a hut or a room reserved exclusively for this work (WHO, 1977, p. 3).

There is increasing interest in the contribution which might be

---

***Exhibit* 6.1 Upgrading the barefoot doctor**

The success of village health workers in various countries throughout the world is well documented (Morley *et al.*, 1983), including the 'barefoot doctors' of China, who have provided so much of the inspiration for these developments (Sidel and Sidel, 1975; Kaplan and Sobin, 1982, pp. 29ff).

However recent developments in China may result in the sacrifice of some of the features which made that country's contribution to practice in primary health care so important (Rohde, 1983, pp. 8, 12). More emphasis is being placed on formal medical training for 'barefoot doctors', and a curative bias is emerging, along with some specialisation. This must result in an unnecessary increase in the cost of the service but, more important, it may erect barriers between the health workers and those whom they serve. There is also a career ladder leading towards full medical training (ibid., p. 9). This has its value in widening opportunities for 'barefoot doctors', but could also bring about undesirable changes from the existing informal and status-free service, with its emphasis on simple remedies.

---

made by traditional practitioners. According to Vuori (1982) they are the main providers of medical care for two-thirds of the world's population. In Africa they include village herbalists, bone-setters, 'witchdoctors', and 'birth-attendants'. Witchdoctors are seen in thousands of African tales as a malign influence, battening on the ignorance and superstition of villagers. They may sometimes be these things, but they are also the bearers of much traditional wisdom – about people, customs, herbs and so on (Morley and Wallis, 1978).

More sophisticated and scholarly forms of indigenous medicine include the Ayurvedic practitioners of India, and Chinese acupuncturists. The latter have now, of course, achieved wide acceptance also in the developed world. Traditional healers are officially recognised in many countries. In Tanzania they are now registered by the government, and in India they have a central role in the government's Community Health Worker Scheme (Bose, 1983, p. 41; Shepperdson, 1985, pp. 2.18–19). They have many advantages over the professional interloper from outside. They are well known in the village and people have confidence in their powers. They are themselves steeped in the local culture and beliefs, and are able to frame their advice accordingly. They know villagers well – have watched some of them grow up – and so can set their treatment in the communal and family context in which it is most likely to be effective, usually enlisting the assistance of other family members in the process.

Control of the CHW by the villagers themselves is now recognised as being of fundamental importance. It ensures not only that the health programme conforms to the community's own perception of its needs, but also that the methods used are acceptable, having regard to local social and cultural ideas. Such local control is well exemplified by the 'village health cadres' of Indonesia (Skeet, 1978, pp. 61ff). These are unpaid volunteers whose work is supervised by the community, and whose expenses are met from a fund built up as a kind of insurance fund by the villagers themselves.

Health Centres

The CHW is to be seen as the base of the pyramid of referral, extending up through a local health centre, to district hospitals and, eventually, to at least one national hospital. Rohde (1983, p. 15) argues that the success of the Chinese system depends, not on the 'barefoot doctors' alone, but also on the back-up provided at secondary and tertiary levels. Indeed the improvements in the health of the community may be even more broadly based than that, in that the efforts of the health services are reinforced by the overall 'political, social and economic milier . . . improvements in food availability, work environments, education and the status of women' (ibid., pp. 13–14). That broader background of support should also include efficient and honest administration – a perennial lack in underdeveloped countries.

The process of referral is connected with the concept of 'progressive care' (Williams and Williams, 1970, p. 9.2). Treatment is provided at just the level required by the condition from which the patient is suffering, on the grounds that any lower level of treatment would be inadequate, but any higher level would be a waste of resources – an indulgence which Third World countries cannot afford. Referral systems have presented some difficulties resulting partly from the distances or the expense involved for patients in reaching thinly distributed health centres or hospitals.

There is also the opposite problem. Patients who are near to a hospital may press for an unnecessarily high level of treatment. If this is to be avoided there have to be alternatives, in the form of clinics within the urban area – even if they are located for convenience within the purlieu of a hospital. Sometimes availability by itself is not enough; in Cali (Colombia) and Manila (Philippines) a campaign to increase awareness of the 'peripheral services' and their role did much to reduce unnecessary pressure on the hospitals (Harpham *et al.*, 1985, pp. 26–7).

Some see the health centre, catering for a population of about 10 000 people, as the real means for the bringing of primary health care to the rural population. In reality the populations for which a health centre provides service is more likely to be between 20 000 and 50 000. This factor, plus the cultural and in some countries the geographical distance of a health centre from many of those whom it was designed to serve, suggests a need for some intervening agent such as the village worker: the centre would give advice and support to the workers in the villages – on environmental health as well as treatment – and provide them with medical supplies. It would also be responsible for taking over their more difficult cases.

One model for a health centre would staff it with medical auxiliaries, who would have a minimum of some secondary education and a couple of years of medical training. This would distinguish them sharply from the village workers. Supervisors would need even more training, including diagnostic skills to enable them to refer in either direction with confidence.

General out-patient treatment would be provided and possibly also a few beds for brief periods of observation. There would be ante-natal and post-natal sessions, and clinics for babies and schoolchildren as well as simple dental treatment. The centre would carry out inoculations, including those which form part of the campaign by UNICEF against the 'big six' causes of child mortality. This might limit the effectiveness of an immunisation programme where patients had to travel along distance or over difficult country in order to reach the centre. In such cases, injections might have to become the responsibility of peripatetic staff instead – or even be entrusted to suitably trained village workers.

Apart from immunisation, the role of the centre in preventive health would be to digest and evaluate directives or guidance from government and other sources on home living conditions, water supplies and sanitation, and make the results available to village health workers in an assimilable form. Equally important, the centre would be the means by which government and national or regional planners could become informed about local conditions.

Hospitals

Beyond the health centres would be the hospitals. District hospitals would make fully trained medical staff available, while more specialised forms of diagnosis and treatment would be provided in regional institutions. Between them they should be able to deal with all except the obscurest conditions or the most complicated surgical procedures.

Though intended to make provision which is accessible to everybody in their region or district, their accessibility would often be only relative. In areas of sparse population and rugged topography much more would have to be attempted by the health centres. To bring the very sick to hospital some form of air transport, such as a helicopter or light aeroplane would be necessary. This may appear to be beyond the financial capacity of poor countries, but it is an ironical comment on our priorities that the army or the police may nevertheless possess them. Where this is the case, they should be made available for medical emergencies – as indeed they are by the police in Guyana.

Then, finally, at the very apex of the pyramid would be the national hospital. It would operate at the frontiers of medical science, and would be the training centre for doctors and nurses; but it should also make room for indigenous practice, and the development of the skills of those with most to offer in this field. It would need to be located at a nodal point of the country's communication network, which would mean either in the capital or, if that were a different place, in the largest city.

The very great financial burden represented by any hospital is not limited to the cost of construction. The running costs are very high (WHO, 1987, p. 35). In a study of the economics of Mityana

District Hospital in Uganda, the running costs were estimated as reproducing the construction costs in a period of a little over two years (Jolly *et al.*, 1970, p. 12.3). The running cost of a hospital at Tamale in Ghana was estimated to be 'more than double the operating budget of the entire Northern Region. For the same cost it would be possible to build 240 health centres at West African standards' (Abel-Smith, 1978, p. 181). Figure 6.1 demonstrates these differences in cost in yet another way.

For a hospital to be given by a rich donor government may not, therefore, be an undiluted blessing if the recipient country cannot afford to maintain it. From the viewpoint of a donor country, however, it is a flagship for a style of medicine which provides it with profitable markets for drugs and equipment. Meanwhile many Third World hospitals work against the handicaps of a

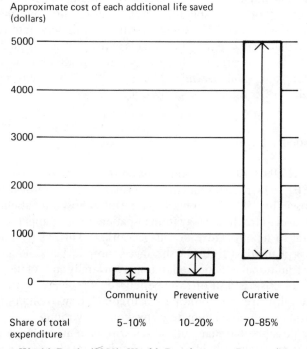

Source: World Bank (1988) *World Development Report* (New York: Oxford University Press).

Figure 6.1 Range of approximate cost of each additional life saved by various health services in developing countries

shortage of drugs and equipment, overcrowded wards and too few doctors and nurses.

Anything which can be done should be done, therefore, to relieve some of the pressure on them (ibid., pp. 115–18). An effective health centre may make it possible to do away with some small local hospitals (Jolly *et al.*, 1970, p. 3.1). In the urban areas, however, with a hospital not too far away, the functions of the health centre will usually be performed by the hospital's out-patient department. In order to prevent the unnecessary squandering of the scarcer and more expensive resources of the hospital (especially those of the central hospital), the principle of progressive patient care should be applied, not only to out-patients, but also to the hospital's in-patients. This would require the use of an efficient procedure for filtering cases.

Williams and Williams (1970, p. 9.3) divide in-patient care into three grades of decreasing intensity: intensive care, intermediate care and self-care. The study at Mityana already referred to showed that 40 per cent of the patients in that district hospital were suitable for self-care, involving only minimal attention from the hospital staff (Jolly *et al.* 1970, p. 12.8). This opens up the possibility of considerable savings in resources.

Community Care

The UN/UNICEF report on *Primary Health Care* (WHO, and UNICEF 1978, p. 36) argues that the principle of referral also implies the possibility of 'referral back' – referral of hospital patients to a lower level of treatment, say from in-patient to out-patient, or from hospital to health centre or village worker. This, as 'community care', is justified partly by the shortage of hospital beds and services. But in traditional societies separation from family and community at a time of crisis is also often experienced as a severe deprivation. Community care enables the patient to complete his treatment in the favourable emotional climate of his home environment.

It is possible that many of the self-care patients at Mityana and in other hospitals would be suitable for discharge home, if a village health worker was in post there. It is pointed out that 112 such out-patients could be treated at Mityana for the cost of treating only one in-patient (Jolly *et al.*, 1970, p. 12.6).

Recent developments in the treatment of diarrhoea (including even cholera) by 'oral rehydration' opens up the possibility of such treatments being administered by relatives of the sick person without any need for medical intervention at all (Bryceson, 1977, p. 112). David Werner's *Where There is No Doctor* (1979), now translated into a number of Third World languages, is a brilliant attempt to provide guidance for such family care but, like all written material, it probably overestimates the literacy of those to whom it is addressed. Like the WHO manual already mentioned, its greatest value may be to village health workers.

It is particularly important to expand community care as much as possible for mentally ill patients. Modern tranquillisers, by their effect in suppressing psychiatric symptoms, have made it possible for many patients who would previously have spent long periods in hospital to return to the community to take up their work and their family lives once again. This is obviously humane, and good sense economically. It is also good from the medical point of view. The lack of stimulation in the hospital environment (no matter how good the hospital) often means that patients deteriorate more quickly.

The cure brought about by the new drugs is usually symptomatic only, so that patients may have to return to hospital or to the health centre from time to time for short periods of further treatment.

Country people, especially in underdeveloped countries, are often tolerant of eccentric behaviour by those living among them, conduct which the urbanised would find upsetting. Lambo writes, on the basis of an experimental Community Health scheme at Aro in Nigeria (1970, pp. 20.3–4), that community care

> is of particular benefit to the African peasant, because not only does he find a hospital ward a strange and disturbing place, but his own close-knit society has exceptionally strong social and human resources which promote his mental health. Among these resources are the natural flexibility and tolerance of village communities, the therapeutic value of traditional cults, and the confessions, dances and rituals that play so large a part in village life. Acting together they all provide strong natural psychotherapy.

Within such a framework, Lambo (1970, pp. 20.6–7) sees a role for the 'witch doctors' in treating the mentally disturbed in the

***Exhibit* 6.2   Community mental health: the Geel experience**

The work carried out at Geel in Belgium over 700 years has proved the viability of community care for mental patients (Roosens, 1979). The patients were boarded out, and a small allowance was paid to the household which volunteered to take them. Many patients still under treatment worked on local farms. There was a day hospital where patients could receive equivalent treatment to that of a residential hospital, while continuing to live a more natural life out in the village. Although the need to maintain contact with hospital limits the area in which such a scheme could operate, Lambo sees it as a model which, given proper supervision of patients by health or social workers, offered even more to a communally-minded Third World country than to the 'loose-knit, critical, "success oriented" societies of industrial countries'.

community, and in supplying information about them on which a diagnosis could be based. No doubt there is an important place for them on the psychotherapeutic side, and in helping relatives to cope with any problems the patient might cause for them. These are very valuable contributions. But if it is a question of maintaining a drug regime, they would need some training. Alternatively, these might be tasks for a social worker. It is difficult not to see advantages in such a programme also for the treatment of the many kinds of physical illness with a strong psycho-social content.

Private Medicine

Any blueprint for a health service in an underdeveloped country which did not take account of the role of the private sector would be very incomplete. It consists of the mission hospitals, and practitioners in private medical practice, the latter being very different from the former in their origins and aims. The mission hospitals play an important part in supplementing the health resources of many poor countries, but the funds collected from overseas, on which they rely, are no longer sufficient to meet the high costs incurred in modern medicine. Payment by patients is becoming more and more necessary.

If the government is providing a health service free at the point of delivery it becomes difficult to integrate the mission hospitals with its own provision without creating injustice between those areas with free treatment and those with a fee-paying mission hospital. Not unnaturally the mission hospitals themselves are not keen on losing their identity in a fully integrated service. On the other hand, the full value of a country's health facilities cannot be obtained unless it can achieve integration, with the mission hospitals playing their part within the referral system. Experience in certain programmes in Indonesia shows that the government and voluntary agencies can find ways of co-ordinating their activities in the field of health (Johnston, 1983, pp. 168ff).

One way of dealing with the fee problem would be for the government to subsidise a mission hospital to the extent of the fees payable. If there were a national system of repayment by patients (preferably according to ability to pay) such a subsidy scheme would fit conveniently into it. In any case, the country would still benefit to the full extent of the mission money expended on the hospital, and the services of medical professionals drawn into the country's service by the work of the mission. Apart from this, every effort should be made to enable the mission to retain its special character, so long as this was consistent with the national plan for health.

Private practitioners are a different proposition. In the nature of things they will be providing service only for the rich, mainly in the urban areas. So long as they remain outside the referral system, they will also lack the back-up available to practitioners within the government service. They may therefore become parasitic on the state system, or seek to duplicate some of its specialised provision, causing further dispersion of the country's professional manpower. There is a case for taking a strong line on private practice. Jolly and King (1970, p. 2.15) suggest that those who leave, or choose not to enter the government service, should be required to pay back the cost of their training, but non-medicals may well ask why private practice should be allowed at all.

Urban Bias

A related problem is that of persuading medical personnel to accept postings away from the towns. The existence of private practice is not the only reason for this. Elite professionals like doctors and nurses, though in the public service, will be no more enthusiastic than others about losing the amenities and society of the urban area.

There are also social-structural reasons for an urban bias (Lipton, 1977): the size of the populations involved, the convenience of locating services in the city, with its network of communications, the financial pressure in a fee-paying or insurance-based system to provide for its customers, and the desire to encourage enclave development by providing facilities. All these work in the same direction. Even a country like Tanzania, dedicated to the interests of the rural majority, has a system of hospital-dominated medical provision which discriminates against the villages (Klouda, 1983, pp. 55–6, 59).

Special steps have therefore to be taken to try to redress the balance to some extent. Ascertaining the needs of various parts of the country, and then permitting doctors only to work where a need exists, would be one solution. Another which would share out the 'discomfort' rather more would be to require all medical personnel to work 'up-country' for a period, after training (ibid.).

Finance

Any suggestion of payment for medical services can be a very emotional question. It would be important to ensure that sick people were not prevented from securing treatment merely by virtue of their poverty. But the finance of a health programme needs to be considered as a whole (Abel-Smith, 1978), rather than issue by issue in this way.

Health education and environmental services such as sewerage, water supply and immunisation, campaigns against disease-carrying vectors and parasites, have to be met from taxation. Personal medical services are in a different category, and could be subject to a fee payable by the patient at the point of service (Salloway, 1982). A somewhat implausible reason is sometimes given for this: that it imposes 'discipline' on the patient in his use of the service and consumption of drugs (Golladay *et al.*, 1977, pp. 176–7). It seems doubtful that more than a minority of neurotic or very lonely people would try to obtain medical services they did not need – the so-called 'moral hazard' said to be associated with low or 'zero-cost' medical provision (Mills, 1983, pp. 71ff). Others suggest an initial registration fee instead, so that any necessary follow-up treatment would not be jeopardised by a charge for each visit (ibid.).

The 'free market argument' is also deployed as a justification for some form of financial nexus between practitioner and patient. A fee, it is said, makes the patient sovereign, enabling him to shop around for the best medical attention for his money (Salloway, 1982, pp. 47–52). But patients do not usually have the knowledge to enable them to choose between the various treatment options offered to them (Titmuss, 1968, pp. 247–68); Abel-Smith, 1978, pp. 41–2). They might be beyond treatment by the time they found out that they needed a change of doctors!

A free-market in medicine would obviously be congenial to neo-classical economists, and arguments such as those outlined above have indeed been advanced by the World Bank (1988, pp. 135–6). However, as in the case of other social services, the Bank is forced to propose special provision for the poor. One way it suggests for achieving this is to distinguish between patients according to their area of residence, especially as between residents of the urban and rural areas. This might also have the doubtful advantage of re-ducing demand in the urban area, making more resources avail-able for the villages (ibid.; Lee, 1983a, p. 99).

The injustice to the urban poor which this would cause demon-strates the simple-minded nature of such a dichotomy between the 'poor' and the rest. It bears little resemblance to the gradations of poverty found among the population of an underdeveloped coun-try. It is doubtful if a means test (and it would also be stigmatising) would be any more effective in the face of the complications presented by subsistence farming or employment in the informal sector in the city.

Certainly without some form of insurance only the rich could make use of a service which charged anything like the economic cost (Mills, 1983, pp. 64ff). This could be run either by the state, by mutual insurance schemes like BUPA in Britain or the American

Blue Cross or Blue Shield, or by commercial companies. Or the service might be entirely free to the patient when sick, the cost being met either by taxation or by the employer (Salloway, 1982). Various combinations of these are also possible – for example, one in which the state, the employer or the insurance scheme met only part of the cost, the rest being paid directly by the patient (McLachland and Maynard, 1982).

Mutual insurance schemes like those of the American Blue Cross and Blue Shield schemes, for example, though non-profit making, limit the amount of cover according to the level of premiums paid. Even the National Health Service in the United Kingdom expects patients to pay towards the cost of drugs, or dental or optical treatment. New Zealand reverses the British system: drugs are free, but visits to the doctor have to be paid for.

In the Third World fees are general, though some countries such as Malaysia provide free basic treatment for the very poor, subject to a test of means. There is also the Chinese system in which the cost is shared by the state, the commune and the family (Mills, 1983, p. 81). The participation of the local community probably helps to make the services provided more responsive to local needs, and to reduce the bureaucracy which many see as a disadvantage of systems like the British National Health Service. Some examples of the methods of financing currently being adopted are set out in the WHO's *Seventh Report on the World Health Situation* (WHO, 1987, p. 56).

The *mode* of payment might also take a variety of forms. It might involve payment at the point of service, or payments per patient made centrally (capitation fees), and covering treatment over a period of time. Or it might be through a directly salaried service, provided by a private organisation or by the state.

The main argument against any large extension of private practice in medical services, or against financing a state service by fees, has already been stated. The very poor might not be able to afford the fees at all, and even those who were not in extreme want might be able to do so only by sacrificing something else which was of importance to them – which they might not always be prepared to do.

There is ample evidence that the demand for medical care declines with an increase in its cost (Cumper, 1983, pp. 36–8). Many factors, such as nutrition and conditions of life, already affect people's health and longevity. Their poverty could then prove an insuperable barrier to treatment when they did fall ill. Nor is it only a matter of equity, important though that is; there is the contribution of a healthy population to development. A country has a large stake in the health of its citizens. It cannot afford to have a section, perhaps a majority of the community, whose health problems are neglected.

Many people, it is true, especially in the rural areas, already spend, in aggregate, substantial sums in cash or kind on treatment by traditional healers. Gish (1975, p. 187) estimated that over a million pounds a year is paid out in this way in Tanzania alone. In Botswana, where 40 per cent of the cost of medical treatment is met by patients, almost two-thirds of that sum is paid to traditional practitioners (Griffiths and Mills, 1983, p. 57). In addition there are usually gifts in kind, such as a cow or a marriageable daughter. But these payments reflect the honoured position which such traditional healers occupy in their communities, and it cannot be assumed that villagers would pay as willingly for modern treatment, or that they can afford to pay, whether treatment is traditional or modern.

Full-blooded state health insurance usually has much lower administrative costs than the mutual schemes. Private profit-making schemes operated by commercial insurance companies are even more expensive. State health insurance also has other advantages. A fund is built up in advance, making health planning easier. The resources thus accumulated can also be borrowed to finance development projects. If these are health schemes of a preventive nature, they may end in actually reducing the amount which has to be spent on curative services. In any case the real cost of a given level of services should fall, with improvements in social conditions over the years, leaving a surplus to support improvements in provision. This is a windfall which should come to the community which has created it. Insurance companies, in their life insurance and other activities, already undeservedly benefit from the improvement in life expectancy which development brings with it; they ought not to benefit yet again from a windfall profit on health insurance.

Finally, as we have seen, it is easy in a state scheme to make arrangements under which contributions can be shared in planned proportions between the citizen, the employer and the state – and perhaps also the local communities.

A great disadvantage even of state insurance schemes in the Third World (Abel-Smith and Leiserson, 1978, pp. 73ff), is that they are so frequently limited to formal sector employees, and in particular that they neglect dependants. For example, in Malaysia, no dependants receive treatment under the state scheme. In Taiwan, schoolchildren and most employees are covered by insurance, but not spouses or very young children. This kind of restriction, especially as it affects the medical care of children, has serious implications for the health of a nation and therefore its prospects of both social and economic development.

The link with employment means that there is also an overwhelming urban bias in them to add to all the other deprivations from which the rural area suffers. And, if the insurance principle is carried to its logical conclusion, it will involve charging higher premiums to those representing the greatest risk of ill-health. This simply compounds the disadvantages of those whose impoverished circumstances already make them more prone to sickness.

In the end the solution which best meets the requirements of social justice and minimises administrative costs will be a health service financed by means of a progressive taxation system, that is, one in which the *proportion* of an income which is taken in taxes increases as the income itself increases.

Political Economy of Health

Some take the Marxist view that any attempt to improve the health of the peoples of the Third World is doomed to failure unless the net is cast much more widely, to take account of the role of the economic system in producing ill-health and in distorting the operation of the health services (Doyal, 1979, 1983; McKinlay, 1984; Shepperdson, 1985). They point to the activities of TNCs like the tobacco and baby food manufacturers and the pharmaceutical companies. They call attention also to the impact on health of urbanisation and industrialisation, the baleful effect of which they attribute, with considerable justification, to the way in which overseas companies seek to maximise the returns from their investments. The persistence of inappropriate forms of health service is seen as part of the same pattern of dependent underdevelopment.

Even more broadly, they see the general environment of poverty, squalor and low morale which is inseparable from under-development as making any general improvement in the health of the community a forlorn hope, until some radical change has taken place in the international economic order.

The nature of the state also enters into these calculations. Many members of groups which exercise power in the state benefit from underdevelopment through employment or trade, or even bribery, and use their power to preserve a *status quo* which is so profitable to them. Others honestly but mistakenly believe that what is happening represents real development.

Where Third World governments are more critical, they face hostility from international capital, and governments in the capitalist countries, which could cause great damage to their economies and their place in the world. International organisations are not immune from this danger, as the recent vicissitudes of UNESCO show. In the face of such structural pressures, it is argued, proposals for reform are bound to be ineffective. Similar arguments have been raised against social welfare programmes in other fields such as education and social work.

If the assumption here is that all progress in social policy must wait until a major reconstruction of the social and economic system has been brought about, this is both callous and unjustified by the course of history. Ways should be found of relieving human suffering resulting from ill-health or deprivation without delay. Experience in Scandinavia, and even to some extent in Britain and the rest of Europe, shows that this is possible.

Summary

Underdeveloped countries will not be able to meet the health needs of the mass of their people if they attempt to base their provision on Northern models. Nor would this necessarily be the most effective approach. An appropriate technology for health is required.

The primacy of preventive and environmental health has already been asserted in Chapter 5. The link between this and curative medicine is represented by primary health workers oper-ating at village level. Though their formal education and training might be limited, they would possess personal qualifications and also acceptability in the local community. Some of them might be 'traditional practitioners'. They would be responsible for the improvement of local and personal hygiene, and also provide the first point of contact for sick people.

They would be supported by a local health centre, staffed by trained medical auxiliaries. The health centre would provide them with advice in the performance of both their preventive and curative functions. Where necessary patients would be referred upward to the health centre, or to hospital where doctors and nurses would be found, but the aim would be to treat them in the community if possible. This would not only be more practicable (more expensive treatment might mean no treatment at all), but in many cases would be more acceptable to patients, leading to a speedier recovery. Placing the emphasis on community care in this way also implies the possibility of referral downwards.

Although the environmental health services are properly the responsibility of the government, there are various ways in which the curative services might be financed: charity (the mission hospitals), insurance (state, mutual or commercial), fees (commonly paid by patients in underdeveloped countries), or state provision financed out of progressive taxation.

The important thing is that treatment should be available to all, irrespective of ability to pay. This is not only required by social justice, but also by the interest which the whole community has in maintaining the health and effectiveness of the population. Only state provision meets both of these criteria. It is also probably the cheapest way of making the necessary provision.

7

The Educational Scene

Educational Underdevelopment

Third World countries are as deprived in education as they are in other respects. Two sets of statistics make this clear: the figures for literacy, and the proportions of children of primary school age who are attending school. World Bank figures for literacy are shown in Table 7.1. Differences in literacy clearly vary between groups of countries according to their levels of income. The exceptions to this are the high-income oil exporters. Although they have made striking progress over the twenty-year period, they still have some way to go before they catch up with even the poorest of the other countries.

In spite of the improvement in literacy rates, it must be a cause for continuing concern that they remain at only just over one-half of those in the North. But these figures, disturbing as they are, tell only part of the story. Because of the continuing rise in populations, the actual number (as distinct from the percentage) who are

Table 7.1   Literacy rates (%) for various groups of countries, 1960 and 1980 (World Bank, 1983, pp. 196–7)

	1960	*1980*
Underdeveloped Countries		
Low-income	34	52
Middle-income	48	65
High-income oil exporters	9	32
Industrialised countries	96	99
Soviet bloc	97	99

illiterate, is not falling at all, but rising. Thus the World Health Organisation (1987, p. 21) reports a decline in the proportion of the population of the underdeveloped countries over the age of 15 who are illiterate, from 48 per cent to 40 per cent between 1970 and 1980, but a 10 per cent increase in the number of illiterates during the same period, from 731 to 800 million. This figure rose to 825 million by 1985. Again the situation is more serious in the poorer countries; in the 'least developed countries' the proportion of illiterates in 1980 averaged 63 per cent for men and 83 per cent for women!

Similar differences between richer and poorer countries are found in primary school attendances (see Table 7.2). The indices as calculated are obviously only an approximation. There is once again evidence of modest progress over the years, confirmed by more recent estimates (see Table 7.3). As Table 7.2 shows, the link with relative affluence is a very close one. Even these figures mask wide differences among the poorer countries. UNESCO (1983, p. 42) predicts that primary enrolments in the year 2000 will still be less than 50 per cent in Bhutan and Upper Volta (now Burkina Faso), between 50 per cent and 59 per cent in Afghanistan, Chad, Guinea, Mali and Niger, and between 60 per cent and 69 per cent in Burundi and Gambia. These countries between them have over one-fifth of the primary school-age populations of the Least Developed Countries.

In contrast there are Benin, Central African Republic, Haiti, Somalia, North Yemen, Botswana, Guinea-Bissau, Laos, Lesotho, Nepal and Tanzania, which together also cover about 20 per cent of

Table 7.2 Primary school enrolment ratios* according to country's per capita income level, 1960–75 (World Bank, 1980a, p. 104)

Income level	1960	1965	1970	1975
Low	42	50	52	56
Lower-middle	47	53	55	58
Intermediate-middle	53	63	70	75
Upper-middle	72	76	80	85
All underdeveloped countries	47	54	58	62
All industrial countries	91	92	93	94

*No. enrolled of all ages as % of total population in primary school age group.

Table 7.3 Primary school enrolment ratios† for 1980 and 1985 and estimates for subsequent years (UNESCO, 1988, pp. 2–34)

	1980	1985	1990*	1995*	2000*
Underdeveloped countries	69	73	75	77	79
Developed countries	92	92	93	93	93

*Projections (UNESCO, 1983).
†See definition above.

primary school children, and have projected enrolment ratios of 100 per cent or more (over 100 per cent because of courses repeated).

Again, however, the facts are worse than the statistics suggest. Because of rising child populations, the number of children aged 6–11 who are out of school is expected to have increased by 11·2 million to 120·5 million over the period covered by Table 7.3. Although this situation is expected to improve slightly by the year 2000, to 103 million, this is more than counterbalanced by an increase in the numbers of secondary-age children out of school. The number of young people of all ages expected to be out of school in underdeveloped countries in the year 2000 is no less than 76 millions above that in 1960 (UNESCO, 1983, p. 42).

In addition, it has to be remembered that the figures given in Table 7.2 are for enrolments, and do not therefore take account of those repeating courses, or the wastage which occurs as a result of absences or pupils dropping out of school. UNESCO reports that only 77 per cent of the children who entered primary school in the Third World in 1978–9 continued to attend for four years (UNESCO, 1983, p. 31). Only 37 per cent of the lower intake of 1970 stayed for the five years which UNESCO considers necessary to establish permanent literacy (UNESCO, 1977). Courses were repeated by one child in six in about half of the Third World countries cited in 1983 (UNESCO, 1983, p. 32) so inflating these enrolment percentages.

Even these estimates of future trends optimistically assume that current rates of educational advance can be maintained. This is an assumption which the rising cost of education and the worsening of the economic situation for many developing countries hardly justifies.

The picture presented, then, is one of severe and growing educational underdevelopment. This hampers economic growth in countries which are already desperately poor and frustrates other possible aims for education, connected with the wider definition of development adopted here. Social justice is one such aim. The personal development of the people of these countries, the position of women, and even levels of sickness and mortality are all affected.

Education and Growth

The 'structural adjustment' philosophy, which now prevails in the policy of the World Bank and other international bodies, means that economic growth takes priority: that social welfare measures in Third World countries have to be justified mainly by their contribution to GNP. The concept of human capital provides a rationale for this. Assessed solely against the criterion of growth, investment in education is amply justified (Colclough, 1982).

Exhibit **7.1   Education and agricultural productivity**

The World Bank has summarised the results of a series of studies on the effect of four years of primary education on farmer productivity. Even without 'complementary inputs' of fertiliser, irrigation, improved seed and transport and so on, productivity rose in five studies out of seven, covering three countries. The average improvement was 8·1 per cent. Where 'complementary inputs' were obtainable, offering more scope to the better educated farmers, productivity rose in nine studies out of ten, covering six countries. The average increase in productivity went up, in this case, to 13·2 per cent (World Bank, 1980b, p. 48).

Research of this kind has been criticised on the grounds that the mere association of education with higher productivity does not necessarily mean that one causes the other. They may be entirely unrelated or, more likely, both be the effect of a common, underlying cause. For example, the getting of an education and the improved efficiency may both result quite independently from a more enterprising attitude on the part of these farmers. Or the causal process may be the reverse of that postulated by the World Bank. Improved productivity, resulting from some factor as yet unidentified, may have raised the life-style aspirations of the farmers, or reduced the subsistence

---

pressure upon them so that they could spare time (and perhaps even cash) for education. This principle – that correlation does not necessarily imply causation – is a commonplace of social research methodology.

These microeconomic studies have, however, been supplemented by macroeconomic evidence about the relationship between various countries' growth rates, and their levels of literacy. On the assumption that literacy was a cause rather than an effect, growth would have to follow along *after* educational progress. Working on this assumption, literacy rates of Third World countries in 1960 were compared with their growth in GNP over the period 1960–7. The ten fastest-growing countries in 1960–7 were found to have literacy rates in 1960 which were, on average and with some individual variation, 16 per cent higher than expected at their income levels.

The World Bank concluded that such results reinforce the microeconomic evidence, to the effect that: 'increases in literacy contribute both to increased investment, and (given the level of investment) to increase in output per worker' (World Bank, 1980b, p. 38).

A noteworthy example is that of the Republic of Korea, whose economic achievements have been partly attributed to the progress it had made in education (Reynolds, 1985, pp. 179–80; Park, 1988). It devoted 20 per cent of its budget to education after the war, raising its literacy rate from 30 per cent to 80 per cent in the period 1953–63, 'by which time South Korea's human resource development had exceeded the norm for a country with three times its per capita GNP' (Reynolds, 1985, p. 180).

Educational expenditure, then, like expenditure on health, should not be looked on as a financial burden, but as an investment. It then becomes reasonable to attempt to quantify the rates of financial return to such an investment (Psacharopoulos, 1973). Personal incomes are used for this purpose, on the assumption that they are a measure of labour productivity (Psacharopoulos, 1980, pp. 41–4). A distinction is made between 'private returns', which charge against incomes only private costs – fees, books, foregone earnings and so on – and social returns which also include public outlays and taxes.

The following summary, being based on the latter, gives a

Table 7.4   Percentage rates of social return to education (World Bank, 1980b, p. 49)

	Primary	Secondary	Higher	No. of countries
All developing countries	24.2	15.4	12.3	3
Low-income (literacy under 50%)	27.3	17.2	12.1	11
Middle-income (literacy over 50%)	22.2	14.3	12.4	19
Industrialised countries	—	10.0	9.1	14

conservative estimate of the benefit gained, as compared with the way in which investments are usually assessed (for example in the private sector), which take the public contribution for granted. For this reason the figures given in Table 7.4 for the stimulus given to growth by education are a more realistic measure than those used for calculating those other returns. An update of these figures in 1981 gives very similar results (Psacharopoulos, 1981).

With an average rate of return ranging from a minimum of 12·1 per cent to a maximum of 27·3 per cent education is clearly a very good investment indeed. It compared favourably, for example, with a '10 per cent common yardstick of the opportunity cost of capital' when Psacharopoulos wrote in 1981 (Psacharopoulos, 1981, p. 326). On a recent calculation, higher education in Third World countries shows an average rate of return of 14·9 per cent as compared with 12·8 per cent for investment in fixed capital such as roads, hydro-electric schemes, irrigation (Psacharopoulos, 1982, p. 155). The rate of return to expenditure on primary education is even higher, as Table 7.4 shows.

Though investment in education is thus seen to be highly profitable, it suffers, like other desirable forms of public investment, from the inability of most Third World countries to finance it. Evidence such as that presented above may therefore play a valuable role if it persuades potential donors of aid, whether governments or international agencies, that making resources available for education can pay rich dividends, even when these are assessed by the narrowest economic criteria.

Equity

Economic growth is not by itself, however, an adequate criterion. If development is the aim, rather than merely economic growth, it is necessary to consider also whether educational policy conduces to social justice. It has long been acknowledged that education greatly affects an individual's 'life chances', and this is confirmed by the high rates of income return to education – higher, as already indicated, for private than for social returns. Psacharopoulos (1981, p. 332) argues that even family influence on a person's advancement in a Third World country is largely achieved through its ability to obtain educational advantages for him.

Richards and Leonor (1981) are led by such considerations to doubt the ability of schools to promote greater equality. In their research in various Asian countries for the International Labour Office, they argue that a favourable family background not only improves chances of access to education, but also the ability to benefit from it. Together with the direct influence of family factors on the availability of the better-paid jobs, they leave little scope for the influence of the school itself. It would seem more reasonable instead to emphasise the undisputed mutual influence exercised on one another by social background and education. In the philosophical cliché, a fairer distribution of education may not be a sufficient cause of greater equality, but it is certainly a necessary cause.

For primary education, Psacharopoulos cites private returns as high as 30 per cent for Nigeria, 33 per cent for Kenya and 56 per cent for Thailand (Psacharopoulos, 1973). Figures for secondary and higher education are usually lower, but still rise for the former as high as 30 per cent (for Kenya); and for the latter to 37 per cent (for Ghana). A more recent study for the World Bank (1983, p. 106) confirms the impact on subsequent income which secondary education can have. The even greater profit gained from tertiary education is shown in Table 7.5. As all of these are 'private returns' they conceal the further inequity resulting from the amount of public money expended in achieving them.

Nor is this all, for education in its higher reaches brings with it not only a return in income, but also in power and status. This is partly through its effect on the financial position of its beneficiaries, but also through the entrée it gives them into professional and other elite groups. The high cost of education at the higher levels (see figure 7.1) is also often at the expense of primary education, reducing still further the educational opportunities, and therefore the 'life chances', of the poor.

Table 7.5 Families of 1954 Indian graduates by average monthly family income (Blaug, Layard and Woodhally, 1969, p. 131)

Income	Graduate families (%)	All families (%)
500 Rs & above	23.3	1.5
200 to 499 Rs	45.7	10.0
Below 200 Rs	29.1	88.5

It is difficult to deny, therefore, that education can be a major contribution to equity or inequity in society. It has been customary in the past, even among socialists such as R. H. Tawney, to see this as indicating a need simply to equalise educational opportunity. The work of Richards and Leonor (1981) confirm the more recent view that it is necessary to go further than this, introducing 'positive discrimination' (HMSO, 1967) in favour of the socially underprivileged in order to counteract the many disadvantages which poverty, rural residence, minority ethnic membership and the rest imposes upon them.

The government of Malaysia has adopted a policy of positive discrimination in education in favour of native Malays (the so-called *bumiputras*) to compensate for the cultural and other disincentives from which they believe this group suffers. Zachariah (1973, pp. 1ff) has described the attempt in India, between 1950 and 1970, to discriminate in favour of the 'scheduled castes', the 'untouchables'. This took the form of special scholarships and maintenance grants, and the reservation of a certain number of places in colleges. Zachariah was convinced that the policy had reduced the educational disadvantages of the 'untouchables', but argued that perhaps poverty rather than untouchability should be the criterion for this kind of discrimination in the future.

In deciding what form of positive discrimination to adopt, the experience of countries which have tried it out should be drawn upon. It does not seem, for example, as if quotas in higher education have been successful in achieving their aims in Malaysia, perhaps because of the lack of motivation among the *bumiputras*. The important question of motivation for personal investment in education will be discussed in the next chapter. What is certain is that gross inequities do exist in the countries of the South, between the rich and the poor, rural and urban areas, and males and females. This is illustrated by the figures given in Table 7.6.

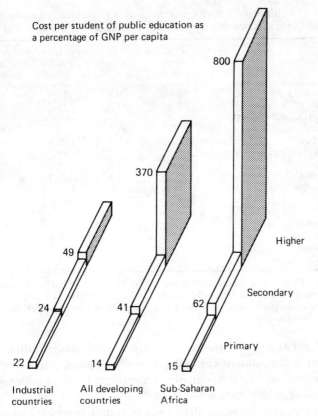

Cost per student of public education as a percentage of GNP per capita

Source: World Bank (1988) *World Development Report* (New York: Oxford University Press).

Figure 7.1 Cost per student of different levels of public education as a percentage of GNP per capita in three country groups, early 1980s

The educational disadvantages of rural areas and of females will be explored after an examination of those disadvantages resulting more specifically from poverty.

Education and the Poor

Although the figures given in Table 7.6 are no more than illustrative, they do show the bias in enrolment towards the richer households – greatest in the case of Nepal, and least in the case of

Table 7.6 Primary school enrolments as a percentage of each income group in various developing countries (World Bank, 1980b, p. 47)

	Boys (aged 5–9)		Girls (aged 5–9)	
	Poorest households	*Richest households*	*Poorest households*	*Richest households*
Sri Lanka (1969–70)	70.3	89.8	65.8	81.9
Nepal (1973–4) (11 towns)	29.5	77.8	15.3	71.2
India (Gujurat state) (1972–3)				
Rural	22.7	53.9	8.6	50.9
Urban	42.1	77.7	30.8	69.5
India (Maharashtra state) (1972–3)				
Rural	24.6	54.6	16.6	52.9
Urban	40.4	86.3	42.1	87.0
	Both sexes (aged 6–11)			
	Poorest households		*Richest households*	
Colombia (1974)				
Rural	51.2		60.0	
Urban	62.0		89.5	
Large cities	69.6		94.6	

Note: Poorest and richest refer (in the case of India, Nepal and Sri Lanka) to the bottom and top 10 per cent of households ranked by expenditure per person, and (in the case of Colombia) to the bottom and top 20 per cent of households ranked by income per person.

Sri Lanka. Even in the latter, there are substantial differences. There is also, almost certainly, a larger drop-out rate among the poor, making the differential even greater. Primary education is very inequitably distributed indeed.

One reason for this is that, even in countries where there is no direct charge for schooling, education is very far from being free of costs to pupils and their families. These costs include the sparing of children for education when they could be otherwise engaged on the land. There is also the expense of sending them to school suitably clothed, finding transport for them, and perhaps even, in the case of younger children, having an adult take the time off to escort them. Quite often, of course, there are also direct costs: school fees to be paid, and even more often books to be purchased and school uniform to be obtained (Preston, 1984, pp. 124–7).

So many poor children do not go to school because their parents cannot afford to send them. At the same time the sacrifices required may not seem very worthwhile to parents if they are not convinced of the relevance of the instruction provided. Only too often the curriculum follows the pre-independence preference for the more academic forms of learning (Watson, 1982, pp. 184–7). Whether this is justified or not, many parents think of it as more appropriate to life in the town than in the country – and most poor people live in the rural areas.

The Rural Areas

In view of what has just been said it is not surprising that the rural areas themselves show up as comparatively underprivileged. This partly reflects the fact that rural families are also poor, and partly the general bias in favour of the towns brought about by the dual economy of the underdeveloped country. The disparity emerges in Table 7.6, and is confirmed by figures for the deprived and mainly rural region of North East Brazil. School enrolments, at 46 per cent, are half the national average. Only 4 per cent complete four years of primary school, two-thirds dropping out before the second year (World Bank, 1980b, p. 47).

The urban bias is even greater at the higher levels of education, as figures from Thailand illustrate. Correlations between level of urbanisation and admission to different levels of education show a leap from 0·14 for lower primary to the significant figure of 0·52 for higher primary, and then consistently upwards to 0·75 for lower secondary and 0·87 for upper secondary (Sudaprasert *et al.*, 1980, p. 255). As far as tertiary education is concerned, a young resident of Bangkok had a twenty-three times better chance of admission than his equivalent in the rural north-east (ibid., p. 240).

The first step towards securing social justice in education would be to devote more attention to the primary, as compared with higher levels. The latter are largely the prerogative of the rich and powerful and the urban resident. Such a shift need not be at any great cost to overall economic growth for, as Table 7.4 shows, the social returns to primary schooling are much higher than those to secondary and higher levels. Psacharopoulos (1981, p. 329) points out that its social profitability is relatively even greater than it appears. This is because the calculations make a general assumption of earnings foregone when attending school, an assumption which is less justified in the case of the younger, primary pupils than at higher levels of education.

There is no encouragement here to those (Ahluwalia and Carter, 1981, pp. 470ff) who see some kind of conflict between the needs of development and the requirements of social justice. What international comparisons demonstrate is actually the very reverse of this. In the poor countries of sub-Saharan Africa, for example, a hundred times as much is spent per capita on higher education as compared with that at the elementary level. This is exceptional, but nowhere outside Europe and the other industrialised countries is the ratio less than eight to one (World Bank, 1980b, p. 46).

In very poor countries it is arguable that the shift in emphasis should be even greater, focussing not merely on the primary stage, but concentrating even more narrowly upon the first four or five years of primary school. Five years is the minimum period, according to UNESCO, in which literacy can become established as a permanent possession of the individual.

UNESCO may here be expecting too much of such a short experience of education. It is also hazardous to leave out of account the possibility that leaving school so soon may rob children from illiterate homes of any opportunity they might have had of continuing to practise their newly acquired reading and writing skills. Nevertheless there is a case for giving priority to the provision of some education for everybody, even if it is at the cost of further education for some others.

Rural Education

Although there are very many desperately poor people in the slums and among the unemployed of the cities, most poverty and deprivation will be found in the countryside. Because of the relative sparseness of rural populations, and the problems of communication which distance and a difficult terrain create, there are severe logistical problems in providing the poor (and incidentally the residents of rural areas) with their fair share of education.

It is reasonable to assume that the accessibility of the school will be an important factor making for its utilisation (Leslie and Jamison, 1980, pp. 118–19). Boarding schools are no solution for poor countries – even if their closely-knit families would allow children to go away, or could spare them for so long from the seasonal demands upon their labour. All-age schools are a common expedient. These are usually assumed in the North to provide a very unsatisfactory learning environment, but this may not necessarily be the case in the more communally-orientated, rural cultures of the South, where children would expect to assist one another. However it would be common sense also to adapt the school time-table to the rhythms or the calendar of agriculture. Fewer children would then be kept away from school at sowing or harvest time.

What the remoter areas probably need is all-purpose education workers, rather like the village health workers discussed in the last chapter. Bearing in mind that their work would mainly be at the primary level, they would not themselves need to have any pretensions to high levels of scholarship (Evans, 1981, p. 35). Nor would they need to be fully qualified as teachers, though they would need training in the difficult art of teaching the beginnings of literacy and numeracy. It would be a particular advantage if they were local residents who therefore understood and were trusted by their neighbours' children.

This sounds like providing Third World village children with an inferior education. There are two answers that can be given to such a charge. The first is that the alternative may be no education at all. The second is that it may not be all that inferior. Northern educationists may have become so hypnotised by the formal aspects of education as to overlook the personal and social influences which may be very potent in a more cohesive society than theirs.

Apart from the local knowledge and acceptability of a village education worker, current research (Simmons and Alexander, 1980; Richards and Leonor, 1981; Psacharopoulos, 1981) points to the importance of home background (at the primary level at any rate) and of teacher motivation (Simmons and Alexander, 1980). These seem to have more influence on the achievements of the schools than the training and qualifications of teachers, or the level of unit expenditure on education (except on books) (ibid., pp. 77–8).

A locally-based education worker would also be able to provide instruction through the medium of the local language or dialect. Failure in this may exclude many rural children from participation in the educational system. However, vernacular education has its own disadvantages. It may have the effect of restricting the 'life chances' of those involved, as well as impairing the performance of the country itself on the world stage.

Another of these research conclusions, which may have more

relevance to urban areas than to the more sparsely populated rural areas, challenges the conventional assumption that larger classes, within certain limits, necessarily mean lower levels of educational achievement (ibid., p. 90; World Bank, 1980b, p. 52). The fact that, in many urban schools, several large classes may share a single room, with a consequent increase in the general noise level and in mutual distraction, does not seem to have received attention from researchers.

All of which underlines once again the importance of well thought-out appropriate technologies for social services delivery (Young *et al.*, 190b). In this connection, some have suggested the use of broadcasting as a way of reaching children in the remoter areas of a country (ibid.; Leslie and Jamison, 1980). This has sometimes been very successful, as, for example, in Latin America (Evans, 1981, p. 41); and in the various mass-education campaigns mounted in Tanzania, specially the health education campaign, *Mtu ni afya* (Man is health), carried out in 1973 (Hall and Dodds, 1974).

Television will have limited utility in poor countries; transmitters of sufficient power would be too costly, and receivers too few. Radios might offer more opportunities, though it is difficult to see already heavily-burdened parents from the villages, even if they possessed a radio, having the time or inclination to insist on their children working away at their broadcast lessons. There is probably more scope for using the radio as a form of enrichment for the lessons provided in the village school by a teacher whose own background may be rather limited (ibid.).

There is, however, a more radical form of 'appropriate' educational provision than any of these: the expansion of non-formal provision. This deserves and will receive more detailed consideration in the next chapter.

Education of Women

The deprived educational status of women, indicated by Table 7.6, is confirmed by figures on illiteracy provided by the WHO (1987, p. 21). Indeed, the evidence from this report is that it is actually deteriorating:

... in 1970 in the developing countries as a whole, 40% of

females and 57% of females aged 15 years and above were illiterate; ten years later the proportions were 32% and 49% ... almost two-thirds of illiterate adults in the developing world are women. In the least developed countries this gap widened ... from 72% of males and 89% of females in 1970 to 63% and 83% respectively in 1980.

Future trends are unlikely to be any better in view of the figures given for female school enrolment over the sixteen years to 1986 (see Table 7.7). These show that there has been no real improvement here either. Not only do girls enter school in smaller numbers than boys, but there seems general agreement also that more of them drop out. Coombs points out (1985, p. 225) that educational discrimination against women – which includes a more limited choice of subjects as well as a lower rate of enrolment – is particularly marked where the general level of participation in education is itself low.

Resistance to the provision of education for them is the result not only of their general state of subjugation, but also of the fact that the role which is assigned to them does not seem to imply any need for education. In addition many Third World women, when they marry, by custom go to live with their husbands' families. To spend time and money in educating a daughter who is going to take whatever she has gained away with her to another family, is not seen as a very sensible proceeding. It has to be remembered that parents look to their children to support them in old age, and would want to see any investment they made in education in this light.

Quite apart from considerations of social justice, there is a

Table 7.7. Percentage of females in total school enrolments in underdeveloped countries (UNESCO, 1984b, 1986, 1988, pp. 2–17, 2–18)

	Primary	*Secondary*	*Higher*	*All educ. levels*
1970	42	34	29	40
1975	43	37	32	41
1980	44	39	35	42
1983	44	40	36	42
1984	44	39	36	43
1985	44	40	37	42
1986	44	40	37	43

strong case on pragmatic grounds for giving some priority to female education. This would release and inform the constructive abilities of half of the population. There is also evidence to show that both the health and nutrition of children are better where women have received some education (World Bank, 1980b, p. 50) and there is also a link, if a rather complex one, between female education and lower fertility (Cochrane, 1977; United Nations, 1985b, pp. 66ff). All of these are desirable for their own sake, as well as having their contribution to make to economic development. The *World Yearbook of Education, 1984* (Acker, 1984a) and a special number of the *Comparative Education Review* (24, 1980) have been devoted to the education of women.

Educational Inflation

This emphasis on the lower levels of educational provision runs counter to the advice which has so often in the past been given to underdeveloped countries. Attention has been focussed upon something called 'manpower planning'. Bearing in mind the importance of the informal sector of employment, it is surprising that the opportunities for training people for work in this sector (Taylor, 1981) have not figured more prominently in such advice. Instead the emphasis has been on higher education, to be given by a country's anticipated need for certain kinds of highly-trained specialist in the future.

Although the estimates of the number of these experts who will be required are apt to be too high in relation to the ability of an underdeveloped country to utilise them (Coombs, 1985, p. 173), this advice has been enthusiastically followed in many countries. 'Africa increased primary school enrolments by 218% during the twenty years from 1960, while higher education increased by 709%. The corresponding figures for South Asia were 128% and 411% and for Latin America, 135% and 831%' (ibid., p. 214, citing UNESCO, 1983).

One consequence of putting higher education in the forefront of attention in this way has been the 'educational inflation' to which Dore (1976, pp. 1ff) and others have called attention. Jobs for the educated, such as they are, arise either in the government service or in the developed urban enclave, where the most senior executive or technical positions go to expatriates anyway. The importation by a transnational of its own people in this way is an accepted part of the exploitation which the dependent underdevelopment of a country makes possible.

In such a buyer's market for local educated labour, employers are in a position to demand higher and higher qualifications. This has generated among the elites of many of these countries a frenzied and competitive demand for advanced training, and for the certificates and diplomas to which it can lead, out of all proportion to the country's ability to provide commensurate employment. Such qualifications become more and more ritualised, more and more unrelated to the real life of the country – what Dore (ibid.) has called the Diploma Disease. Meanwhile a serious unemployment problem now includes a major (and politically dangerous) element of 'educated unemployment and underemployment'.

This phenomenon is manifested in many countries (Coombs, 1985, pp. 194ff), but especially in certain countries of Asia. Taking Sri Lanka as an example, Dore (1976, p. 4) writes:

> At the beginning of the seventies, the schools were producing annually about 70,000 children with eight years' education, nearly 100,000 with the first 'Ordinary Level' secondary certificate, and another 12,000 with higher level certificates. At the same time the total number of wage and salary jobs coming available was *altogether* probably no more than 70,000 – and there were all the disappointed aspirants of previous years joining them in the competition.

Coombs (1985, pp. 195–6) points to the widespread gap between the aspirations of such students and the reality confronting them. Disillusionment with education is one outcome to be expected. Another is an alienation of educated young people from society, which is potentially threatening to the structure of social order itself.

The blame for all this is not, of course, to be laid at the door of the highly educated sections of the population. It arises out of the stagnation of an underdeveloped economy. Psacharopoulos and Sanyal (1981, pp. 37–40) show that the 'middle levels of education are especially hit by unemployment ... unemployment clearly peaks at the secondary or college drop-out level' This gives support to the view already stated that, so long as the economy is underdeveloped, the highest return is going to be obtained from making at least some primary education available to as many people as possible.

Meanwhile the need to train enough specialists to meet the realistic needs of the country cannot be ignored, even if the returns to that investment must come later. More will be said about this later.

Summary

The yawning gap in education between the North and the South is only too obvious from the figures for illiteracy and for school enrolments. Some limited progress has been made in both of these indices over the years, but not enough to counter the large increases in population, especially among children. The number of illiterates and of children 'out of school' is still increasing.

Meanwhile the colonial tradition of an over-academic form of education, with its urban bias, has been continued, resulting in the 'diploma disease' – an overvaluation of paper qualifications. Nevertheless the returns to investment in education are considerable, and often greater than to investment in physical 'productive' assets. As investment in human capital, education is a strong contender for overseas development aid.

There is great inequity in the distribution of such education as is available – between rich and poor, rural and urban residents, and men and women. This discrimination increases at the higher levels of education. As educational inequality preserves existing inequalities in power and wealth, its reduction would represent an important step towards greater social justice.

8

Ends and Means in Education

Cultural Change

Some educationists in both North and South have seen the greatest contribution of education in the effect it might have in the modernisation of attitudes, which incidentally would mean the weakening of traditional beliefs and customs. It is not at all clear that such a replacement of the 'economy of affection' by our individualistic and self-seeking way of life is going to be a gain. Maybe there is a stage in the industrialisation of a country at which this becomes unavoidable, but much would be sacrificed in the process. In particular, the 'mutual aid society' of family and community would be lost, calling for a massive expansion in public social provision in its place.

A number of countries which have travelled even a little way along this path are already beginning to try to retrace their steps, notably, for example, the government of Fiji in its Eighth Development Plan (Fiji, 1980). Even a country as modernised as Singapore, but with the strong Chinese family tradition behind it, has been urged by its Prime Minister to reject a welfare state solution in favour of a combination of family care and occupational social services.

Then there is the dislocation which arises as one system slowly replaces another. Desperate needs would remain unmet, but this would be by no means the only consequence. Traditional ways of life are not simply a collection of behavioural prescriptions. Such prescriptions are embedded in a matrix of beliefs which play an important part in holding the society together. Experience shows that, during periods of cultural transformation (as in the 'melting-pot' of the United States, among the Indians of both North and South America, among the indigenous peoples of New Zealand and Australia, and even in old Europe at present), there is usually a lengthy phase of value conflict and confusion before a new equilibrium is found.

One example of the way this is affecting the Third World is the form taken in many countries by corruption (see Chapter 13). Another is the alarm engendered in Malaysian villages by the changes in the behaviour of Muslim girls when they migrate from the countryside into the city (Fawcett, Khoo and Smith, 1984, p. 139).

If it is through the schools that the new life-style is propagated, this anomic state is likely to be further compounded by inter-generational problems. No extraordinary prophetic powers are required, in these circumstances, to predict an increase in many social problems, including delinquency and other forms of aliena-tion among young people, and uncertainty about, or even disre-gard for social norms. It may be that this alienation is already under way (see Chapters 10). Modernisation may be inevitable, but if it has to be brought about it will require a more community-based approach than that which the school provides.

The conflict between modern and traditional values, however, is only part of the tangled ideological skein which Third World countries have to try to unravel, and which have important bearings on educational policy. There are at least two other elements which must be brought into the reckoning. The first of these is the idea of the nation, cherished by all governments of new countries. The second is what Freire called 'conscientisation'.

Nation-Building

Beset as so many governments are by conflicts between tribes and other linguistic groups or between different races, many of them see the unity among their people which consciousness of nationality can give as an essential condition for any significant progress, whether in the economic or the social spheres. This is not a new idea. The Americans have long used ceremonies around the raising and lowering of the national flag as well as more specific teaching about the significance of American nationality as a way of fusing its melting-pot of immigrant nationalities into a unity.

Such a policy will not work, however, where divisions arise out of deeply-rooted differences in religion and culture which are able to call up strong emotions. If they are also backed by formidable structural barriers, such as historical segregation in residence and occupation, differences in power, and economic and other vested interests (Bullivant, 1981; Jones, 1981) the search for any kind of simple unity must be doomed to frustration. It took a civil war to underline this fact in Nigeria. Events in Malaysia and in Fiji, Sri Lanka, Kenya and Uganda have shown that ethnic hostility can survive many generations of living side by side.

It must be possible to create proud and self-conscious nations around a full acceptance of differences. The failure to do so is a sign either of an unnecessary lack of confidence in the governments concerned, or of unwillingness on the part of the dominant group to share some of its privileges. For there is no law of nature that says uniformity is strength. Rather the reverse. A nation which can rely upon many and varied contributions to its life is a fortunate one.

If particular steps need to be taken to ensure that racial or ethnic minorities (or even majorities who are politically weak) do not receive a worse education, either as a result of an attempt to 'assimilate' them in the interests of nation building, or because of undue privileges given to members of a dominant group. This would not preclude 'positive discrimination', like that exercised in favour of the dominant *bumiputras* in Malaysia, if social justice required it, though sympathetic attention would have to be given to the feelings of grievance which this might provoke among other groups.

Sometimes the achievement of equity between ethnic groups has to take account of segregation in areas of residence. For example, the Tamils of northern Sri Lanka live in clearly demarcated areas. The East Indians of Guyana live in the country, while the politically dominant Afro-Guyanese are mainly urbanised. To allow differences in educational provision to persist between these different localities is to produce a form of unjust ethnic discrimination.

The special cultural needs of ethnic groups may also be insufficiently provided for. A traditional language, for example, may have ritual or religious significance, or may be the only way members have of maintaining contact with their history or literature. If it is excluded from the classroom, the group's willingness to participate will be at risk. East Indians, who are ethnic minorities in so many countries, often find themselves in this position. There is, of course, the opposite danger. Lack of facility in the dominant tongue because of exclusive use of an ethnic language may cause the future life chances of a group to be severely restricted. There are many other cultural requirements besides language. The turban of the Sikh, or the Muslim requirement of prayer at fixed hours during the day, are only two such. All seem divisive to the determined unifier, but none more so than the outright challenge of a rival language.

Tokenism is a great temptation, but it would solve nothing. Bullivant (1981, pp. 218ff) points out that the *ad hoc* introduction of minor ethnic elements into schools may in fact merely have the effect of establishing the cultures in question as subordinate. They may also be used to distract attention from inequalities in power and life chances. Instead they should be incorporated within what he calls a 'polyethnic' curriculum. This would ensure that all were on an equal footing at least as far as education was concerned.

A nation-building programme which focusses mainly on the school would in any case be too narrowly based. Either the influence of the school would be too weak to contend with the many cultural pressures emanating from the child's family and indigenous community, or it would be successful and alienate him from his own people. The occurrence of such alienation was observed in the United States by Thrasher, many years ago, in his study of juvenile gangs in Chicago (Thrasher, 1937).

This is not to say that an education which is tolerant of differences cannot play a part in inculcating in children a sense of being members of a nation, but it can only do so if the society itself is no less tolerant, making such a national identity acceptable to their elders also.

Conscientisation

During the years when countries were struggling to free themselves from colonial subjection, the idea of a 'free nation' was in the forefront of attention, providing a powerful symbol around which support for independence could gather. Often, however, there was also a subsidiary theme: that of relieving the poverty and other social ills from which so many people suffered. These were usually presented as a consequence of colonial exploitation, and therefore remediable by the achievement of independence.

Some of the new leaders, Nyerere prominent among them, understood that political independence did not necessarily mean the end of economic exploitation by the North, and adopted radical socialist policies in the quest for a more genuine independence, one in which an improvement in the lot of the poorer sections of the community might be aimed at. In other countries, mainly in Africa, disappointment among the people because that independence had not led to the expected improvement in their condition, led to political instability, and an increase in the expression of socialist sentiments among the hard-pressed governments concerned.

Latin American countries have a much longer history of independence, and some had higher GNPs per capita than most of the newly emancipated countries. Nevertheless they all had serious problems of poverty, whether regional, as in north-western Brazil, or on a national basis, as in Honduras or Bolivia. It was not surprising, therefore, that there should be a similar swing to the left, at least in popular feeling. Many Roman Catholic priests moved to the left with their people, becoming a powerful radical force. Writers like Freire (1972) and Fanon (1980) preached an eloquent revolutionary message.

In few of the countries of South America did this find any expression in government policies. Many of them were ruled by dictators or juntas backed by the great landowners. Where elections made a shift to the left possible, military coups, often backed, alas, by a United States which was too concerned about American capital invested in these countries, soon brought about a return to the old oligarchies. One successful coup of this kind was the removal from power of Allende in Chile, but more recent happenings in Nicaragua and in El Salvador show that the same forces are still powerfully at work.

Nevertheless socialist ideas have had much influence on educational thinking, rooted in many cases in Marxism. This has led to a view of the school as a means by which capitalism produces a 'false consciousness' in the working population, so that they accept their deprivations as unavoidable or in some way justifiable. The schools thus become important in the political struggle.

Freire (1972, p. 31) saw the proper role of education as the 'conscientisation' of the population. By this he meant opening their eyes to the oppression from which they suffer, and to the way in which this is sustained by dominant beliefs and ideas. When they have thrown off these blinkers, education becomes at last a 'pedagogy of all men in the process of permanent liberation'. Ideas like these have been widely influential, being reflected, for example, in the image of the 'new man' in Cuba, and in much of Nyerere's thinking about the role of education in Tanzania.

But Freire was writing from a non-socialist Brazil, and therefore was assessing the education of the poor as a potentially emancipatory force. The situation would be different in an African country, already socialist, where the need was for the stabilisation of the social order.

It is the same sense of the political significance of schools which accounts, among other things, for the suspicion among some socialist development theorists about the views (to be examined shortly) of Philip Foster. He argues that curricula are less important than the motivation for education which arises from the availability of employment. There appears to be a curious reversal of roles here. For example, one would have expected a socialist like Carnoy (1975), while regretting Foster's enthusiasm for market forces (Foster, 1975) to agree with the latter at least in his claim for the fundamental importance of the economic factor.

Many may balk at the suggestion that the classroom should be used (as they see it) as a means of political indoctrination; but others will argue that it is naive to pretend that political ideologies of one sort or another do not always play a part. Just as education overtly hostile to capitalist values would be inconceivable and dysfunctional in a capitalist society, so would education with a capitalist orientation in a self-consciously socialist Third World country.

Marxists argue that each economic system produces and propagates its own self-justifying ideology, and this dominates what is taught in the schools. Thus in capitalist societies, private property and individualistic motivations for effort are legitimated, not merely by the content of lessons, and the readers and other texts which are used, but even by the school's mode of organisation and its structure of incentives. On this assumption, radical changes in the ideals animating education, such as those sought by Freire, as well as a more equitable distribution of educational opportunities, must await a shift towards socialism. History suggests that this is unduly pessimistic. Incremental improvement can gradually bring about desirable changes. As Freire's own experience in Brazil shows, attempting too great a leap forward may serve to alarm powerful vested interests and actually set the clock back.

Though ideologies are thus inescapable, facts and fact-based theories should remain inviolate if education is not to consist simply of a form of brain-washing which could be as harmful to the future of the country as to that of the children themselves. The purpose of education is to open minds, not close them.

Ideology may also make its own contribution to education. The collective motivations engendered by widespread acceptance of the socialist ethic can in their turn help to marshal public support behind national educational campaigns. The 'nation' by comparison may seem remote from the daily realities of village and family life, and so make a weak appeal. In particular it appears rather hollow in the face of a reality in which extremes of wealth and poverty are, it appears, to continue to be tolerated between national 'brothers'.

The examples usually cited are the successful adult literacy campaigns carried out in Cuba, Tanzania and China. Castro set aside 1961 as the Year of Education and, closing all the schools, sent the teaching staff and pupils into the country to teach illiterate adults. The aim was to abolish illiteracy within a year. This was a carefully planned scheme, involving the identification of illiterates, the training of instructors, and the provision of incentives to people to accept instruction by holding out to them the prospect of more scope within the co-operatives. The outcome: a rise in the literacy rate from 75 per cent to 96 per cent, meaning that 70 000 more people were enabled to read and write (Noor, 1981, p. 13).

Even a poor socialist country like Tanzania could marshal enough support to make a million literates a year over a four-year period (ibid.). China's achievements in reducing illiteracy have been no less impressive, though they seem to have taken rather longer (ibid.). According to a tentative estimate by the World

Bank (1982, p. 196), she managed to raise the level of literacy between 1960 and 1980 from 43 per cent to 69 per cent of the population aged fifteen and over.

With some exceptions (for example, Korea) literacy campaigns in countries which have not been able to draw on imagery about greater social justice and the building of a new society have achieved less impressive results, with high costs in relation to the number of people becoming literate, and with many either dropping out or relapsing afterwards. Except in times of national emergency it has proved impossible for the more pluralistic, non-socialist countries to bring about the kind of national mobilisation that marked mass literacy campaigns in Cuba and China.

Non-Formal Education

Particularly relevant to literacy campaigns is the distinction drawn between formal, informal and non-formal education. The first of these, the formal, is that involving classes in school. Informal education proceeds through the ordinary relationships of everyday life – within the family, the community or the various organisations to which the individual belongs. Informal methods as so defined have, of course, always been important in traditional education and socialisation.

The third, the non-formal type, differs from the informal in the fact that it is *organised*, either by the state or by churches or other non-official bodies. Like informal education, however, versions of it have always been part of socialisation in traditional society. These include 'apprenticeships' to craftsmen, hunters and healers, the organised instruction of age-grades in their social obligations and so on. Also like informal education, it is distinguished from formal approaches in making use of unorthodox ('appropriate') techniques and in being more decentralised and therefore less authoritarian and standardised. This means that it can be conducted through the medium of the local vernacular language, making it a more authentic and manageable experience than education conducted in, say, English, or in some equally alien 'national language' promoted by the government in the interest of nation building. This has its disadvantages, of course, for those who want to continue their education to a higher level, or to use it as a stepping-stone to work in the civil service or the modernised sector.

The localised nature of non-formal education also facilitates participation by 'consumers' in the shaping and management of the programme. This constitutes a form of education in itself, and also ensures that the instruction provided more nearly meets their perceived needs. To that end, it can be flexible and very varied, and offer new scope to ethnic minorities and other disadvantaged groups. These features of non-formal programmes must help to increase the motivation to engage in education, so long as the rewards for so doing are commensurate with the effort and opportunity costs involved.

Although missionaries and other pioneers in Third World education have utilised non-formal approaches for many years, it has been mainly the 'deschoolers' (Illich, 1971; Reimer, 1971) and the followers of Freire who have made us aware of the emancipating potentialities within this type of education. But in many poor countries its relatively low cost (Iraq appears to be a high-cost exception) figures largest, opening up the possibility of education on a wider scale than such countries could otherwise have afforded:

> Facilities will normally be simple and low-cost, while more use is made of educational and non-educational settings designed primarily for other purposes, and of staff who are not professional educators, including part-timers and volunteers. Since part-time study dominates, the opportunity cost of student time is kept low, and costs to the public budget may be reduced through community self-help and, sometimes, by the sale of commodities produced during the educational process. (Simkins, 1977, p. 16)

Its classification into complementary, supplementary and replacement modes (Evans, 1981, pp. 19ff) is an aid to understanding. In its *complementary* form, it is used to enrich formal schooling at the primary, and less commonly secondary, level, through a wide range of leisure, cultural, vocational and other life-centred activities. Social agencies and factories may be encouraged as in Cuba, to involve themselves in the work of the schools and children may be given attachments within these settings.

Cuba took a step further with its 'schools to the countryside' programme. This involved all junior high school students in a forty-five-day stint in rural camps, combining a limited amount of academic study with farmwork. This was to progress to 'schools in the countryside', with the intention that all junior school education should take the form of an integrated programme of work and study (Leiner, 1975).

Supplementary non-formal education is a way of extending the education of those whose formal schooling has ceased, usually because they have dropped out or been unable to meet the academic or financial requirements for continuing in school. They include a variety of vocationally orientated learning activities within practical settings, ranging from apprenticeships and other in-service forms of training to the practical education provided for unemployed young people in organisations like the Brigades of Botswana, described in Chapter 10.

The Village Polytechnics of Kenya (Anderson, 1971; 1973, pp. 282–301) are another variant. The following brief account of their aims is culled from a Kenya government publication (Kenya, 1971):

A Village Polytechnic is a low-cost training centre in a rural area. It aims at giving primary school-leavers from that area skills, understanding and values which will make them able to look for money-making opportunities where they live, and to contribute to rural development by building up the economic strength of their own community.

In its *replacement* mode, non-formal education is intended to provide compensatory opportunities for those who would otherwise miss out altogether. It includes the kind of 'appropriate' arrangements to be made for children of school age in remote areas, where formal schooling is difficult to provide, such as radio study groups, and the village education worker already mentioned. The work of village health workers, social workers and community development staff may also incorporate a considerable amount of education.

Community development (to be discussed more fully in Chapter 10) has considerable potentiality for non-formal education. It encourages intellectual and personal growth through participation, as well as more specific forms of learning by groups engaged in understanding and solving the problems met in their communities.

Literacy Campaigns

As the figures given in Chapter 7 show, there has been an improvement in literacy rates in most countries, but population trends cause the horizon to recede all the time. Nobody would question the need for more effective campaigns with adults in an attempt to catch up, but what form should they take? Although it is taken for granted that they should be non-formal in their methods and content, they can make their own contribution to the formal system by enabling the newly literate adults to provide the kind of domestic environment in which children, made literate in school, are able to practise their new skills and thus preserve them. One of the most serious problems of Third World education is the frequency with which so-called 'established literacy' is lost when attendance at school comes to an end. Relapses are not confined to the graduates of the adult campaigns.

In return, children at school may have much to offer informally to adults in their families, and even to a wider circle as teachers in non-formal programmes. The chain-reaction could extend further: the missionary activities of children at home could strengthen their own grasp of what they have learned in the classroom.

Exhibit **8.1 Shortcomings of literacy campaigns**

Noor (1981, p. 14) has listed the following reasons for the relative lack of success of adult literacy programmes:

teaching adults as if they were children;
providing too little subsequent scope for using the skills gained (as with the children);
giving too few opportunities to women who, it seems from the statistics, are the better prospects for success;
failing to offer incentives which would make people willing to make the necessary sacrifices or face local scepticism.

In developing a literacy campaign, it is important (extending the ideas of Foster in a way which he might not accept) to convince potential trainees that the benefit to them in the end will be enough to justify the personal and financial costs to which they are committed by taking part. At least some weight was given to this in the experimental Functional Literacy programme conducted jointly by UNESCO and The United Nations Development Programme (UNDP) between 1967 and 1974 (UNESCO 1980; UNESCO/ UNDP, 1976). 'Briefly the idea was to combine literacy and numeracy with a programme of education in basic vocational skills directly linked to the occupational needs of participants' (ibid., p. 120).

Teaching shifted between the classroom and a variety of practical settings: demonstration plots, fields actually under cultivation, poultry houses workshops, and so on. This sometimes had the effect of improving agricultural or workshop practice, as well as advancing literacy (ibid., p. 167). There were also favourable effects upon wider aspects of social behaviour – interest in further education, management of personal finances, participation in co-operatives, clubs, political parties, village councils and so on – though perhaps rather less than had been hoped for (ibid., p. 176ff).

This non-academic approach has often been challenged, mirroring a wider debate in which Philip Foster among others has questioned the value of vocational education (Foster, 1966). In fact, Foster's objections are to education which is directed narrowly towards vocational training, particularly in agriculture. He offers no opposition to the use of the rural setting as a basis for literacy and numeracy training, which he sees as merely a proper use of pedagogical method (Foster and Sheffield, 1973, p. 7).

Overall the experiment was felt to have justified itself. Table 8.1 gives, for those countries for which suitable data is available, some indication both of the overall achievements of the programme and of the difficulties it encountered – particularly its high drop-out and even higher failure rates. The figures hardly suggest that the project had discovered any final solution to the problem of either motivation or pedagogical method. There is also the question of how to retain such gains as have been made. The relating of literacy and numeracy to daily work seems as hopeful a way as any of achieving that.

Table 8.1   Results of UNESCO/UNDP literacy programme, selected countries (UNESCO/UNDP, 1976, p. 174)

	Enrolment	Examinees	Passes
Tanzania	466 000	293 600	96 900
Iran	97 400	46 900	13 900
Ethiopia	36 800	21 700	9 300
Ecuador	17 500	10 000	4 100
Sudan	7 400	2 400	600

Cost, also, is a not unimportant consideration for such poor countries and it has been estimated, for the eight countries concerned, that in only one (Sudan) would primary school have been cheaper. For the other countries the savings over orthodox schooling varied: 2 per cent in Ethiopia, 28 per cent in Ecuador, 55 per cent in Madagascar, 63 per cent in Iran, 85 per cent in Tanzania, 86 per cent in Algeria and 89 per cent in Mali (ibid., pp. 188–9).

Relevance of the School

The apparently favourable influence of a curriculum which was oriented in this way towards the real world brings into the centre of attention the much debated question of whether the school should not also be less academic than it often is. The contention is that, in spite of the introduction of non-formal elements into the curricula of many schools, former colonies have often continued the tradition of predominantly scholastic education which they inherited from their imperial masters (Watson, 1982, p. 184), although such forms of study bore little relevance to the daily lives of the rural masses. Hence the reluctance of many to send their children to school in the first place, and the high drop-out rates. Indeed those children who enrolled and stayed on would do so because their families wanted 'more' for them than simply returning to the village afterwards, resulting in an in-built resistance to change among those who used the schools.

In so far as the more academic kind of curriculum had any practical relevance at all, went the argument, it was going to be in the towns. The less practical kind of curriculum thus merely exacerbated the problem of excessive urbanisation. Children would continue at school in order to obtain certificates to enhance their chances of success if they did migrate. Not unnaturally they would then feel that remaining in the village was a waste of this superior education of theirs.

Finally it is not beyond the bounds of possibility that the abstractions and other intellectual preoccupations of the more academic forms of schooling make children impatient with the limitations of rural life. There may be something here like the distinction made by Saul Bernstein (Lee, 1973) between the linguistic usages of the middle and working classes. The former Bernstein saw as more concerned with concepts, and therefore as functional in a middle-class world where direct physical action often took second place to the manipulation of ideas. The latter, on the other hand, with its predominance of active verbs and concrete nouns, had special value in a life-style in which action in the present was the overriding objective.

The damage done by an excessively abstract curriculum might then not be confined to its effect in augmenting the flow of urban migrants. It could also have a selective effect, seducing away from the country-side the more ambitious and able children: those who had not only stayed on at school, but had also coped best with its abstractions.

Perhaps it is time to give up slavish adherence to Northern educational ideas, developing instead curricula which are related to the needs of people living in the villages and working on the land. This is the view which has been so stoutly contested by Philip Foster in a series of books and papers (1965, 1966, 1975 and so on) which have had considerable influence on the policies of bodies like the World Bank and UNESCO. He writes in the following passage about what motivates children and their parents when making decisions about education:

Their vocational aspirations are almost exclusively determined by factors which lie outside the schools. No amount of technical, vocational or agricultural instruction taken alone within the formal educational system is going to check the movement from the rural areas or reduce the volume of unemployment. The crucial variables lie in the structure of incentives within the economic system and the degree to which [it] supports entrepreneurial activity. (Foster, 1965)

It should be noted that what Foster is rejecting is any claim that the curriculum is the whole answer – 'taken alone'. He must surely be right in this. How could anybody doubt that the 'structure of incentives' is important? In those countries in which an affluent life-style has already been achieved and the marginal rate of taxation is substantial, there will be people who are willing to undertake an education purely for reasons of recreation or self-realisation. The sacrifices, the marginal opportunity costs, are not high in relation to the expected benefits from the education.

In a Third World country, on the other hand, the expenditure of time or money on education may mean genuine material deprivation for a whole family group which traditional culture expects to be placed first. In such circumstances, prospective students will have to feel that a course of study will open up new opportunities for them. They will have to see it as an investment – for them and their families.

The bearing of the condition of underdevelopment upon all this is only too obvious – even if Foster has not been prepared to acknowledge it (Foster, 1975, p. 430). So long as the dual economy persists, so long as a growing army of landless peasants and of the mass unemployed in squalid, overblown cities, continue in juxtaposition with highly profitable expatriate exploitation, opportunities for improving one's circumstances will remain too few to motivate the uneducated millions.

No doubt neo-classicists, with their faith in the market economy, would urge them to educate themselves, so as to be equipped to compete for the jobs which are going. This, 'taken alone' (to borrow Foster's phrase) would not provide more jobs. In the unlikely event that it gained any credibility outside the groups with power and influence who are already caught up in this contest, its effect could only be to intensify the struggle for those jobs which exist, with that accompanying further proliferation and devaluation of qualifications against which Dore has warned us.

In other words, the enemy is still underdevelopment. Human capital is still constrained by the limited opportunities for its application which the underdeveloped economy can provide. The revival of the rural economy could motivate people to seek an education, but even then not of the more academic kind. To appeal, education would have to be relevant to the opportunities which rural life was then able to offer them.

Basic Education

Doubts about both the relevance and equity of formal education in the Third World has led to the emergence of the concept of 'basic education' (Noor, 1981; Coombs, 1985, p. 54). As education for life it should comprise more than basic literacy and numeracy, or even the wider studies encompassed in a primary school course. And for all the reasons of equity given in Chapter 7, it should be available to everybody irrespective of nationality, ethnicity, sex or income.

Part of the 'basic needs' philosophy, it implies a major shift in educational expenditure in favour of the deprived and disadvantaged. The idea of giving priority to four years of primary school for all has emerged from this school of thought. The wider horizons adopted by those adult literacy campaigns which have a functional perspective involve them also in providing what amounts to a 'basic education' for adults – and could also set in train the parallel process of 'lifelong education', which so many see as also necessary if the educational backlog is ever to be made up.

Noor (1981, p. 9) divides 'basic education' under three headings:

(a) Communication skills and general knowledge, including 'literacy (if possible [sic]), numeracy, and general civic, scientific, and cultural knowledge, values and attitudes'.
(b) Life skills and knowledge, embracing 'hygienic practices, sanitation, nutrition, family planning, the environment, management of the family economy, and creating and maintaining the home'.
(c) 'Production skills, which embrace all forms of activity directed towards making a living or the production of goods and services, at whatever level of sophistication.' (Also see Coombs, 1985, p. 54.)

This underlines what has been a major theme in this chapter: that education needs to reflect more closely the concerns of everyday life. The argument so far has been that this justifies it in the eyes of those who are being invited to partake of it, but it is more than a question of motivation, important though this may be. There is a sense in which these various aspects of preparation for life, like Siamese twins, cannot be separated without harm to all.

It has been pointed out, for example, that literate mothers are more likely to provide their families with a satisfactory diet and commit their families to better health and hygiene practices. They also tend to space their children more rationally. Improved agricultural methods also result from progress in literacy and numeracy. These gains in their turn strengthen motives for education and the opportunity and ability to benefit from it. At the policy level, lower rates of reproduction also play their part, making more manageable the country's task of raising levels of literacy and numeracy.

A knowledge of political and cultural conditions in the country is also required if increasing social competence is to be accompanied by a fair share of power in the state. And political power may be a precondition for persuading the 'haves' in the society to embark on something as potentially dangerous as the education of the 'have nots'. If these sound like 'chicken and egg' problems, so they are. A little progress in one respect will facilitate a little progress in another, and so slowly but steadily forward. On such assumptions, village workers in health and education, agricultural extension workers, social workers, community developers and even party organisers have tasks to perform which are intimately interrelated.

Exhibit 8.2   A 'basic education' educational system

Some commentators have questioned whether an effective 'basic education' policy could be implemented without rethinking the nature of Third World education from the ground up, and supporting it by equally drastic reforms in society as a whole (Simkins, 1977, pp. 54ff). It would require a massive shift of investment to the non-formal sector, probably at the expense of formal schooling.

This would not only be for resource reasons. If non-formal education coexisted with a substantial and prestigious formal sector, it would soon come to be seen by the educationally ambitious as 'second best'. Those who could would opt for orthodox Northern-style education, and those who could not achieve this would press for changes in the direction of formal schooling, examinations, certificates and so on. There is already some evidence that this is happening in non-formal developments like the Botswana Bridgades, and the Village Polytechnics of Kenya.

Such a process would have to gain its credibility from the structure of incentives in the country as a whole. The non-formal system would be mainly directed at the needs of a stagnant countryside, while employers in the modern sector would always give preference to those with a Northern type of education and paper qualifications. The indebtedness of this kind of thinking to Foster is obvious enough, though it is unlikely that he would approve of the solution which is proposed.

This solution would be a major shift in the centre of gravity of the education system, so that non-formal education became the norm; accompanied by a parallel social and economic policy seeking to achieve development rather than under-development. The latter would include policies for the revival of the countryside, and for taking back control of the country's resources and industry so that they might enrich the people themselves rather than transnationals from overseas. It is no accident that the most striking advances in non-formal education have been made in countries like China, Cuba and Tanzania, where educational reform has been part of a wide-ranging transformation of society itself.

Giving a prominent role to non-formal approaches does, of course, mean that education becomes much less stable as a system, with growing points springing up all the time. This does not have to be a disadvantage. It can mean that education has become more creative and dynamic. To represent such a situation, Coombs suggests replacing the term 'education system' by 'education network' (Coombs, 1985, pp. 27–8).

The Elite

Beyond basic education are the secondary and tertiary levels of the formal system. As already pointed out, some of the functions they perform must be provided for in order to supply the administrators and technicians upon whom the progress of the country depends. They are also important in enabling those who are gifted to realise their potentialities.

A study in Kenya and Tanzania, reported in 1983 (World Bank,

1983, p. 106) confirmed earlier findings by Psacharopoulos (see Table 7.4, above) that secondary education can also produce substantial returns in productivity, and that this is especially so if it concentrates on skills rather than credentials. As for tertiary education, reference has already been made above to Psacharopoulos's demonstration of a return greater than that to investment in the physical infrastructure.

Such opportunities in a poor country are bound to be very limited, and a vexed question will be how to select those who are to have them. Current methods are obviously inequitable. This situation would not be improved by the adoption of the free-market proposal in respect of higher education made by the World Bank: '. . . in many cases excess demand is so great that fees would have little effect on enrolment' (World Bank, 1988, p. 136). It is astonishing that the Bank does not seem to have understood the effect that fees would have on *who* would be able to offer themselves for enrolment.

There is no reason to believe that selection by means of formal academic examinations, as proposed by Philip Foster (1975, pp. 388ff), will be socially more just, or more effective in choosing the most able. The influence of family and cultural background on performance in such examinations is well known. Foster, tongue in cheek perhaps, sees a lottery as an alternative to them.

Nevertheless some way has to be found of tapping the real reservoir of ability in a country, wherever it is to be found: in town or country, in the formal or informal sectors of the educational system, among men or women. Much new talent should be revealed as opportunities to begin the educational process are widened.

Finance

There are two ways in which the financial commitment of a country to education may be measured: as a proportion of GNP, and as a share of the national budget. A given proportion of the national income is of course a heavier burden for countries with a lower GNP. Nevertheless most Third World countries have allocated an increasing proportion of GNP to the improvement of educational services. Simmons (1980, p. 28) estimates that the growth in educational expenditure between 1960 and 1973 was usually twice and in some instances three times that of GNP itself – but despite these increases, the demographic race was still being lost. In the more adverse conditions since 1973, even this expansion has ground to a halt (World Bank, 1982, p. 198).

The share of education in the national budget is an even more challenging statistic, for it demonstrates how high a priority a country gives to education as compared with other forms of state expenditure. It is a sad comment on the times in which we live that even the poorest countries spent, on the average, over six times as much as on defence as on education, and nearly nineteen times as much as on health (ibid.). So long as such priorities are accompanied by underdevelopment and high rates of natural increase the educational gap in Third World countries is bound to widen, no matter how desperate the need, or ingenious the 'appropriate' devices adopted.

There is no acceptable way out in Foster's proposal (supported by the World Bank (1988, pp. 139–40)) for the greater use of private schools. Already a large proportion of the school system of countries like Lesotho, Swaziland and Burundi are in private hands (World Bank, 1980a, p. 125). This makes any real educational planning impossible. Moreover private schools are fee-paying and therefore both an inefficient sieve and socially unjust. Still less could one justify Foster's suggestion that the demand for government-provided primary education might be reduced by charging fees (1975, pp. 382–3).

At the secondary level, fee-paying schools provide a resort for middle-class children who have been unable to meet the academic requirements for admission to state schools. Such schools absorb limited teaching resources, and often maintain lower standards than those within the state system. In an achievement-oriented society like that of Hong Kong, many unacademically-minded children are pressured to continue their education in this way. They have little chance of academic success, and even less scope for subsequent 'educated' employment than their more able peers in the state system. It is probably no accident that they have a reputation for hooliganism, and that research shows them to be convicted of significantly more than their share of adolescent law-breaking (Chow *et al.*, 1985, p. 103).

The current panacea for financing the health services as well as education is 'cost recovery' (World Bank 1988, pp. 136ff). There is no indication that the complications involved in fixing the cost to be recovered (that is the opportunity cost) have really been worked through. Lip-service is also paid to the need to protect the interests of those who cannot afford to pay, but in general terms which give no reason to believe that the difficulties of achieving this (referred to in connection with health in Chapter 6) have really been understood.

Summary

Education is much more than a matter of acquiring skills and accumulating information: it operates in an ideological context. Many governments stress its role in giving heterogeneous populations a sense of common nationhood. Others look to it to help the masses to an understanding of their social predicaments, and how to escape from it.

Its appeal must depend, however, upon its perceived relevance to the kind of life which most people lead. On these grounds it has been argued that it should make more use of non-formal methods, and be related more closely to the needs of the rural majority. Adult literacy campaigns have been able to demonstrate the advantages of such a 'functional', non-formal approach, especially where they have also been able to draw on the support of a powerful ideology.

But in the long run the need is for a 'basic education' for all, in which (as some would argue) there should be a wholesale moving of the centre of gravity away from formal towards a predominantly non-formal system. Such an education would not be concerned only with the 'three rs' but would encompass a broad spectrum of topics, including social and political ideas, health and hygiene and occupational skills over a wide range. Even such changes as these, however, will not be enough, unless they are accompanied by the incentives which only a revival of the rural economy can provide.

Beyond this, selection for secondary and higher education poses difficult problems. Academic examinations are socially inequitable and do not make the most of a country's reserves of ability. Underdeveloped countries cannot afford to waste talent in this way.

The willingness of governments to expend an increasing proportion of their countries' national incomes on education has suffered a setback as a result of the economic crisis since the seventies. The increase in the school-age population has made the situation even more difficult. Some governments also give greater priority to military expenditure.

Yet, as judged by the narrowest of economic criteria, education (especially at the primary level) is a highly profitable object for public investment. This becomes an even more plausible argument if the world economy shows signs of becoming more conducive to development in the underdeveloped countries than it is at present.

9

Role of the Social Worker

What might be called the 'human face' of welfare is represented by social workers, and in certain important respects by community development workers. For this reason they are sometimes said to offer different and competing solutions for the same problems. As will become apparent, though both are of great importance they are dissimilar in both their methods and their functions.

Social Work

Social work is commonly understood to mean finding a solution to a person's difficulties through personal discussion with him. Its critics see this kind of individualised casework as unrealistic because the human problems it seeks to tackle are social in nature, arising out of social conditions and relationships, and having consequences which extend beyond the individual immediately concerned.

This might be particularly the case in the countries of the South, where people are more used to discussion within a family or other group than in the one-to-one privacy which characterises an individual interview with a caseworker (Shamsiah, 1981). Djamour (1959) writes: 'To be surrounded by members of his family helps give a Malay a sense of security ... and there was a particular dread of solitude.' In South Africa, there is a Bantu saying, 'Umuntu ungumuntu ngabantu', which means 'Man is man through, with and in association with other persons' (Dlamini, 1984) and expresses the group-mindedness of the African with enviable clarity.

Because social work method concentrates on the individual and adjustment to society, it is also charged with being manipulative and supportive of an often unjust *status quo* as against social reform. Pearson writes in this connection about 'social work as the privatised solution to public ills' (Pearson, 1973). In Third World context this bias is seen as even more harmful in distracting attention and precious funds from social policies aimed at reducing poverty and improving health services and environmental conditions.

These strictures are based on an out-of-date conception of social work. Modern social workers are only too well aware of the importance of the family and the community, and have developed techniques of groupwork and community care which give expression to it. Nor are they blind to the contribution made to the problems of individuals by injustices in society, and so they accept responsibility for ensuring that clients gain access to such welfare resources as are available. But they go beyond this, seeing political action to change social conditions as an important part of their professional function. There certainly is no doubt about the need for such improvements in social provision in the Third World. That will already be obvious to anyone who has read this far. The case has been made in earlier chapters for even more radical forms of social restructuring, directed against the evil of dependent underdevelopment.

At the same time, it has to be recognised that the social reform activities of social workers will be limited by their relationship to their employers. They are public officials and as such are expected to implement the policies of their political masters, not to engage in political activity against those policies. Fortunately another route is open to them. They are often able to 'reform the system' through the recognition of their expertise within that system, perhaps even to influence the formation of policies from the outset.

Meanwhile there are many tasks for them to perform with clients. Suppose there were no social caseworkers to accept responsibility, for example, for the abandoned or orphan children found wandering around Third World cities, like those in Malawi referred to by Kadzamira (1975)? Some of them find work in the informal sector, shining shoes, hawking, working as guides to blind or crippled beggars and so on. Others beg for themselves, become prostitutes or roam the streets in gangs. Many other people in need – widows, the elderly, the disabled – would also remain unnoticed and unhelped as the traditional support system weakened with the advance of modernisation, and the family and the community became less and less capable of keeping a benevolent eye on their members.

Unless social workers took over this obligation, the prospects for such groups would be grim. No matter how good the other social services may be there has to be a means by which individuals can be helped to gain access to them. And if the other social services are not good, which is usually the case, people are going to need even more help, in order to make the best of what there is.

Considerable expertise is required to track down what help is available in a complicated situation in which impoverished public services are intertwined with mission and other voluntary agencies. It may not be easy even for social workers to find their way

---

Exhibit **9.1   Duties of social workers**

An indication of the range of essential functions which, as long ago as 1969, social workers found it necessary to perform in a country as traditional as Fiji are given in the Annual Report of the Social Welfare Department. The Department could say of its staff (Fiji, 1969):

... in addition to the preparation of social enquiry reports for the courts and probation supervision work, their duties included preparation of information in respect of children in need of care and protection; child custody, prison welfare, and after-care for boys released from the approved school, general youth service, participation in rural extension work, assisting in finding homes for the aged, assistance for full legal aid liaising with the voluntary organisations, and assisting in the finding of free place in schools for children of poor families, adoption placement and supervision of legal custody of children, matrimonial conciliation, supervision, placement and financial administration of all children in foster homes and institutions, payment of family assistance, and issuing certificates for remission of medical fees.

through the maze. For clients, especially Third World clients, many of them illiterate and unused to the ways of modern bureaucracies, it would be impossible.

Acting in this 'gatekeeper' role, however, the social worker also needs to be able to help clients to assess their needs, in order to match these up with what is available. One can perhaps use the term 'social diagnosis' (the title of a past classic of the social work literature by Mary Richmond (1917)) to refer to this, without implying any other than a metaphorical connection with the practice of medicine. It is nevertheless a highly skilled activity, requiring a knowledge of the social and personal factors which have brought about the problem confronting the individual.

Community care

This discussion has been based so far on the assumption that mutual aid within the extended family, what Hyden calls the 'economy of affection' (Hyden, 1980), is on the retreat, and this is usually taken to be the inevitable result of economic growth and its accompanying modernisation. Leaving aside the example of Japan, where some of the traditional functions (and some of the emotions) of the family seem to have been taken over by the employer, there is evidence from countries like Taiwan and Hong Kong that a good deal of family cohesion and support can survive economic development.

That also seems to be the view of a number of Third World governments, which are seeking to recover some of the traditional ground lost in recent years without sacrificing economic progress. Thus Fiji's Eighth Development Plan (1980), while fixing ambitious targets for growth, and admitting that traditional institutions were themselves evolving and were therefore less able to play their former role, nevertheless goes on to argue: '. . . the present system of providing destitute allowances is not appropriate to the needs of communities which still retain strong traditional institutions. . . . Reliance on traditional institutions should be encouraged where desirable, and generally acceptable.' This would not be confined to material support, aimed at replacing or supplementing 'destitute allowances'. An ambitious programme was projected, in which many who would usually have been in residential institutions would be cared for instead by their families. This alternative of 'community care' was proposed for deprived children and the elderly in homes, physically and mentally ill patients in hospital (who might then be discharged earlier) and even prisoners.

In case this kind of programme might be thought to be confined to countries like Fiji, in which modernisation has not progressed very far, it should be noted that Lee Kuan Yew, Prime Minister of Singapore, one of the most highly developed of the countries of the South, has expressed similar sentiments, admittedly against the background of the strong filial traditions of the Chinese family. For Lee, the charm of family support resides partly, at any rate, in his frankly expressed distaste for the Welfare State. He flirts also with the other alternative to the state – the Japanese solution of occupational welfare provided by employers.

In the case of other countries it is (in contrast to affluent Singapore) their poverty which has caused them to rediscover their traditions. They cannot afford the expensive public social provision which the decay of the 'economy of affection' makes necessary. But whatever the reasons, many countries, at various levels of development and under development, are now becoming more aware of the value of the family 'mutual aid' system, and are no longer willing to see it drift into desuetude.

But even if a substantial traditional welfare sector has been preserved or revived, there is still an important role for the social worker. The scale of the human problems generated in an under-developed society are such that relatives and friends can no longer be expected to cope with them without expert advice and support – including some financial support. Otherwise women members of a family would be the main sufferers – with the exception, perhaps, of the clients themselves.

To see community development as a substitute for social work with clients, even in the form of community care, is to misunderstand the nature of both activities. The problems of individuals can only be tangentially approached through an approach in which the community is the 'client'. On the other hand, the importance of community development for health and education, and for improvement of agricultural methods and the reduction of rural poverty has already been demonstrated. It will be considered in more detail later in the next chapter.

Training and Organisation

Like their Northern counterparts before them, Third World social
workers seek professional training, and the status and pay which
this can bring with it. Most of them see this as requiring training
abroad – in Europe or America. Although this gives them a career
advantage over untrained or locally trained colleagues, there is
bound to be some doubt as to whether this is the best kind of
training for the job that has to be done in the circumstances of an
underdeveloped country.

Midgley (1981) argues that the individual casework approach
which he believes to be central to it is inappropriate for Third
World social workers, and a form of cultural imperialism.
Although, as we have seen, the casework so criticised is more of a
stalking-horse than a reality, there are other grounds for justifiable
criticism. The work to be done in the underdeveloped world is
very different from that in affluent countries, with their high living
standards, good communications, extensive public social services
and literate populations. And populations, one must add, with few
traditional resources of mutual aid to fall back upon.

The alternative of local training, in countries where the methods
of social work in use are still not very advanced, might well prove
to be a case of the 'blind leading the blind'. Nor would the problem
be satisfactorily solved by using the resources of those Third
World countries in which social work methods are more sophisticated, like Hong Kong or Singapore. They are mostly countries
which, in becoming modernised, have also adopted the Northern
model of social work training.

Perhaps this problem has been exaggerated. There is growing
sensitivity in Northern countries nowadays to the special nature of
the problems presented by underdevelopment, and by the cultural,
geographical and demographic characteristics of underdeveloped
countries. If they are prepared to design courses which are
informed by these insights, little will be lost by those countries in
the Third World which use them for the training of their social
workers – at least until there is enough local expertise to make
their own courses viable.

In any case the number of professional welfare workers who
would be required to perform the duties envisaged for them here
would be too numerous for underdeveloped countries either to

train or to pay. But, if a local health service can be provided by village health workers, who have received only a limited amount of training, why should not many local welfare services be provided by part-time social welfare aides?

There is a case for combining health and welfare in one person if suitable local workers can be found: these functions do interrelate at a variety of points. Thus it is assumed later in this chapter that social workers will find themselves giving practical advice on baby or child care, on the management of old people, some of whom may be senile, or on the care of the disabled.

Another example is the employment in Barbados of former psychiatric nurses as welfare aides. In addition to their social work, they were used to administer regular injections to patients who were thus able to go on living in the community with their relatives, instead of being hospitalised. Many other routine health duties could be carried out by them. Another activity which comes to mind is family planning advice, though that may call for medical facilities and more specialised knowledge than social workers usually possess.

The use of local residents as social work aides would help to solve the problem created by any reluctance to live and work in the rural areas on the part of professionally trained social workers. But such trained workers (like doctors and nurses in the health service) would still have to deal with the more difficult cases in those areas, and make sure that the standard of the service was maintained at a high level.

Social work in former colonies is usually conducted under central rather than local government. As 'social welfare' it some-times has its own ministry. More often it shares a minister with some other social service – health as a rule, though housing, education or community development are sometimes paired with it. The Welfare Department is also frequently responsible for means-tested forms of national assistance (though not social insurance schemes). This makes sense, as it enables the needs of an individual or family to be assessed as a whole.

Such a Welfare Department has a range of benefits both in kind and cash to bestow, making it attractive to politicians anxious to win the favour of their constituents. It is this more than any question of administrative efficiency which accounts for the fact that social welfare shifts from ministry to ministry as the balance of power fluctuates within the cabinet. The 'particularistic' attitudes of people in many Southern countries enables a politician to provide a welfare benefit as a form of patronage, a kind of personal favour in exchange for support.

To dismiss this clientalism as corruption is to be guilty of an oversimplification (see Chapter 13). It may not make for the fairest and most effective distribution of welfare services, and indeed sometimes results in a minister, in effect, usurping the role of the social worker. It is therefore important that it should be replaced by a more professional approach. But this is more likely to be achieved if its origin in the traditional network of mutual obligations is understood, so that a distinction can be drawn between the occasions when it is defensible and those when it is not.

Social Problems and Social Change

The range of duties which need to be performed by social workers operating in such a context varies greatly from one country to another in accordance with differences in circumstances and in way of life. A country with a stable system of collective land tenure, in which most people obtain their food, clothing and shelter mainly by means of agriculture, will be one in which the extended family is still alive and well. The social problems of people in such a situation will be very different from those of a country in which agriculture is moving into private ownership, and becoming highly capitalised. In the former case it is also still possible for social workers to look to the traditional mutual aid system for solutions.

Where this system has begun to break up, creating a class of landless and often unemployed labourers in the countryside, the number of people in distress increases rapidly. Meanwhile the deterioration of the mutual support system, exiled from its basis on the land, gathers pace. Many people migrate into the towns, but this merely adds other problems to those from which they are trying to escape. From being unemployed in the villages, most of them now find themselves unemployed in the towns. At the same time their arrival gives a further boost to urban congestion. They will almost certainly find themselves living in overcrowded and probably squalid living conditions.

As their exodus gradually administers the *coup de grâce* to the rural kinship structure, to which they had previously turned for help when in trouble, there develops a welfare vacuum which only the state can fill. As must be apparent by now, social services in the poorer countries of the world cannot be adequate to the level of need from which their populations suffer. The social worker's task becomes one of helping individuals and families to survive, with the assistance of such help as national policy and the activities of domestic and foreign relief agencies can offer.

Child Welfare

Children and women will be the worst sufferers: the women because of their social undervaluation, but also because they will often voluntarily deprive themselves of food and other necessities in order to supply their families. This is one of the reasons for malnutrition among them. But children are more vulnerable than adults to malnutrition and other sicknesses, which can have serious effects on their later development. Also, as in the North, a minority of parents may shift their own despair and anger onto their large families, who may be seen as just another burden added to what, even without them, is an intolerable load. In a disintegrating society ill-treatment and neglect of children will be on the increase.

Some of these children will run away; others will be abandoned. Such children, roaming the streets of Third World cities, have always been a cause of serious concern to welfare agencies. Malawi, already mentioned, is merely an example of what is a very serious general problem. Acosta (1976, pp. 233–4) writes:

In Colombia, neglect and abandonment of children are among the worst problems. The street child, called *gamin*, is a universal phenomena. These children live in the streets 24 hours a day, subsisting by stealing, moving in groups called *galladas*, and sleeping on the sidewalks, covered with old newspapers. Police estimates give a number of about 9,200 children living under these conditions ... Beside this population, there are about 400,000 abandoned children in the whole country.

A UNICEF spokesman, quoted in the *South China Morning Post*, Hong Kong (27 November 1984), estimates that 'there are

10 million children in Brazil living on the streets, fending for themselves anyway they can'. According to the same newspaper,
'Brazil's Globo TV network estimates that in Rio de Janeiro and
Sao Paulo alone there are 4·5 million abandoned or semi-
abandoned children.'

Many underdeveloped countries have child welfare legislation
and among former colonies it usually follows closely the lead given
by the laws of its former imperial overlords. In former British
colonies, British child care laws may have been copied almost
verbatim, though the principles on which they are based would
probably have been jettisoned in the United Kingdom by that
time. Former French possessions often continue the tradition
under which Paris, in pursuit of its objective of turning all people
into Frenchmen, applied laws to them at the same time as they
were introduced in metropolitan France. They may therefore be
more up-to-date.

In one respect the policies adopted are all very similar. In the
few cases where they recognise the existence of a child welfare
problem, they tend to 'solve' it by placing children, whether from
the villages or the towns, in residential homes. This is obviously
not the best way of socialising children for normal family life,
especially (though not only) when the homes are large and
impersonal. It is also a very expensive policy to adopt. And it
leaves wastefully unused such communal and kinship resources as
may still be available. This is ironical at a time when the rich
countries themselves, where the disintegration of the extended
family has gone much further, are nevertheless looking to community care as the best way of caring for their deprived children.

There is in many countries a wealth of goodwill to be drawn on
by social workers as they, as part of a community care policy in
child care, set about the task of preserving or reviving the
traditional sense of responsibility towards children in need. Thus
in Malaysia children are valued and loved, and a childless woman
is pitied. For this reason a large family is a source of satisfaction
even to quite poor families (Shamsiah, 1981, pp. 44ff).

Similarly, the extended family in Malawi takes great care of its
orphans and other children in need. Kadzamira (1975) describes
how this obligation is usually assumed by the father's eldest living
brother in patrilineal areas, and a maternal uncle in matrilineal
families. Before entrusting a child to such a relative, the family

would want to be sure about the security of the guardian's marriage, the kinds of personalities involved, and whether the child would be fed adequately. And great care would be taken to safeguard any rights of inheritance which the child might have.

In the English-speaking Caribbean, the prohibition of marriage among plantation slaves has made the family a more fluid institution than in other parts of the world. The women relatives of many children are the only permanent features of their lives. Even there, however, rich resources for the community care of children are available. A woman related to children would expect to take care of them if their parents died, or were unable to assume their obligations because of illness or poverty. Many such children have been brought up entirely by an aunt or a grandmother. Women relatives will even take responsibility for children whose mother has gone abroad for work or education – a less common occurrence nowadays, with the proliferation of racist immigration laws in the 'host' countries. The extended family in the Caribbean is an extended family of women – mothers, aunts, grandmothers and even big sisters.

In spite of the general acceptability and the effectiveness of this form of familial care, Children's Homes are still widely used by Caribbean governments. Yet social work with the female king-group, especially if accompanied by financial assistance to help meet the additional expense, would make it unnecessary in many cases.

In Britain those willing to become foster-parents have, for very many years, received an allowance from the government. This has never been a form of remuneration, but only a grant towards the additional cost of adding the child to one's family. It has been assumed that foster-parents are fond of children, and are willing to make sacrifices in order to have the opportunity of looking after them. There would be resistance in most Third World countries to paying relatives even a small sum towards meeting the extra expense incurred in taking in a child. Many people will contend that relatives have obligations towards a child which they should not be allowed to shift onto others. That may be true, and in a country in which traditions are still strong and economic life is not too harsh, it may be a viable policy. In all too many countries, however, neither of these preconditions exists. To people living already on the margins of subsistence, an extra mouth could be just the last straw. If customary imperatives have begun to lose some of their power such people could refuse to help without too much guilt or loss of face.

It would, in any case, be a self-defeating sort of social policy which achieved a family placement for a child only at the cost of abject want for everybody concerned, including the child himself. It should be borne in mind that, although the present discussion is concentrated on social work, these aspects of child care cannot be separated in practice from nutrition, health care and general living conditions, all of which might be at risk in a very impoverished foster home. Cost would also be raised as a fatal objection to such payments, even in countries which spend substantially more *per capita* in caring for children in residential institutions. What makes even subsidised foster care so much cheaper, of course, is that part of the input of foster parents which is not paid for – the 'care' element itself.

But the main arguments in favour of fostering are not financial. First or all, it is a practical way of cherishing and strengthening a faltering system of kin-based welfare. Secondly, it is a more sensible and humane way of training the next generation to assume the responsibilities of adulthood than residence in a home, where the atmosphere is bound to be more impersonal and the way of life more modernised than the children will usually encounter when they do go out into the world.

In a plural society the ethnic affiliations of children have to be taken into account in placing them. If they are boarded out with members of their own family or with foster-parents who share their cultural background, their upbringing will be much more likely to make for a good social adjustment in later life than that in a culturally alien or at best neutral Children's Home.

There is a price to be paid for reliance on traditional institutions: it will bring with it beliefs and practices in child care which may not be very acceptable nowadays. Reference has already been made in Chapter 6, for example, to traditional beliefs about feeding and illness which are not good for the child's development. Similarly some traditional groups are very authoritarian, limiting a child's activities and his intellectual growth. They may even seem cruel by the standards of Northern social work.

The danger in making judgments of this kind is that of assuming that modern ways are necessarily the best. The nurture of children in a society is usually such as to produce personalities which are well adapted to the kind of life which people have to lead in that society. It is for this reason, among others, that the word 'indigen-isation' has come to figure prominently at international confer-ences and elsewhere when the special features of Third World social work have been under discussion (Yasas, 1974). Traditional child-rearing practices are an important part of a traditional way of life. Changing one impoverishes the other, bringing nearer the decay of those very customary institutions which it is desired to foster and to utilise.

But does the rough necessarily have to be taken with the smooth? Customs do differ in their centrality for a culture. There is no reason, for example, to believe that the survival of a trad-itional society will be jeopardised by improvements in nutritional practices, or by persuading people to go to a trained health-care worker if a traditional practitioner is having no success.

Such issues loom particularly large in making provision for girls – for widowed or deserted wives. Unmodified traditional solu-tions, in many societies, would result in a continuance of the discrimination from which females have historically suffered. The role of social policy as it affects the position of women is the subject of Chapter 11, but the removal of some of the disadvan-tages from which they suffer (for example by increasing their freedom of choice, and reducing the exploitative use of female labour) may have dramatic (and desirable) effects on economic and social life without greatly weakening the norms on which the 'mutual aid' system rests.

Care of the Elderly

In purely economic terms, the old may be no less of a burden than children, but they are often felt to make their social contribution through their experience and wisdom. This is particularly true in oriental countries influenced by Chinese or Japanese culture, where they are positively venerated.

In much of India, where the traditional joint family is still domi-nant, the oldest male is the head of the family, and has great authority. When old people are too frail to exercise such power any longer, there is a clear understanding as to who has the responsibility of looking after them: first of all sons, then daughters, brothers, uncles, and finally other relatives (Desai and Khetani, 1979, pp. 101).

In many other countries, for example in Africa, old people are listened to with great respect, and properly provided for. Their prestige and experience enables them to solve many family problems (Gotip, 1983). There is a sense of mutual obligation between the generations which links the care of children with the care of the elderly: the younger generation recognise the debt they owe to their elders for their upbringing, and rely upon their own children to feel the same way when they are old. Such attitudes are reinforced sometimes by superstition, such as the fear in some Kenyan country areas that, if old people are neglected by their relatives, they have the power to bring misfortune down upon those who are defaulting upon their responsibilities.

But all this could change. With urbanisation and the decline in traditional land tenures the physical basis on which the prestige and care of the elderly has been founded is disappearing. At the same time life expectation is increasing because of improvements in environmental conditions, nutrition and health services. Between 1965 and 1984, life expectancy at birth in low-income developing countries (excluding the exceptionally good figures for India and China) rose from 44 to 52 years, and in the middle-income economies from 52 to 63 (World Bank, 1988, p. 222). Although these figures are still scandalously low, they represent a great increase in the number of people surviving to a dependent old age, and this at a time when the family's ability (and perhaps motivation) to care for the elderly is being sapped.

For old people who have no other resort but the welfare services the commonest solution, as in the case of children, is a residential home. In some countries, like Colombia (Acosta, 1976, p. 235), most of the homes are run by religious or charitable organisations. There may sometimes be, as in Hong Kong in 1973 (Little, 1979, p. 154), a bewildering array of them, 'many ignorant of the other's existence', and calling urgently for rationalisation. Elsewhere, there are state homes – austere relics of an earlier Poor Law-style relief system, inherited from the colonial era.

Invariably the homes are large, impersonal and regimented. Nothing could represent a greater contrast to the honoured position of an old person in the care of his kin. Voluntary

---

***Exhibit* 9.2   Care of the elderly: an indigenous experiment**

Old people's homes are almost always based on a Northern model which bears little resemblance to the kinds of homes the old people have been used to. They cater more to the vanity and modernising ambitions of local politicians than to the preferences of the elderly themselves. Little (1979, p. 154) describes an interesting, more indigenous approach in Kenya: 'This church-sponsored project consists of a semi-circle of native thatched roof huts, in each of which lives an otherwise homeless old man with his chickens and his kitchen garden.'

---

charitable organisations sometimes show what can be done, by building more modern homes, divided into villas which house smaller groups in a more homelike atmosphere. One problem, as ever, is that of cost. Old district hospitals or poor law institutions already exist, while new bright homes would cost a good deal of money.

But there are objections to the widespread use of homes as such. Residential care wrenches an old person from the environment in which she (it is more often she) has lived throughout her life, where she could do familiar things in the company of her friends and relatives, and could enjoy the rights and dignity appropriate to her age. Also old people in the rural areas only gradually withdraw from home duties or work on the family plot. There is none of the trauma of 'retirement' suffered by old people in the North, or which follows on institutional placement anywhere.

A residential unit consisting exclusively of the aged is also very likely to engender feelings of fatalism and pessimism among them, and would lack opportunities for the varied activity and social interaction which are necessary if their physical and mental capacities are to be kept alive. Little (1979, p. 155) describes attempts in Hong Kong to avoid these disadvantages by locating supervised hostels for the elderly in all-age housing estates, but these do not go far enough. There is a very strong case for developing boarding-out programmes for the isolated elderly, but they could not be made effective without social work support.

Simple placement is not enough for them any more than it is for children. A home needs to be found in which the old person can enjoy the privileges of age much as if living within her own family. This will call for the careful matching of foster family and old person. Just as the ideal foster-parent is somebody who wants a child, so the ideal foster family would be somebody who wants a father or mother. Subsidies will probably be necessary. If given to members of the old person's family they will probably, because of the strength of the feeling that younger people have obligations to the old, meet with even stronger opposition than subsidies to foster parents.

It may not only be a matter of money, but partly of services in kind. Space is one problem. If a family are already living in overcrowded conditions, an old person may have either to share a couple's conjugal bedroom or sleep in the same room as the children. In the worst cases she may have to share a room or a hut which already has to serve as sleeping and living room for the whole family. This will conduce neither to the dignity of the old person, not to the willingness of the family to meet their customary responsibilities to her.

Where the extended family looks after an old person, the burden of personal care, which could be very onerous, can be shared and is not likely to be much of a disincentive. It is going to loom larger where, say, her children or grandchildren, who are expected to receive her, have moved to the town where they live with their own children as an urbanised nuclear family, with one or possibly both partners going to work outside the home. Providing relief, in the form of a holiday home, a club and voluntary visitors to entertain or 'keep an eye on' grandmother, would then be very welcome. And where such services do not exist, a boarding-out subsidy might enable a working wife to take time off to provide care for the elderly relative. It goes without saying that, in such cases, regular visits by a social worker would be vital to success, to give moral and emotional support, advice and help in the mobilising of any other resources which might be needed.

The availability of medical services is another factor. This is, of course, important to everybody, especially those with children; but it derives special significance from the frailty and proneness to illness of the aged. Indigenous practitioners whom old people will have long consulted, and village health workers whom they know, will probably be more acceptable to many of them than doctors or nurses practising 'new-fangled' forms of health care. Some of their complaints, due to the hypochondriasis of age, will be well within the competence of para-medicals, but others will not, and the availability of transport to clinic or hospital then becomes crucial. This essential interrelatedness of the various social services has always to be borne in mind in social policy planning.

The Sick and Disabled

This is even more obvious if, as is proposed in Chapter 6, policies for health also place more emphasis on community care, for the sick, or the mentally or physically handicapped. The need for medical services to be available goes without saying, but we are also at last beginning to realise the important part which social factors play in causing illness, and in promoting or retarding recovery. Social work, whether provided by a welfare aide or by a village health worker, is therefore needed in order to help families and the patient to deal with their anxieties and fears.

Superstition is rife (and not only in the underdeveloped world) in people's ideas about what causes sickness and how it should be treated. Having a sick person around can also lead to all kinds of family tensions. There is also the need for guidance from somebody who knows about the social services, and can bring them into the picture where required. As already suggested, a local health worker may be equipped to satisfy these needs. Somebody certainly must if community care is to have a chance. This is particularly true in the case of mental illness, which (in spite of the tolerance referred to earlier) can cause social embarrassment and arouse primitive fears.

It has been estimated that, of a world total of 500 million disabled people, two-thirds live in the poor countries, most of which have no rehabilitative services (Doyal, 1983). They are often also more neglected by their kin than other dependent family members. Many of them resort to begging – where of course their disability can be a positive asset.

It is usual to describe degrees of disadvantage, in order of increasing severity, as impairment, disability and handicap. The last mentioned, the most severe, is where disability is of such a degree as to prevent disabled persons from doing what is normally expected at their age. Obviously the degree of physical or mental deficit will be the primary determinant of whether there is impairment or disability, but it does not settle alone the vital question of whether there will be handicap. The absence of rehabilitation services and of aids will mean that many an impaired or disabled person will regress to handicap who might otherwise have lived a rewarding life, and perhaps even earned his own living.

The care of a loving family is no less important. If they are prepared to go to the trouble, they can reorganise the work to be done on the family land so as to find a role for an impaired or disabled member. A little family encouragement would also motivate such members to try to achieve to the limits of their capacity, rather than to sink back into apathy and failure. As soon as they are once more contributing to their own maintenance, their image (and indeed their self-image) will change. They are no longer 'useless', imposing on their relatives.

This is asking a good deal of a poor family, and could only be expected if the family had the support and guidance of a social work aide. Such a worker (or the health worker) might also find that work needed to be done with the disabled person, in order to bring about the initial improvement which will make everybody concerned feel there is something to strive for. Where state rehabilitative services do exist it is the responsibility of social workers to know about them, and to ensure that they are utilised by disabled clients. Where they do not exist or are inadequate, workers have a professional obligation to make this clear to the government. Otherwise they can hardly deny the charge that they are merely servants of the *status quo*.

There has also been, in recent years, some interest in low-cost aids, many of which a family could construct themselves (Hogg, 1983; Caston, 1982). These might help to alleviate the situation until state services arrived on the scene, but getting families to make such an effort would be a formidable social work task.

Meanwhile the only provision made in many underdeveloped countries is residential care, and that only for the more 'fortunate' few. Such residential institutions are usually for long-term placement. Those who can work are put to some kind of activity, but for the rest the institution is a breeding-ground for hopelessness and dependence. As in the cases of deprived children and the elderly, this is the wrong answer, both from the financial and the welfare points of view. It is difficult to see boarding-out other than with relatives as a practical alternative. There will probably continue to be a need for institutions, though as with the elderly there is plenty of scope for institutions of a more indigenous and stimulating kind.

Summary

A case has been made for a social work service, suitably indigenised, in developing countries. There are strong arguments for supplementing the services of fully-trained social workers with the services of part-time aides working in the villages in close co-operation with village health workers. The emphasis would be on 'community care', in order to utilise, and perhaps give new life to, the caring traditions of Third World communities. Provision for the care of children, the elderly and the sick and disabled have been discussed within this framework.

10

The Community and its Youth

Community development (Dore and Mars, 1981; Evens, 1977; Henderson, Jones and Thomas, 1980) has long been employed to co-opt local populations behind new practices, ranging from, say, health and hygiene, on the one hand, to farming methods on the other. Its use in this way, though pragmatically useful, will probably be no more important in the long run than its value in two other respects: (a) strengthening the sense of communal solidarity in a locality in order to make community action more effective; and (b) increasing local participation in the formulation and implementation of official policies.

The first of these is community development in its most literal sense. In a city, for instance, it may be directed towards a squatter settlement where neighbourhood cohesion has still to emerge. In rural areas, it could help towards the revival of a traditional sense of mutuality which economic and social change had undermined. The aim in either case would be to help local residents to become more aware of their membership of a local community and of ways in which they could benefit if they gave each other neighbourly support and co-operated in common endeavours. The slow progress made by *ujaama* in the new Tanzanian villages (Hyden, 1980), suggests that they will calculate the benefit to them and their families very carefully before deciding that proposed changes in their way of life are worthwhile for them.

The community development worker, then, would help them to understand their problems as a community, and to find ways of approaching these constructively. This might involve the worker in action within the community, or approaches to the authorities, local business organisations, or whoever it was felt might hold the key to the situation. The emphasis would be on finding indigenous solutions through self-help.

The second long-term aim, that of increasing local participation is a contribution not only to grass-roots democracy but also to better decision making. A policy which is going to have important consequences for local people will be more effective and fairer to them if they play a part in developing it and carrying it out. After all, they are the experts on local conditions and local needs and also know where the shoe pinches.

There is a vein of radicalism among community development workers in the North (Craig, Derricourt and Loney, 1982) which has led some of them to emphasise its emancipating role. They see community development as a means by which residents of deprived areas can be made aware of the injustices from which they suffer, and combine to resist further encroachments upon their rights. Those who take such a view will often contrast it with what they see as the establishment bias, even the 'social control' function of the social worker.

There is no gainsaying the conformist orientation of the social worker, and the need to balance this by a concern for social reform; but it is doubtful if community workers are any freer from the constraints imposed by conventional norms and the structure of power. They are mostly employed by public bodies to change what the latter see as undesirable situations, not to stir things up and make more problems for them.

This is particularly true among the new nations of the Third World, where the achievement of national unity in ethnically or tribally divided populations is an overriding aim. As community workers (like social workers) are civil servants, they will be expected to help to achieve that aim. Stimulating local self-consciousness and demands for differential treatment will not be seen as a helpful contribution.

Sometimes community development is used even more blatantly as an instrument of government. Of certain Latin American countries, Gilbert and Ward write (1984, p. 770):

For the state the main aim of community action programmes is less to improve conditions for the poor or to modify forms of decision-making, than to legitimate itself. The main object of community action is now to help maintain existing power relations. The aim is less to change conditions for the poor than to make sure they cause no problems.

The other side of the coin is the claim that giving so much weight to the views of conservatively minded peasants may hamper desirable development. Hyden (1980, p. 225) states categorically that 'if governments were to rely on participatory and grass-roots approaches alone, there would be no modernisation, no development'. According to Moore (1967) the peasant has always had to be coerced in order to achieve change.

Studies like that in India by Mehta (1984, p. 75) confirm that peasants do not always accept the view of government about what is in their interest, but this may only underline the need to make a reality of participation, in order that their voice may be heard. It should not be taken for granted that they are always wrong and the government always right. As Chambers (1985) points out, their views are highly rational when judged in the light of their own criteria. These criteria may include non-material considerations related to their customary obligations within the 'economy of affection' but can also give due weighting to very shrewd calculations of economic advantage.

The kind of governments to be found in some underdeveloped countries suggests that coercion in decision making may predominate as much in the immediate future as Moore found it to have done in the past. Military and other tyrants, supported often by powerful economic interests, have every motive for riding roughshod over any dissenting views held by poor peasants. Even more benevolent rulers may be too intent on getting on with their policies for development to accept the delay and, as they see it, obstruction, which goes with participation. This is particularly likely in one-party states where political opposition has always been minimal.

Yet the idea of participation continues to show its durability. There is the quest for the 'new man' in Tanzania and Cuba, and the prominence given to personal growth and dignity in Chinese development aims, both unrealised but still beckoning. Can one speak of real development if the mass of the people are to remain helpless cyphers, meekly doing what they are told by 'those who know best'?

Self-Help

The aim in all these activities is to stimulate self-determination through self-help. By self-help, members of a community can also provide themselves with amenities such as a schoolroom, better roads and so on, which might not otherwise be available to them. Governments are frequently able to furnish materials and technical advice, where lack of resources or the necessary political will has long hindered them from providing the amenity itself. For the poorest countries, on the other hand, even self-help projects may be difficult to finance.

There is always the possibility of conflict between a self-help project and the ministries which usually provide these services. There are issues of co-ordination to be faced, and some of these will be taken up in Chapter 13. But destructive civil wars of this kind arise more often out of the competing ambitions of politicians and should be firmly suppressed by governments.

Midgley (1981, pp. 162ff) has seen the organisation of self-help activity as a very suitable addition to the social worker's role, where it fits in with a country's needs. On the basis of developments in Sierra Leone, he even envisages that they might acquire practical skills in mixing concrete, digging wells, constructing roads and the rest. The range of new abilities called for seems unrealistic, in view of the skills which are already needed in order to carry out the social work tasks outlined in the previous chapter – plus, in some cases, further functions in the field of health.

Two-Way Communication

The community development movement in the Third World (Ruttan, 1984) took off in the late 1940s with the Etawah project in North India (Mayer *et al.*, 1958) and flourished throughout the 1950s. Food crises in many countries in the sixties however, seemed to some to call for more decisive and speedy action than the participative procedures of community development made possible. Governments and aid agencies alike concentrated their efforts on centralised action in pursuit of what became known as the 'green revolution'. For some governments this seemed also to have offered a welcome escape from the inconvenient habit, which community development encouraged, of the people taking things into their own hands.

There is, of course, a serious point here. Sometimes urgent action is required. There is also an inevitable tension between the decentralised decision making inherent in community development and the reconciliation of divergent local trends and interests in a national plan for development. Moreover, as the conflicts over agricultural reorganisation in Tanzania showed, even governments with a commitment to communal values are not going to abandon what they believe to be essential schemes because of 'wrong-headed' or 'reactionary' local opposition.

For such reasons the initiative for action will usually come from above. Indeed to leave villagers with an open agenda may be a recipe for dissension or inaction. Cosio found, in his study of community development in the Mexican village of Carbajal, that people became bored in the absence of leadership, and stopped attending meetings even before agreement had been reached on what should be done (Dore and Mars, 1981, p. 31). Leadership can provide the inspiration of a great national crusade, as well as guidance on the more mundane aspects of policy.

These contradictions can only be resolved by incorporating in the planning process a strong vertical line of two-way communication, and a clear hierarchy in which decisions of different degrees of generality can be made at different levels, in consultation with the people themselves at village level or with their representatives at higher levels. China has shown that structures for national integration need not be inconsistent with a high level of local autonomy (Aziz, 1980, pp. 50–1).

Such an interchange of information, while improving decision making at the centre as well as increasing the influence of the local community on those decisions, will also put the government in a better position to explain its policies to those most affected. There is a danger that it might then be tempted, as indeed so many already have been, to use this opportunity merely as a means of propaganda and indoctrination, or even coercion. Influence upwards must be a reality also, and if the government overrides this, it must make it clear just why such action is necessary. There is much discussion in the social planning literature about the relative merits of 'bottom up' and 'top down' development planning. The need is to unite both in an integrated plan.

The traditional local leadership often cannot be by-passed, but the result may be less authoritarian than it appears. Chiefs or heads of families often have to be very sensitive to the views of their people. Where there is tyranny, as so often in matters concerning women, it is not enough simply to erect representative institutions on the Northern model. Experience has shown that they often do not travel well. The old power structure will take them over, causing them to lose any credibility they might have had as a way of getting at grass-roots opinion. What emerges must be an organic offshoot of the traditional way of doing things, providing scope and 'face' for the traditional leaders, while making sure that other voices also receive a hearing. Even liberals in the North usually fail to understand how the African 'one-party' political system really works.

The words 'parish pump' are often used as a term of derision, implying an inability to understand the larger issues of public policy – not to see, as it were, any further than one's own back yard. For many Third World country-dwellers, their own back yard is the true, omnipresent reality. The capital city and the government are a long way off, with concerns which often seem unreal to those engaged in the daily struggle for survival in the more distant areas. Social control, effected through the family and the community and the influence of the 'big man', is largely a local matter. If social change is to occur, it must start here.

Problems of Youth

The demographic trends discussed in Chapter 12 ensure that teenagers and young adults will represent a large and growing proportion of the community – invariably well over a half (see Figure 10.1). A population policy may help as far as the next generation of young people are concerned, but this large increase in numbers is already in the demographic pipeline. They are therefore a force to be reckoned with as far as governments are concerned. They have often been to the fore in riots and demon-strations, and have sometimes played a significant part in bringing a government down. Finding a way of integrating them with more stable elements in the community is thus high on the political agenda. Although this is a community development task it pre-sents special difficulties as such.

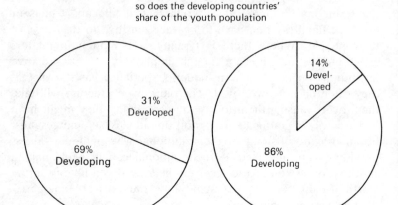

As populations grow,
so does the developing countries'
share of the youth population

31%
Developed

69%
Developing

14%
Devel-
oped

86%
Developing

1950

2025

Source: *United Nations Chronicle* January 1986 (United Nations, 1986b).

Figure 10.1   Share of youth population: developing countries

These young people are disproportionately concentrated in the cities for it is they, less bound by tradition, and more impatient of the limitations of rural life, who are most likely to shake the dust of the villages from their feet and migrate to the towns in search of excitement and wages. Few of them will obtain jobs: most of the long-term unemployed are to be found among them. The United Nations, in its documentation for International Youth Year, 1985, gave an illustration of this problem of growing youth unemployment. Between 1980 and 1990, the number of *extra* job-seekers in Mexico will be 6·3 million, with a further 7·223 million in the ten years from 1990 onwards (United Nations, 1986a).

These unemployed young people became a familiar feature of the street scene in the cities of the South. Thronging, idle and angry at street corners or outside betting shops or bars, they are a constant reminder to politicians of the reality of underdevelopment and of their own failure. It is not surprising if they are also seen as a kind of human volcano, which could erupt into a riot or worse at any time. This fear is given credibility by their prominence in the crime problem (Clinard and Abbott, 1973, pp. 12–13).

As the age group itself expands in size, so does its contribution to these problems, including the perception of youth crime as a threat to social order. Other problems of youth, such as drunkenness, the use of drugs, or sexual promiscuity, exacerbate these anxieties. Like the crime problem, they are probably more widespread among the youth of the North, but the latter, as a group and as deviants, are less numerous.

The challenge to public order from demoralised young people may seem remote. It could become more real if they began to see their troubles as the fault of a government of the 'haves'. They might then gain that sense of being in a common plight and having a common enemy which Marx and Engels (1846) rightly saw as required for united action in the class struggle. Young people so aroused have sometimes played an important part in past coups, though the outcome has rarely been an improvement in their own situation or that of their country. This may be because such coups often change merely the composition of governments and not the vested interests behind them. Nor do they have much impact on the condition of underdevelopment from which those interests benefit at the expense of everybody else.

Youth Organisations

Regional policies aimed at developing the countryside would do much to stem the rush of youths to the town. This would not only ease the urban problem for the future, but would also mean that more young people would stay within the ambit of their families and of traditional restraints, at least until these, in the course of development, also yielded to newer ideas.

Instead, governments have relied largely upon the Northern expedient of the youth organisation. This has its value, but as a solution to the problem of alienated youth its utility in the rich North has been found to be marginal. Over the years since they became independent, underdeveloped countries seem to have been slow in learning that lesson from their own experience.

All countries outside the Russian and Chinese spheres of influence have voluntary societies which provide service for youth. These include in the former British colonies such nationwide youth organisations as the YMCA, the Boy Scouts, and the Boys Brigade. Churches have youth wings with a denominational flavour. Many governments encourage and subsidise these. In addition political parties have their youth sections. There are also youth clubs or centres provided within the framework of education or community work programmes. On the whole these have not appealed to the poorer sections of the community. In particular they do not appear to attract delinquents and other alienated young people.

The alternative in some countries has been a national youth service, sometimes obligatory for all young people, sometimes voluntary, and sometimes highly selective and elitist. It would often be based on the youth wing of the governing party and therefore would have a political flavour. In some countries it was intended from the beginning as a way of coping with a political problem. During the struggle against colonialism many adolescents and young adults became politicised and militant. Independence when it arrived did not immediately bring the Utopia which the idealism of youth had perhaps caused many to expect from it, and the new government became the target for much of their dissatisfaction. Agitation, often backed by the threat or even the use of violence, had been functional during the colonial period. Now it was a threat to political stability.

Ghana as the first black African state to achieve independence, met this unrest ahead of the others. In 1957, unemployed youths in that country assaulted their national leaders. Others were soon to encounter the same hostility. It was hoped that a paramilitary youth service would bring discipline to these turbulent youngsters and that, if the service was also linked to the governing party, this would channel their political ardour into support for the government and its policies (Graaf, 1982, p. 7). These expectations were not realised. Graaf writes of 'continued protest, resistance and "gross indiscipline" among trainees. In Ghana and Zambia trainees turned to political thuggery' (ibid.). Members of the Zambian Youth Brigades began to misuse their position to intimidate members of the public, and in Kenya members of party youth wings campaigned and plotted against their own leadership (Coe, 1973).

It became apparent that unemployment was the root cause of much of this kind of behaviour, and youth policy changed accordingly (Graaf, 1982, p. 8). The political biases of the youth movements were sharply reduced, in favour of programmes of vocational training (UNESCO, 1982). These it was hoped would lead to better prospects of employment for many members at the end of their period of service. At the same time there was a deliberate shift in recruitment towards a lower age group, which cut out the more politically minded.

Although national youth movements vary from one country to another, most of them have certain features in common. Service is undertaken away from home, under military-style discipline in camp. But the standard of these camps varies from the relative comfort of those of Zambia to the spartan austerity of Malawi Youth Pioneer camps. The primacy given either to vocational training or to encouraging members to assume leadership and community development roles, also divides them.

Where the latter elements loom large, as in the case of the Malawi Youth Pioneers (Graaf, 1982, pp. 16–21), the youth service becomes almost a missionary arm of the government. This is emphasised by the direct and personal interest taken in the movement by the national President for Life, Dr Banda. Members of such an organisation are bound to consist of government supporters. The political element, in other words, has not been abandoned, but preserved in a fairly safe form. In order to reduce tribal and class divisions in the movement, regional origins and educational level are ignored.

The training itself includes some academic subjects, but otherwise is directed towards rural life and work in agriculture. The aim is not only to turn the trainees themselves into successful farmers making use of up-to-date methods, but through them to influence other people. Camps are located in the poorer rural areas, and even during their service trainees are expected to make contact with the local people. And with their future missionary task in mind, they are trained in youth leadership. Unfortunately the young are at the bottom of the 'pecking order' in traditional rural society in Malawi, so members are increasingly collected together in rural settlements where they can provide each other with support in attempting to influence their neighbours.

The Brigades of Botswana (ibid., pp. 22–46) differ from the Malawi Pioneers in many ways. They are not run directly by the government but by a number of voluntary organisations operating in different parts of the country. And although they carry out some non-formal educational work, including literacy classes, their concentration is more on the work training aspect. In spite of the egalitarian and social reform ideology which inspired their formation (Van Rensburg, 1967, p. 23), most trainees join 'to get higher-paying jobs in the modern sector' (Pearson, 1974, p. 84). Not surprisingly in these circumstances, the Brigades have been more successful in training in urban skills (particularly in the construction trades) than in those required by agriculture. They are not even liked in the villages.

A feature of the Brigades is the way which they combine production with training, with the aim of covering their costs. They do not achieve this aim; they are heavily subsidised by the government. Some critics have argued that the requirements of commercial production are nevertheless damaging to their training. This need not be the case, of course: the training of young workers through apprenticeships has long been a successful feature of Northern industry.

The contribution of the Brigades to the meeting of the training needs of the country is not inconsiderable. Trades referred to by Graaf (1982, p. 22) include 'building, forestry, carpentry, electrical work, plumbing, printing, textiles, tanning, dressmaking, panel-beating and welding'. Nevertheless their contribution to the youth problem has been minimal. Up to the end of 1981 they had trained 3500 young people, of whom about three-quarters had found employment of one sort or another, but this is a drop in the ocean compared with the number who are unemployed and unoccupied in the country as a whole.

The Development Alternative

Most of these national youth movements, in fact, face a dilemma. They can set out to train and find employment for a relatively small proportion of the young people who need them, in which case, whatever else they may achieve, they will have made themselves largely irrelevant either to the needs of youth as a whole or to the law and order problem which is the main concern of so many governments. Or they can become a form of compulsory (and very costly) national service for all within a particular age group, as in Tanzania (Morrison, 1976). In such an event, young people will certainly be withdrawn from the streets in large numbers, but the relief will be temporary. There will be no jobs after training for such large numbers (Bettenhausen, 1971, p. 139).

Philip Foster's strictures on vocational training are very much to the point here. There is no viable alternative to regional planning aimed at reviving the economic and social life of the village. Youth settlement schemes will not achieve this, no matter what value they may have for the young people directly involved, for they are separated from the mainstream of rural life and can only have a marginal effect upon it.

There is every justification for giving special attention to the needs of rural youth, and not only to preserve law and order. After all, they represent the majority of the population, the majority of the unemployed, and the future of the country. But it is vital to remember that these needs and the threat to law and order are both by-products of more fundamental problems. A few countries, in their youth programmes, have begun to see where this leads. Burkina Faso and Guinea-Bisseau have both begun to involve the villages in their training work with young people (UNESCO, 1982, p. 62). Rural society in the Third World is often based on age-grading, providing both peer group support and a means by which the young may be inducted into the skills traditionally thought necessary for the adult. Governments ought not to allow an infatuation with modernisation to prevent them from using this indigenous 'youth service', as a means for bringing about desirable forms of development in the villages.

The assistance of the indigenous leadership of the village communities, the chiefs and elders, should also be enlisted; and the young people should be trained in activities directly relevant to the villages' own development aspirations, and if possible in roles which they can continue to perform within the village after their training is completed.

Almost every underdeveloped country which took part in the conference at the end of the UN International Youth Year, 1986 saw training and jobs for their young people as major priorities for them (United Nations, 1986a). The training and employment of the next generation is in fact an integral part of the development process, especially if, at the same time, it can help to maintain the cultural continuity which has been seen to be so important for both development and social welfare.

Summary

Community development is distinguished from social work in the community by its concentration on the needs of communities rather than on those of individual clients or families. Its aims are twofold: (a) to strengthen the sense of community, and help members to find common solutions to their problems, some of which might (perhaps with government help) be tackled by self-help activities; and (b) to encourage greater participation by members of a community in the making and implementation of decisions which affect them.

Community development workers in new countries (like most social workers) are usually civil servants and they are therefore often used as a means for securing the wider acceptance of government policies. Although this may often be legitimate, it may sometimes be motivated by political, or even exploitative or corrupt aims.

There is in any case a natural divergence between local pre-occupations and the nation-wide concerns of central government. Turning this divergence into a creative 'top down, bottom up' interaction should be the aim of community workers, and of those governments which recognise the advantages such an interaction could bring with it.

Politicians are inclined to see the growing number of un-employed young people on the streets of their cities as a threat to public order and their integration within the community, there-fore, as a priority. Originally it was thought that compulsory recruitment for a period into a quasi-military youth movement, perhaps with a link to the governing party, would occupy them and inculcate in them both loyalty to the government and the habit of discipline. When this proved unsuccessful attention shifted to youth organisations whose aim was vocational. While more con-structive, such organisations could not guarantee that members would obtain jobs afterwards. Countries participating in UN International Youth Year also emphasised the value of education and training to young people, but insisted that it was also essential to find work for them.

In a world in which mass unemployment is no longer the unhappy prerogative of the poor countries of the South, this is a tall order. But at least they have opportunities not available to the industrialised countries. They can still try to find a place for many of their young people in a labour-intensive agriculture within revived rural communities.

11

Women's Rights

The World Health Organisation referring mainly to the Third World, reports: 'although women constitute one-third of the world's official labour force, they are responsible for nearly two-thirds of the hours worked, receive only one-tenth of the world's income, and own less than 1% of its property' (WHO, 1987, p. 24). Economic discrimination is thus added to the other forms of disadvantage from which, as previous chapters have shown, women in underdeveloped countries suffer simply because they are women.

Not that women are treated as the equal of men in the developed world either. Although the situation has improved in recent years, many inequities still persist. Women are still expected, except in the more enlightened families, to do the greater part, if not all, of the housework as well as being responsible for the care of children, which places severe limits on their social activities and the opportunities available to them for employment. As if this were not enough, a job market dominated by men also imposes all sorts of further restrictions on the admission of women into certain occupations, especially those giving high pay, or power and status.

Meanwhile the work within the home, although of course of great importance, is not usually given a market value and is not therefore esteemed as it should be (Benston, 1969). To employ an outsider worker simply as a housekeeper and baby-minder would in fact be very costly, and that would be without the irreplaceable emotional contribution to home life which a wife, mother or daughter also makes. Another way of assessing the monetary value of the work element would be by means of the economist's concept of 'opportunity cost'. What would a woman be able to earn, if she devoted to gainful employment the time she now spent on her home?

Third World Women

The domestic functions of Third World women are much more onerous than those of women in the North (Rogers, 1980, pp. 152–8). Thus, apart from child-care, they spend many hours every day in fetching water, especially if there is no well, collecting firewood and preparing food such as maize, which they have themselves previously grown, for storage or consumption. Combined with frequent child-bearing and their inferior diet, the workload of women in the Third World is beginning to cause them to suffer serious health problems (ibid., pp. 154–6).

Women also contribute directly to family subsistence by their gardening or fishing activities. Indeed they usually do most of this work, but because what they produce is not sold but consumed by the family it is treated as having no economic value (Rogers, 1980; Sacks, 1983, p. 212; Beneria, 1982b). Thus if the male 'bread-winner' is unemployed it is this which is salient; society (and its statistics) attach little importance to the fact that this, and indeed the whole family's, bread is actually being 'won' by the subsistence activities of the woman.

Where (as is often the case) women also share in the work involved in growing 'cash crops', their labour, because it is equated with domestic work, is often not acknowledged as having economic value (Rogers, 1980). And in such cases it is nearly always the man who is seen as the 'grower' or 'farmer'. He receives the money, and any development aid or training which is available (ibid, pp. 125ff). This is so even if, being a migrant worker, he is rarely there, and the holding is left in the hands of the woman (ibid., pp. 63–8).

The demand that governments should find a way of quantifying the value of the domestic and productive contributions of women was potentially one of the most radical results of the Nairobi Conference with which the UN Decade of Women ended in 1985 (United Nations, 1985a). The limitation of work opportunities outside the domestic circle is also important, not only because the alternative of work in the home is undervalued, but also because it

---

Exhibit 11.1   Women's Share of Work

The International Labour Office's *World Labour Report*
(ILO, 1984, p. 2) describes the economic role of women as
follows:

> Women, especially those who are poor, work hard.
> Women's productive work is often underestimated because
> of the many tasks they perform, some of which are not
> visible, and because a household's status may be lowered
> by appearing to depend on women's earnings. Yet in Nepal,
> for example, women contribute 50% of household income
> compared with 43% by men, and the balance by children.
> Even secluded women in Nigeria and Bangladesh engage in
> extensive productive work. In the Andes rural women per-
> form a substantial part of the agricultural work despite the
> image to the contrary given by census data. And in Africa
> women are the principal producers of food. The contribution
> that women make to total household earnings is significantly
> higher in poor households. Many women work for pitiful
> returns as wage labourers or traders. When all work is
> counted, paid and unpaid (such as collecting water and fuel,
> preparing food etc.), data from the Third World as a whole
> indicate substantially longer working hours for women than
> for men, especially in poor rural households. That women's
> work is of marginal importance is a lingering and dangerous
> myth.

---

constricts a woman's personal development. It also perpetuates
her personal dependence on her male relatives.

The toleration of this state of affairs by women is at first sight
difficult to understand. Women, after all, do play the central role
in the early socialisation of children and are in a position to
inculcate more egalitarian attitudes in them. The fact that they do
not do so is evidence that they themselves accept their own
subordination as legitimate, or at least inevitable. Sometimes this
complaisance seems to be based on the assumption that the world
has always been so, that it is part of a natural order of things,
expressing itself throughout the ages in every aspect of society:

marital relationships, the division of labour, the law, education, the arts, social rituals, and even the view of the world expressed in religious beliefs. In many cultures, notably Islam, the role of religion in legitimising male dominance has been central.

Even in the Soviet Union, where discrimination on the grounds of sex is illegal, there persists a widespread belief (shared by younger as well as older women) that certain jobs are more suitable for men while female occupations should draw on women's 'expressive' qualities. Nearly all Russian teachers, for example, are women. In marital relations also, it is taken for granted that the wife should adapt herself to her husband's needs: as one Russian woman, speaking of relationships between the sexes, said in a recent television interview, 'A women must always be an actress'.

Feminism

There is often a quasi-biological assumption that women, as the weaker and more passive sex, have an 'expressive' role as contrasted with the 'instrumental' role of their menfolk (Millet, 1971). Their main functions are the bearing and rearing of children and the provision of a warm and secure emotional refuge for the men after the latter's daily forays into the world outside the home are at an end. This has always been, even in the industrialised countries, a fiction as far as working-class women are concerned. As a picture of the relative work loads of men and women in the Third World, it is wildly inaccurate. Nevertheless it has helped to underpin this belief that women are destined by nature to rely on the more active and dominant males.

If an ideology is defined as a system of ideas which have evolved to support the social *status quo*, these beliefs may properly be described as ideologies. Together with the institutional arrangements through which they are made effective, they constitute the social system which feminists call 'patriarchy' (Millet, 1971; Eisenstein, 1979; Coward, 1983). All sections of the women's movement – liberal (Friedan, 1965; Charvet, 1982, pp. 6ff;), socialist (Women's Studies Group, 1978) or radical (Firestone, 1971; Koedt *et al.*, 1973a) – have seen their first task as being to raise the consciousness of women about the effect of these ideologies upon their position in society (Mackinnon, 1982). They see biology as determining sex only and not gender roles, that is, the behaviour expected of women because they are women. Though it may be going too far to dismiss biological differences entirely, they are right when they go on to say that it is society which has created gender inequalities and which can also remove them (Rosaldo, 1983; Chodorov, 1983).

Liberal feminists (Friedan, 1965; Charvet, 1982, pp. 6ff) assume that an improvement in the status of women can be brought about by rational arguments of this kind. If women can come to understand how their subjection has occurred, they can convince those who control the levers of power, and thus bring about the reforms which they seek. This approach has met with some, albeit limited, success in the industrialised countries. Discriminatory laws have been changed. Occupations formerly closed to women have become available to them. They have gained more control over their own property and income. And, in government employment at least, equal pay for equal work is becoming the rule.

Yet underlying social attitudes have not changed very much. Many men, even in the North, do not accept the feminist case, and even among women, those who feel strongly about it are still in a minority. As a result access to many kinds of employment, in the professions and in senior positions everywhere, are still restricted to men. Although these biases in recruitment and promotion are not openly acknowledged, they enable many sceptical male employers to nullify the effect of equal pay rules. Even the social activities of women are often curtailed by social conventions about what it is proper for them to do, or to do without male escorts.

None of this will surprise those feminists who take a socialist stance. The liberals, they say, assume that people can be persuaded by argument, and that society can therefore be changed in accordance with the joint dictates of conscience and reason. But such a belief in the power of reason ignores the dominant role in society of capitalists, with their vested interest in the subordination of women, and also the way in which the climate of ideas is shaped by its capitalist nature. 'It is not the consciousness of men', wrote Marx in a famous passage, 'that determines their existence, but, on the contrary, their social existence determines their consciousness' (Marx, 1859, pp. 11–12). The conclusion is that an improvement in the position of women cannot be brought about so long as capitalism itself remains intact.

Early Utopian socialists like Fourier and William Thompson (a follower of Robert Owen), had linked the oppression of women with capitalism as early as the beginning of the nineteenth century. Socialism would emancipate them because of its ethic of equality and social justice. But in 1884, Engels offered a less purely ethical rationale, in his *The Family, Private Property and the State*. Writing from a Marxist point of view, he argued that the subjection of women began with settled agriculture and the emergence of private property, especially in the form of animal herds. The men were able to appropriate this property, and the power in their households which went with it, because they had always controlled the tools of food production, as the women had those of the household. The rest followed with inexorable Marxist logic. Now privately owned, capital became concentrated in fewer and fewer (though still male) hands, with the result that property-less men now joined women to form an exploited majority.

Biological Explanations

Although this theory has played an important part in feminist thinking, it is based on the nineteenth-century anthropology of Lewis Morgan (1877), whose account of the stages of social development is no longer accepted. It also overlooks the genuine role which has probably been played by the biological differences between the sexes. The bearing and nursing of children is an obvious disadvantage for a woman, in that it interrupts both her social life and the continuity of her employment. The fact that she may withdraw from work for a period when pregnant also puts her at a disadvantage in competing with men for work or promotion (Rosaldo, 1983; Sanday, 1983).

This is used as a justification for locking women into low-grade, low-paid forms of employment, where, it is argued, their occasional absences and preoccupation with family affairs would do 'less harm' (Chodorov, 1979, p. 88). The related belief in their 'expressive' nature limits their work opportunities in a similar way. They are seen as better suited to jobs as aides to men, or as receptionists, shop assistants and so on, in which their qualities of personality can be drawn upon.

Nor is it possible to overlook the greater physical strength of the male. One view of this is that it causes him to be more important for the survival of the species in a hostile environment, and that it is for this reason that he is more cherished. Even liberal writers sometimes give credence to this narrow view of the qualities which are serviceable for survival (Coombs, 1985, p. 228).

Others argue that the superior strength of the male enables him to establish his ascendancy by *force majeure* (Collins, 1975). The suggestion (Whyte, 1978, pp. 31–2) that the frequent absences of the physically aggressive males, because of their involvement in warfare, actually allowed women to gain in power and status, seems to be an oblique confirmation of this. In the more sophisticated North, physical violence against women is not now tolerated (wife-beating is an offence), though in more subtle ways, physical dominance undoubtedly still plays a part. In many underdeveloped countries, on the other hand, force is not only still practised, but sanctioned by public opinion. In such a matter, legislators often need to be ahead of public opinion, and a number of countries have laws to protect women from this kind of abuse.

The traditional approach by women's rights campaigners has been to minimise the differences between the sexes, with the aim also of minimising socially imposed gender differences. This 'androgynous' view is rejected by some radical feminists, who want instead to emphasise the importance of women as women. Women, it is contended, do not need to try to be like men. Being

---

Exhibit 11.2   Female separatism in the Arab world

The emphasis on a female identity is found not only in the North, but has surfaced also, perhaps not surprisingly, in the Arab world, where

> a number of feminists have sought a way forward within the Islamic tradition rather than through its rejection ... arguing that a strategy for 'Liberation' in the Islamic context should build upon rather than reject the separateness of the male and female worlds... Within this approach there is an attempt to re-evaluate the 'private sphere' of women. (Cammack *et al.*, 1988: 210)

female is better. For example, radical feminists contrast what they see as the uncertainty of males about their sexual identity, resulting from the little boy's dependence on his mother in early infancy, with the security which that same contact gives to women. This was a problem which gave great difficulty to Freud, leading to a rather tortuous solution through his theory of the Oedipal situation.

This concentration on femaleness has not always led to an emphasis on the complementary nature of men and women. The sexual bond itself, especially where institutionalised in marriage and the family (Coward, 1983) has sometimes been seen as a major factor in the preservation of unequal power relationships. The response of some radical feminists is to try to cut men out of their lives entirely. They argue that, with the development of sperm banks, artificial insemination and *in vitro* fertilisation, males are only marginally necessary for the procreation of children; and that the emotional and sensual needs of women can be met through lesbian relationships (Koedt, 1973b; Rich, 1981). Nor in these days of scientific formula-feeding should any woman need to be hampered by the obligation to feed her child.

Women with a heterosexual orientation, and those who find having and nursing children a rewarding experience, will not be enthusiastic about such an agenda. They will want better job opportunities, pay and conditions of work, as well as equal rights to hold and dispose of property. At a more personal level, safe and effective contraception will be high on the list, so that they may choose the timing and frequency of their pregnancies, especially if this can be combined with generous arrangements for maternity leave and legal protection for their career prospects during these absences. They will also want to see more crèches, with affordable fees, so that they can leave their babies, when they are old enough, with an easy conscience.

Many of these issues are of less importance in the South, as was made clear by the deliberations of the Nairobi Conference (United Nations, 1985a). The differences in priorities are well illustrated by a recommendation from the Conference that better stoves should be designed to relieve the women of some of the burden of gathering fuel. It will be a long time before issues such as maternity leave and career prospects can have any meaning for Third World women, many of whom still have little chance of doing any paid work at all. Nor is there any baby-minding problem. At present women often take their young babies with them when they go to work in their gardens (Hammond and Jablow, 1976, pp. 54–5). When the children become too old for this, they will be looked after quite readily by grandmothers or other relatives, or by women whose own pregnancies are at a stage where they are still immobilised in the village. Factory work, and other paid employment outside the home, could change all that, especially if the tradition of mutual aid suffered attrition, as it has in many places.

Contraception, to be dealt with in the next chapter, and bottle-feeding are much more significant. The great convenience of bottle-feeding for hard-pressed women, together with the sales pressure of the formula manufacturers, have caused something of an explosion in the use of these products, much to the detriment of their babies' health and nutrition. The water with which the formula has to be mixed is often not pure enough and, because the formula itself is so expensive, these poor mothers give it to their babies in too diluted a form. There is also the possible emotional deprivation for the babies if the activity of feeding is separated from physical intimacy with the mother, which bottle-feeding makes only too easy. Psychoanalysts have pointed out that this warm sensual contact may be important for a baby's sense of security and future ease in social relationships.

There seems very little doubt that the physiological differences between the sexes have played their part in subordinating women to men, but there is also reason to believe that this effect has been reinforced by economic factors. Engels may have got his anthropology wrong, but his instinct (like that of Fourier and of Thompson) that capitalism had something to do with it was probably sound. This theme will now be examined.

Economic Exploitation

Because of the low valuation attached to their work, women have always been used by employers as cheap labour. This, besides being a source of profit on its own account, also tends to depress the wages of male workers. But women also make other less direct contributions to the productive process. As mentioned earlier, there is the unpaid work which they do in helping to sustain and feed the household. Also, as mothers, they recruit and socialise the next generation of workers. As wives, they provide a stable and satisfying domestic and emotional haven for their menfolk in the labour force, reconciling them to the alienation and powerlessness which they experience in their daily work. Sacks (1983, p. 222) adds an interesting gloss on this: that the dominance of men over women may in itself help to make the working lives of the men more tolerable. None of this enters into the supply price of labour, or what Marxists call its cost of reproduction, and so makes it possible for men to accept lower wages.

In all these respects women correspond very closely to what Marx (1967) called the 'reserve army of labour' (Benston, 1969). Any improvement in their position would threaten the capitalist with increased labour costs. Low wages, it should be remembered, according to neo-classical theory, are an important 'comparative advantage', encouraging capitalists to invest in the countries of the South. If women do function as a 'reserve army of labour' in the industrialised countries, they are hardly required for this purpose in the Third World. For a 'reserve army', adequate to such limited opportunities for employment, can still easily be found among the men, in the large numbers of peasants who are being impoverished or deprived of land by consolidation.

However, the role of women in keeping down wages may become critical as the demand for male labour exerts pressure on the supply. It may already have become so in middle-income countries like Taiwan or South Korea. Women may still have the refuge of the extended family but, as this is weakened by underdevelopment, they will be forced by family hardship to seek a livelihood in competition with the men, either on local farms or, failing that, by migration to an urban centre. Capitalism, it appears, has even more interest in a depressed status for women in the underdeveloped countries of the Third World than in the industrialised North.

These arguments are not accepted by all feminists, implying as they do that workers of both sexes share a common predicament under capitalism. As against this, some feminists contend that women are a separate class in society, exploited by the male patriarchy, which includes the capitalists. As Acker (1984b, p. 70) puts it, patriarchy is an 'ancient form of oppression with its own logic and its own beneficiaries and victims'. A very different objection is raised by O'Kelly (1980, pp. 247ff), who suggests that in its later stages Northern capitalism has actually improved the situation of women, by opening up new job and educational opportunities to them. They have also secured the vote and a good deal more freedom of movement and expression than they had before. These may be the exceptions which prove the rule, however, for they arose mostly at times of labour shortage, especially during the two world wars, when the bargaining power of women was at its height. The limits imposed on their subsequent progress, especially in the critical area of employment, are only too apparent.

Nevertheless it would be idle to claim that, if underdevelopment could be ended tomorrow, that by itself would bring discrimination against women to an end. One has some doubt, for example, about the picture often painted of an age of sex-equality among the hunters and gatherers of pre-industrial society. O'Laughlin's account of gender relationships among the Mbun Kpau of Chad in Central Africa (O'Laughlin, 1983) is instructive here. Certainly in existing traditional societies, the powers of women are strictly limited, and often only decisive in relation to children and the home. Male dominance, presumably based at this early stage on an exploitation of the biological influences referred to, preceded any involvement in a world economy.

Traditional Roles

Among the Melanesians of the Western Pacific, for example, many of whom have a tradition of communal sharing which is the antithesis of capitalist acquisitiveness, women are expected to be obedient to their menfolk. They do much of the gardening and fishing in addition to their domestic chores, while the men, who used to spend their time in tribal fighting, now gossip in the Men's House. If the possibility of waged employment arises it is the men who take advantage of it, with all the enhancement of their power which this monopoly of cash gives them, while the women continue with their customary task of securing the family's livelihood.

Women are excluded from tribal rituals. Indeed they are

prohibited from even entering the Men's House, where most of these ceremonies take place. The assumption is that they are ritually unclean. Consequently, before a youth in some tribes can be admitted to manhood and to the Men's House, he is required to take part in a ceremony in which he symbolically washes away the pollution derived from his mother during childhood. As an anti-dote to any feelings of lofty superiority in the North about such customs, it is worthwhile perhaps to recall the similar attitude towards women displayed by the Christian churches, particularly the Roman Catholic, the Orthodox and some Anglican commun-ions.

Melanesia is in no way exceptional. Practices derogatory to the status of women are found throughout the Third World. In many parts of Africa, a man's wealth is closely connected with the number of wives he has to cultivate his gardens. Women, who have often grown the food, eat last, even if this means that they become malnourished. Marriage customs commonly favour the men. Thus a barren wife, or one who has borne no male children, may find herself supplanted or sent back to her family in disgrace. Although poverty prevents many men from taking advantage of the social custom of polygyny, the fact that it is so widely accepted demonstrates the low statues of wives.

This is even more powerfully shown by the opposite practice of polyandry, in which one woman is married simultaneously to a number of men. This never means that a woman has decided to take more than one husband (as would be the case if it were a counterpart to polygyny) but that two or more men, often brothers, have decided to share a wife – perhaps because of the cost of having a spouse to themselves.

Already located at the bottom of the social pyramid, it is women who suffer most from family poverty, whether brought about by drought or disaster – or by underdevelopment. Even in areas in which traditional land tenure remains unimpaired, the effect of underdevelopment in drawing the younger menfolk away from the village into the industrial or mining enclave, which occurs particu-larly in Africa, greatly increases the women's burdens. For, to the work they do in cultivation they now have to add the heavy task of clearing land and the tending of animals, for which the men had usually taken responsibility.

Most men return home faithfully at the end of their contracts, and spend some of their earnings for the benefit of their families, though much of the money may go on buying pigs or cattle for reasons of status, or on gambling or beer. The latter may certainly be seen as selfish and wasteful, but in the language of Chapter 2, it may also be seen by the men concerned as necessary for their survival as socially significant persons within the culture in which they live. But in some cases the men cut off contact with their families altogether, establishing new unions in the urban centre. Then the family's only resort is what is left of the traditional system of mutual aid.

The traditional way of life, then, imposed many disadvantages on a woman. She would often have little status. She would defer to her husband. Working hard, she would nevertheless have no independent income and little acknowledgment of her contribution. She would bear many children, seeing many of them die young. At the same time, in accepting her lot as not only inevitable, but right and proper, she had a degree of security in her life arising from the stability of a subsistence economy and the support and approval of her kinsfolk. Even her hard labour on the land often played its part here, for with it sometimes went traditional rights to control the use of the land.

The incursion of Northern capitalism worsens even this situation. The woman's family and kinship links and the familiar way of life, her land rights (Rogers, 1980, pp. 134–5) and the subsistence they provide – all are threatened by this new dynamic. It preserves and exploits her social inferiority for its own purposes, greatly worsening her material situation in the process. Many women are forced into employment by poverty, and these jobs do not fulfil any emancipating role at all. They are a form of underpaid drudgery, often carried out under deplorable working conditions (International Labour Office, 1984, pp. 203ff). This is when the function of female labour as a 'reserve army' becomes most obvious.

Plantation work in countries like Sri Lanka and Malaysia provide an example: women 'constitute more than half the labour force, but they receive lower pay than men for the same work, face extra burdens because of inadequate child-care facilities and the long distances between home and work, and often see others collecting their pay' (ibid., p. 206).

Female Migration

It is not surprising, therefore, that women are themselves now abandoning the rural areas in increasing numbers. This is not an entirely new phenomenon. Women have often left their home areas on marrying. This commonly resulted from customary rules of exogamy, requiring a woman to marry outside her own group, often combined with an obligation to go to live in her husband's village. Women have often also moved 'for marriage', that is, in order to find husbands where demography made this necessary, or to find husbands with better life chances than the local men. These are the main reasons for the very limited amount of female migration which takes place in India, for example.

With the decay of the rural way of life, moving for marriage has begun to mean rural–urban migration. But women are now also moving to the cities on their own account, in the hope of getting jobs in the modern sector and of benefiting from the better facilities they believe will be available to them there. An important further reason is to escape from traditional hardships imposed on them as women in the villages. The exceptions to this trend are the Arab countries, India, and Central and East Africa (Fawcett, Khoo and Smith, 1984).

Rural–urban migration by women in Latin America already exceeds that of men, as may that in the Philippines. The same is true of Thailand as far as migration to the capital, Bangkok, is concerned, though not to other cities. Indonesia displays a similar pattern of migration to the larger cities (ibid.). Although males still predominate among rural–urban migrants in Malaysia, the rapid increase in the proportion of women is beginning to cause alarm in that Islamic country. Somewhat unreliable data suggest that industrialisation may have caused a similar increase in Taiwan and South Korea. In West Africa, where women have always been economically active (Cammack *et al.*, 1988, pp. 184ff), they move back and forth between the villages and the towns (Fawcett, Khoo and Smith, 1984), but elsewhere in the continent most migrants are male (ibid.).

Increasing female migration is bound to have a decisively adverse effect on the prospects for traditional rural society. It will also further exacerbate such problems of the burgeoning cities as unemployment, housing, and health and hygiene. And in spite of the gain in independence and standard of life which some female migrants will be able to achieve, many find themselves faced with a whole set of new hardships which social policies will have to try to confront (ibid., pp. 397–406). The low level of education of most of them, for example, places them at a disadvantage in competing for urban employment both with their better-off sisters and with men, for such employment usually requires some degree of literacy. As we have seen (Chapter 7) sex differences in literacy are already great, and are actually widening. This makes women fair game once again for exploitation and low wages. Prostitution is a not uncommon outcome. Housing and health are other areas of concern, especially where children are also involved. Women and their children often find themselves in situations in which they have need of the traditional support which they left behind in the rural area.

The doctrine applied to escaped serfs in medieval Europe, that 'town air makes free' has its own resonance for women in the Third World. So there is no reason why migration to the city should be less justifiable for them than for men. But perhaps migration by both might be lessened with advantage if rural development received the degree of attention it deserves.

Reforms

The case for greater equality between the sexes on the grounds of social justice is easily established, and this also makes its achievement part of what is meant by development. The World Bank has pointed also to the economic return to be obtained from the fuller development of human resources. To allow the potentialities of women to remain, as at present, largely unrealised is to waste the human resources of half of the world's population.

Any attempt to remedy this situation will appear irrational under the conditions of underdevelopment. What point is there, after all, in encouraging large numbers of women to enter a labour market which is unable to employ those at present offering themselves for work? Which is rather like saying, why try to improve the nutrition of women when the diet of some men remains inadequate. The answer is of course, to take steps to increase the supply of food – and work. This could be achieved only if a country could escape from the underdevelopment trap, which would be no small task.

Much has been said in earlier pages about the transformation of traditional ways of life by economic change, and the suffering which this has brought in its train. A policy for development rather than underdevelopment would throw existing social arrangements into the melting-pot also, but would allow them to be remoulded in forms which increased the prospects for growth and social justice, rather than the reverse. The dissolution of traditional attitudes which are prejudicial to women could well be one of the gains.

In practice what pass for development projects may often have the reverse effect, formalising male hegemony in accordance with Northern ideas, and in the process eliminating such traditional rights as women's access to land, and their control over its use. Such programmes are invariably focused on men, and when provision is made for women it is separate and residual rather than main-line provision (Rogers, 1980, pp. 79ff). Women are defined as marginal, in spite of the central economic function which they fulfil in traditional society.

The damage done is not confined to the status of women. For example, economic incentives in such schemes are usually directed at men rather than women (ibid., pp. 181ff). If most of the work on the land is done by women such measures are unlikely to be very successful in stimulating production.

The millennium, by definition, is not going to be achieved overnight. In the meantime social policy must attempt to achieve what it can within the existing socio-economic environment. Education must come first. Providing better educational opportunities for women will do much, as we have seen, to improve standards of health, nutrition and child care. Better educated woman also exercise more control over the size of their families (Cochrane, 1977) – with the apparent exception of Indonesia (Superlan and Sigit, 1980, pp. 29).

The whole issue of family planning will be taken up in the next chapter, but it might be noted here that the rescue of Third World women from the burden of constant pregnancy, however brought about, would be a major step forward in their emancipation. But as important as any of these arguments is the contribution better education in itself can make towards achieving more equal status for women in society. Literacy alone will open many windows onto the world for them. As education proceeds it will help them to develop as more self-dependent individuals, able to think through things for themselves, rather than to leave everything to the men. It will also enable them to be more critical of the traditional practices and beliefs which have held them in subjection for so long.

Educational equality must also include the content of the education to be provided. Only too often, in planning the 'basic education' of women, the schools concentrate on 'female' subjects like housekeeping, child care, cooking and nutrition, and family planning (Rogers, 1980, pp. 81ff). There is no doubt about the value of teaching them such subjects, and not only for the benefit of their families. For it is they who suffer most from inefficient domestic routines and a deficient diet, and are burdened by frequent pregnancies and large families. Education in such subjects also makes its own contribution to economic growth; it is part of what is meant by investment in human resources.

But such investment is incomplete if it does not help women to develop any capacities they may possess for work outside the home. This may relate simply to teaching them better techniques of gardening. The Nairobi Conference laid stress on this, together with the more ambitious matters with which feminists in the North are concerned (United Nations, 1985a). For even in gardening, where women are already active, it often seems to be assumed (perhaps because of the general underdevelopment of women's abilities) that men will take over when improved methods of cultivation are adopted. Beyond this, however, such education should introduce women to paid occupations currently monopolised by men. In either case the vocational education of women would be as profitable for the country as that of men.

Foster's contention that appropriate work opportunities must be available if vocational education is to be other than a frustrating experience for its recipients and a waste of time and resources for the country is valid, but only underlines the importance of achieving more non-exploitative job opportunities for women (Kelly, 1984, pp. 84–5). The solution for both sexes must be found elsewhere than in the curtailment of educational opportunities.

Opening up such opportunities for women to secure paid work

which does not simply take advantage of their inferior social position can in itself do much to improve their status. It achieves this through the greater bargaining power which an independent income gives, but also through the changes in roles within the family which the exigencies of the work situation necessitate. For many centuries Chinese women had been dominated by their fathers or husbands (Kaplan and Sobin, 1982, pp. 304–5). The transformation brought about in their position since the passage of the Marriage Law of 1950 has been attributed partly to the subsequent female literacy campaign, but mostly to the government's success in getting women into jobs (ibid.). The improved position of women in North Korea has similarly been attributed to their increased employment as a result of labour shortages (Molyneux, 1984, p. 275).

But women in many countries are also the core of a traditional social system, some aspects of which, it has often been argued in these pages, will be needed for the foreseeable future in order to meet the subsistence and welfare needs of the rural population. If the form assumed by the outside employment of women does not take account of that fact it may do more harm than good.

What role, if any, can the law play in all this? It cannot be great in the villages. Even the physical abuse of women by men, if it is sanctioned by custom, will be only marginally affected by laws against it, and at the cost of widespread resentment – perhaps even sometimes on the part of the women themselves: consider the support for their own subjugation given by Islamic fundamentalist women in Iran. The status of women in a more general sense is even less likely to be advanced by legal coercion. The way forward must be through persuasion within the local community, in the course of which the indigenous leadership, the chiefs and headmen, will also have to be won over. If women are receiving some education they are more likely to be supportive of these efforts on their own account.

Laws can serve a more useful purpose in the modernised sectors of the economy. This is one case in which the weakening of traditional solidarity will be a positive advantage. The nature of urban life, and the kinds of ideas associated with modernisation itself, will also play their part. So in the developed enclave it will be more possible to enforce legislation to protect females against assault or undue restrictions by their husbands or fathers and (to some extent) against economic exploitation by either their male relatives or their employers. As children they can be given an equal right to education, and as adults equal civil rights, although, as experience cited from the Soviet Union shows, older attitudes may still prove very durable.

Although the application of laws against discrimination may only be enforceable in the towns, they can serve an important symbolical function over a wider area. They present an image of the way women should be treated, an image to which the country as a whole will gradually become accustomed. Such ideas will no longer seem strange and outlandish, and community workers in the villages will be able to point to them as the national ideal, from which present customs diverge so lamentably.

The status of women arises within many local contexts: education, health, agricultural extension and so on. Workers in all these fields will have to have regard for it in the way they do their work. This includes the social worker. Her activities in connection with children, the elderly, social aspects of sickness and disablement, and indeed the cohesion and stability of the family as a whole, will give her influence over a broad front on the future role of women in the families with which she works.

Powerful resistance to change will continue to emanate from the values of the community. Work to change relationships within families will have to go hand in hand with efforts to change attitudes on a broader front. Nevertheless experimental work on cognitive dissonance (Brehm and Cohen, 1962) has shown that, where a belief conflicts with what actually happens, the belief tends to change to conform with the practice. When women have achieved more equality in fact, it may not even matter whether the long-standing belief to the contrary does change, or merely becomes an empty myth.

Summary

In the Third World, where so many are underprivileged, women are the most underprivileged of all. Although they give birth to and rear large families, and work hard at domestic chores and in the fields, often to the detriment of their health, their status is low. Power is monopolised by men, to whose welfare and domestic comfort they are expected to devote themselves. If they receive any education at all, it is very limited.

Various explanations for this state of affairs have been offered: the greater physical strength of the male, the burden of bearing and nursing children, the male control over property in a capitalist society, or even a historical patriarchal despotism arising from these or other sources. Whatever its causes, one reason for its persistence is undoubtedly the fact that it is widely accepted as proper by women themselves.

Underdevelopment has tended to worsen the situation of many women by weakening the supports provided by traditional society without opening up alternative opportunities for them. Employment outside the home, where it is available, is often exploitative. Joining in the flight to the urban areas in order to escape from the poverty and restrictions of village life often presents them with new problems which they are ill-equipped to face.

If their position is to be improved within the traditional social framework, their burden of work will have to be eased by the introduction of 'appropriate' domestic aids, and more productive gardening and agricultural methods. Education and family planning also have a central role to play. Where outside work could be accommodated to their traditional functions, it would open up new vistas for them.

But first attitudes have to be changed. This would be a stepwise process and therefore slow. For example, changes in attitude towards family planning leading to smaller families or better education for women would put them in a position to make further gains. In advancing this process of grass-roots social education, social workers and community development workers have an important job to do. And their first and perhaps most difficult task will be to convince the women themselves.

12

Population Policies

The fear that population will outstrip food supplies has haunted human beings throughout history, and has been periodically vindicated by disastrous famines. Malthus put this fear into the form of a theory and Britain reacted by establishing, in 1801, the world's first systematic population census, which has been repeated every ten years ever since. Other countries in the then industrialising North followed suit, and as a result the rapid growth of their populations became apparent. Nevertheless Europe did not starve. The agrarian revolution of the time made the land very much more productive, and the opening-up of rich farmlands in North and South America and Australia made assurance doubly sure.

The process by which this increase in population was itself eventually brought under control was referred to by the French demographer, Landry, as the 'demographic transition' (Kosinski, 1970, pp. 5–6). It is seen by some as a natural accompaniment of development, and is usually expected to occur in the Third World, as it has in the First. It falls into four stages. During the pre-industrial period, there is high fertility accompanied by high mortality, and therefore equilibrium in the size of the population. During the second stage, improvements in the conditions of life associated with modernisation lead to a fall in deaths, but fertility remains high, with a consequent escalation in the size of the population. At the third stage, the gap between birth and death rates narrows, as fertility itself declines. Finally the gap between the two rates disappears entirely, and the population is at an equilibrium. Although the population is no longer increasing, it has, of course, become stabilised at a much higher level than before.

Third World Trends

What is now causing alarm, however, is the steeply upward population trend in the newly independent countries of the Third World. Since 1950, the average annual rate of population increase in the South has been well over two per cent (in some countries much higher), as compared with less than one per cent in the North (United Nations, 1986b, p. 52). This is not the result of any overall increase in birth rates in the underdeveloped countries; they have actually fallen, as Table 12.1 shows. However, as in Europe, improvements in diet, sanitation and water supply, and the introduction of modern medicine caused mortality rates, particularly infant mortality rates, to fall even faster. The effect of this is clearly shown in the table.

While the birth rates of the 'less developed' countries fell by 30·2 per cent between 1950–5 and 1980–5, the decline in their death rates was almost twice as high, at 55·4 per cent. Over the same period birth rates for the 'more developed' countries fell by 31·7 per cent as compared with a fall in death rates of only 5 per cent. Indeed the latter have not fallen at all during most of the period in question.

In some circles in the North the anxiety about these trends was racialist in character, similar to the feelings which had caused such people to refer to the growth in the population of Japan before the Second World War as the 'yellow peril'. But to be fair, the population explosion in the South was on a much larger scale than anything previously experienced anywhere. How much concern should there be about this? Is the Malthusian nightmare of a world

Table 12.1   Crude birth and death rates per thousand of population for the more developed and less developed countries, 1950–90 (United Nations, 1986b, pp. 78, 90)

	1950–5	1955–60	1960–5	1965–70	1970–5	1975–80	1980–5	1985–90*
Less developed countries								
Birth rate	44.4	42.0	41.9	40.5	37.2	32.9	31.0	29.4
Death rate	24.2	20.9	18.3	15.1	13.4	11.8	10.8	10.0
More developed countries								
Birth rate	22.7	21.7	20.3	17.9	17.0	15.9	15.5	15.1
Death rate	10.1	9.3	9.0	9.1	9.2	9.4	9.6	9.5

*Projections

population controlled only by 'war, famine or pestilence' in danger of becoming reality?

Pestilence, as we have seen, still causes many deaths, and wars (as currently in the Sudan) kill more people from disease and famine than die on the battlefield. The question of world hunger has been discussed in Chapter 3; the 'green revolution' has not yet provided an answer to it. Meanwhile the populations of the poor countries are still rising, if at a diminishing rate. Present forecasts by the United Nations are as shown in Table 12.2. This shows that the Third World share of world population, which was 67·3 per cent in 1950, had increased to 74·5 per cent in 1980. By 2025 it is expected to have risen to 83 per cent.

The annual population *growth rate* for the 'less developed' countries as a whole is expected to decline from 2·0 per cent to 1·1 per cent between 1980–5 and 2020–5, but little comfort should be taken from this because of the large absolute numbers of people to which they refer. Thus South Asia, despite a reduction in the rate of increase from 2·16 per cent in 1975–80 to 0·93 per cent in 2000–25, will add 666 millions to the population of the world between 1980 and 2000, and another 740 millions in the succeeding 25 years, constituting respectively 39·8 per cent and 35·5 per cent of the increase in world population during the two periods in question (United Nations, 1986b, pp. 48–50).

Overall figures also conceal wide differences between different parts of the world (ibid., pp. 48–9). The highest population growth rate is in Western Africa – 3·12 per cent per annum in 1980–5, reaching 3·35 per cent in 1995–2000, but expected to be still running at 2·16 per cent in 2000–25. This will mean an increase in the population of Western Africa from 144 millions in 1980 to 558 millions in 2025.

There is nothing in figures like these to suggest that a 'green revolution' (of an appropriate kind) is not needed, but they must

Table 12.2   Populations in 1950 and 1980, and population forecasts to 2025 as assessed in 1984, more and less developed countries (millions) (United Nations, 1986b, pp. 48–9)

	1950	1980	1985	1990	2000	2025
Less developed countries	1 684	3 313	3 663	4 036	4 845	6 809
More developed countries	832	1 137	1 174	1 210	1 277	1 396

raise serious doubts as to whether, by itself, it would be enough. The Malthusian threat would be postponed perhaps, but no more, unless policies to limit the growth in Third World populations are also adopted.

Social Consequences

The Third World food situation is not the only reason for adopting such policies. It is generally agreed that a large population can be a powerful generator of poverty. It has been demonstrated earlier how an increase in GNP is converted into an actual decrease in per capita GNP when population rises. But the decline in the incomes of the poor families themselves will be even greater, for it is they who usually have the largest families. An increase in population worsens the position of poor families also in another way. As Ahluwalia has shown (1976), it decreases the return to labour by comparison with capital (because of the increase in the supply of labour), which means lower wages. That is if a job can be found, for a growing population combined with underdevelopment will mean high levels of unemployment.

At the same time, government income from taxation is constrained by widespread poverty, even though the inflation of population calls for more expenditure on social services such as education, housing, sewage, water supply, medical services and welfare. The result in badly funded and therefore inadequate public services is bound to bear hardest on the poor, whose need for such services is greatest.

At the personal level women are the main sufferers. They endure one pregnancy after another, to the detriment of their health. Pregnancies and child care take up what time is left to them from their many chores, perpetuating their dependence, and preventing them from widening their experience. They have much to gain from an effective population policy.

If social justice is one of the criteria of development, then high population rates are seen to be its enemy, but the threat they offer to purely economic development will be every bit as great. Investment in human and infrastructural capital is limited by lack of funds. High levels of unemployment involve a waste of resources and low labour productivity because of the relative shortage of usable land and of capital. The lack of capital is exacerbated by the inability of most of the population to save anything from their already inadequate incomes.

The Opposition

There are also, it is true, problems associated with a static or declining population (Council of Europe, 1978). These arise from changes in the age composition of the population. In the absence of an epidemic or a catastrophe, mortality can be expected to fall. The boost this gives to the population can only be cancelled out by a decline in the birth rate. These two together – more old and fewer young people – mean an ageing population, with possibly a decline in vigour and enterprise. They will certainly mean a less flexible and occupationally mobile population, making the economy less able to adapt to new products or production methods (ibid., pp. 77–8). In the Third World context there would also be a strengthening of those traditional forces in the community which are hostile to the changes necessary for development. But with present rates of natural increase in the underdeveloped countries there is no danger of any of this happening. The emphasis has to be placed on the dysfunctions of over-rapid growth.

In a few countries, it must be admitted, there may already be too few people to occupy and cultivate the land properly, given the level of mechanisation which the country prefers or can afford. There would then be, in economic terms, increasing returns to labour, making an increase in the working population a profitable proposition. Such rich but unexploited and, possibly, largely unpopulated areas might also be a temptation to invasion by other less well-endowed countries. As shown in Chapter 3, the countries which are in this happy position of having good land to spare are few and becoming fewer.

More radical objections have also been raised (Bondestam and Bergstrom, 1980). It is argued that population control in the Third World is sought by the industrialised North to protect its own employment and food supplies (Bondestam, 1980, p. 23). This brings to mind another argument raised by some groups in the South: that the developed countries are concerned about the population issue now only because their own period of growth is over. They want to restrict the expansion of population in the South to protect their economic dominance and racial and political supremacy. Others contend that population policies in the South would not be necessary if it were not for underdevelopment (Egero, 1980, pp. 197ff).

There is probably some truth in these arguments, but apart from the last they would seem of little importance to governments concerned with the welfare of their people rather than with racial or nationalistic aggrandisement. The need to escape from the strait-jacket of underdevelopment (including agrarian under-development), on the other hand, is undeniable, but this is not an argument against an effective population policy.

Development, as we have seen, aims at a more balanced demographic structure, within which crisis action to limit the size of families, leading to coercion or undesirable forms of persuasion, would be less likely. Experience in Europe suggests that, given real development, people might need less persuading: that they would themselves begin to limit their families in order to protect their better conditions of life.

Finally there are the ethical and religious objections. Being matters of personal values and theology they are not open to challenge from the point of view of even long-term expediency. They are nevertheless very influential in determining the outcome of the debate about population policy, and will be examined in the next section of this chapter.

Government Policies

It is surprising that so many countries appear not to have recognised the dangers in present population trends. Of 134 countries reported on by the Population Council in 1984 (Nortman, 1985, p. 32), only 37 accepted the need to reduce their population growth rates. Another 33 had birth control policies for other reasons, such as the welfare of families, but 64 had no pro-grammes of any kind. Indeed a few took the opposite view: that their national populations were too small.

The global situation appears less worrying if populations, rather than the number of countries, are taken into account. Seventy-six per cent of the total on which data has been collected are in countries which are attempting to control the growth of their populations, as compared with only 7 per cent with no programme at all. This is because of the teeming millions in those Asian countries, like India and China, which have active population policies. In the light of what has already been said, however, the global aspect may not be the most important. Even the issue of whether there is enough food is more local than that. Issues of poverty, women's rights and development certainly are.

The reasons why countries are hanging back are very varied (ibid., pp. 42ff). In some, particularly in Latin America, the influence of the Roman Catholic Church, with its well-known opposition to birth control, predominates. It had caused some countries:

> to make a distinction between birth control and family planning, supporting the latter but not the former. Birth control, according to this distinction, corresponds to a fertility-reducing population policy, while family planning is part of a family welfare policy whose purpose is to eliminate abortion caused by multi-parity and too close spacing of births. (Urzua, 1978, p. 19)

As we have seen, 33 out of the 134 countries in the Population Council sample adopted non-demographic policies of this kind. It is no accident that many of these are in Latin America (Nortman, 1985, p. 34). The Church has sometimes had an even more drastic effect, leading to restrictions even on welfare-oriented family planning. An example is Bolivia, with its 'pronatalist policy'. It is worth noting that, in contrast to the rest of South America, its birth rate has hardly fallen at all in the last 30 years (United Nations, 1986b, p. 80).

In some Arab countries, Muslim attitudes to women and the government of the family have also had restrictive effects. Ayatollah Khomeini, speaking for Iran, expressed a view which is undoubtedly powerful in the Arab world when he said, 'According to the religious laws, women can avoid pregnancy if their husbands allow them to do so and if application of medical procedures does not endanger their health' (Nortman, 1982, p. 45). Some Arab countries take an even more austere view. Saudi Arabia is pronatalist and encourages early marriage. Oral contraceptives are available free, though all others are forbidden.

Many countries in Africa (Angola, Cameroons, Guinea, Ivory Coast, Madagascar, Malawi, Niger) reject any idea of restricting their populations (Nortman, 1985, p. 33). Traditional attitudes in the general population probably play some part in shaping such reluctance on the part of governments, including the view that a large family is necessary in order to ensure support for the parents in old age. The United Nations, in its World Population Monitoring Report for 1979 (United Nations, 1980, p. 12), points to another factor: that a number of these countries 'had no adequate data base with which to formulate policies (and, presumably, could change their perception when such data became available)'.

In a number of these countries, and of course in others elsewhere than in Africa (for example, Brazil (Nortman, 1982, p. 50)), the governments contention is that the population is at an optimum level or even too low in relation to the economic needs of the country. The problem of defence, already referred to, will sometimes, no doubt, also be a consideration. The validity of these arguments is probably confined to those countries (already referred to) with large areas which are still thinly populated. In addition there are some governments which equate a large population with national prestige.

Singapore, which has claimed to suffer from a labour shortage in spite of recession and unemployment elsewhere, is probably a special case. Limitations of space have caused that country nevertheless to place much emphasis on trying to achieve a zero population growth rate (ibid., p. 47), while tackling her manpower problem by a shift away from labour-intensive industry.

Birth Control Methods

Those who are concerned about the rate of population growth in certain parts of the Third World but reject contraception on religious or other grounds will place the emphasis either (rather optimistically) on voluntary abstinence from sexual relationships or on delaying marriage. It will be recalled that the latter has been one of the factors in the demographic transition in the North. 'Thus the average age of women at marriage in developing countries today is under 20 years, whereas in Europe it is about 26 years' (Killick, 1981, p. 76). It should perhaps be pointed out that in the

Northern countries there has been a return to rather earlier marriage in recent years.

In some societies marriage already occurs at a later age than elsewhere. In Eire, where younger sons do not inherit and the influence of the Roman Catholic Church has inhibited the use of contraceptives, economic necessity led to the custom of delaying marriage (Kennedy, 1973, pp. 139ff). In the Third World, the Masai of Kenya are a well documented example of a community who traditionally permit marriage only to mature men who have served for some years as *murran*, or 'warriors'. During this period they live in the warriors' kraal with the immature girls. The girls are of course in no danger of unwanted pregnancies, and are said to gain experience which will enable them to be better marital partners when they do marry (Lowie, 1953, pp. 47–8; Shorter, 1974, p. 33).

In spite of the fact that the circumstances which led to late marriage in both Eire and Masailand have largely disappeared since the war, the custom has shown considerable survival power. Early marriage can be expected to be equally durable in countries where it is the practice (see Figure 12.1), especially if it is rooted (as late marriage used to be in Eire and Masailand) in socio-economic realities.

Where the legal minimum age for marriage is raised in the absence of a birth control campaign, the danger is of a possible increase in extramarital pregnancies. Social prohibitions on these are weaker nowadays. Also to be taken into account is the prevalence of consensual unions (the so-called 'visiting relationship', or even the more permanent 'common-law' marriage), especially in Africa and the Caribbean. These mean that marriage is delayed, but not conception (United Nations, 1985b, p. 55). There may also be a catching-up tendency among those who marry late. Nevertheless campaigns urging later marriage, or laws to that effect, seem to have had some success in countries such as India, China, Tunisia, Malaysia and Sri Lanka. In China, the national minimum age of marriage (22 for men and 20 for women) may be, and indeed sometimes has been raised still further by provincial governments, like that of Shanghai.

At the other extreme is the legalisation of abortion. This has been credited with responsibility for the dramatic fall in the Japanese birth rate since the war, but it may merely have succeeded in legalising what had been a previously high postwar rate

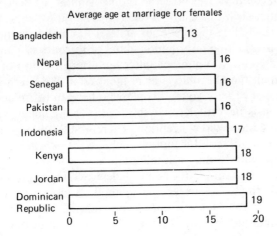

For many young people –
particularly females –
the responsibilities of adulthood come early.

Source: *United Nations Chronicle*, January 1986 (United Nations, 1988a).

Figure 12.1 Average age at marriage for females in various underdeveloped countries

of illegal abortion. Even if legalisation does not always have the effect on fertility which had been anticipated, it may be justified if it does thus cease to criminalise women who seek the termination of their pregnancies, and saves them from the risk and suffering which accompany unrecognised and therefore uncontrolled backstreet abortions. Such methods used in underdeveloped countries are likely to be even more dangerous than those of Northern abortionists.

The debate about abortion arouses strong feelings on both sides, often centring upon the question of whether the embryo is a person or not, or at what stage it becomes one. 'The right to life' is a phrase often used by religious or other groups who are opposed to it. On the other side, apart from the population argument and that of relieving the hard-driven or poor mothers of large families, is the contention of the feminists that women have the right to the control of their own bodies. The opposition is seen by them as still another (and very intimate) attempt to assert the control of women by men.

From another angle abortion may be seen as a confession of failure by a country to develop the use of effective contraception within the country. This criticism probably takes too little account of the difficulties, especially in the Third World – the pressure of tradition (including the power of males!) – and also the problems met in disseminating information about birth control in an under-developed country. Young people everywhere are also often less prudent than they become later in life, and in the South it is the large number of very young people who have to be influenced.

Abortion is nevertheless no substitute for a campaign to per-suade people to avoid conception. There is still some support for natural forms of contraception, such as the so-called 'rhythm method', among Roman Catholics and others who cannot accept the use of mechanical or chemical devices. There is very little doubt that this is an unreliable method, leading very often to unwanted pregnancies – ironically enough the kind of situation which is likely to result in the even less welcome demand for an abortion.

There remain condoms, the pill and inter-uterine devices (IUDs) (United Nations, 1985b, p. 109), the last two being the methods most widely sponsored by Third World governments (ibid., pp. 104ff). In the last few years the medical dangers associated with the use of the pill have received a good deal of attention, but the dangers involved seem to be much less than those associated with pregnancy itself, especially in an under-developed country with high rates of maternal morbidity and mortality. The World Health Organisation reports that 'maternal mortality accounts for the greatest proportion of deaths among women of reproductive age in most of the developing world... Rates in countries where the problem is most acute are as much as 500 times higher than the lowest rates in industrialised countries' (WHO, 1987, pp. 74–5). The further contribution to ill-health and deaths among mothers which results from their being overburdened by a very large family is probably impossible to assess. Such risks as there is from use of the pill can be reduced further by medical research and examination to sort out those who are most vulner-able.

The pill's chief drawback is not the medical dangers associated with it, but the fact that it has to be taken every day. Among peoples who are not accustomed to regimenting themselves in this way, it will probably be missed more often than it is taken. Even after present efforts to develop a once-a-month pill have succeeded, the IUD will have advantages from this point of view. It requires the insertion of a physical barrier into the neck of the uterus, to prevent sperm from entering, and therefore remains effective until it is removed. The daily decision required by the other methods becomes unnecessary.

Some versions of the IUD have proved dangerous, and all may cause occasional complications for wearers, but they usually require little attention once they have been fitted. Their permanence and trouble-free character are invaluable assets in Third World countries where the punctilious adherence to a daily regime might be difficult to obtain. However they do make demands on scarce medical and nursing resources, and for anatomical reasons some women cannot wear them. A mixed system including both the pill and the IUD therefore seems to be called for.

Because sterilisation has an even more permanent effect than the IUD, particularly female sterilisation which is irreversible, it has special attractions for those Third World governments which are most impatient for results (United Nations, 1985b, pp. 104–9). It is now generally recognised, for example, that compulsory sterilisation was for a time imposed on large numbers of men in India. Male sterilisation is a much simpler and safer procedure than that of women, and fertility can usually be restored if desired at a later stage. At the same time it does call for action by the male partner, who may have less of a stake in contraception anyway, and be prey to all kinds of unjustified fears about the effect which sterilisation will have on his potency or sexual gratification.

The obvious first step for a government which has been convinced for the need for birth control, whether for social or demographic reasons, is to ensure that the necessary appliances or procedures are readily available and provided free of charge. Because of the possibility of medical complications they should be distributed by medical or paramedical personnel. Traditional beliefs about the proper relationships between the sexes, as well as personal delicacy on the part of women, means that they would have a strong preference for appliances to be fitted by women (Rogers, 1980, p. 109). Also the work should be done on as local a basis as can be arranged. Those who are fearful or reluctant about using the appliances will not travel long distances to have them fitted.

Education and persuasion are another matter entirely, calling for an understanding of the community life and personal circumstances of the people concerned. The problems may sometimes run deep. For example, long-established customs or beliefs, already discussed, or the ideologies of ruling groups, may limit the acceptability of birth control or the use of a particular method (Polger and Marshall, 1978). In Africa, the lack of knowledge of contraception must be a factor making for high rates of reproduction, but the even lower levels of utilisation suggest that attitudes are also very important (United Nations, 1985b, p. 96). This may indicate a job for the village health worker, perhaps in co-operation with social or community workers. The success of the Chinese programme is due to the fact that a national campaign was combined with grass-roots persuasion in the workplace and the neighbourhood.

The task is twofold: to change public attitudes through group educational activities and also through casework with individual families. Various forms of opposition can be expected. Roman Catholics will object on religious grounds, but could be made aware of the greater willingness among their co-religionists in other countries to see birth control as permissible. Male attitudes and traditional beliefs generally will have to be countered. This will be easier to achieve if the custodians of tradition, the chiefs, headmen and medicine men, are the first won over. Myths about the effects of using birth control techniques have to be dispelled.

When infantile mortality in a country is declining this becomes a powerful argument against those who are afraid that they may otherwise lack children to enjoy, give them standing, and maintain them in their old age. It is another of those reciprocal relationships. As the caption to Figure 12.2, in the UN report on *The State of World Population, 1988* (United Nations, 1988), puts it: 'Contraceptive use rises as infant mortality falls. But success in encouraging family planning also helps lower infant mortality'.

Because many underdeveloped countries are also plural societies, ethnic rivalry sometimes raises its head when the limitation of births is under discussion. It is not unusual for a group to feel that their influence will be less if their numbers are reduced. Where the government actually discriminates against them, they may even see birth control as a genocidal plot by the authorities.

Assuming that contraceptives are both conveniently and cheaply

Contraceptive use rises as infant mortality falls.
But success in encouraging family planning
also helps lower infant mortality.

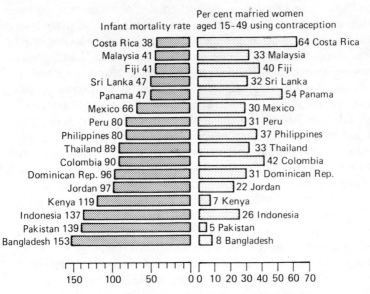

Per cent married women
Infant mortality rate aged 15-49 using contraception

Costa Rica 38 — 64 Costa Rica
Malaysia 41 — 33 Malaysia
Fiji 41 — 40 Fiji
Sri Lanka 47 — 32 Sri Lanka
Panama 47 — 54 Panama
Mexico 66 — 30 Mexico
Peru 80 — 31 Peru
Philippines 80 — 37 Philippines
Thailand 89 — 33 Thailand
Colombia 90 — 42 Colombia
Dominican Rep. 96 — 31 Dominican Rep.
Jordan 97 — 22 Jordan
Kenya 119 — 7 Kenya
Indonesia 137 — 26 Indonesia
Pakistan 139 — 5 Pakistan
Bangladesh 153 — 8 Bangladesh

150 100 50 0 0 10 20 30 40 50 60 70

Source: United Nations, *State of World Population, 1988.*

Figure 12.2 Contraception and infant mortality

available, use may be made both of rewards to encourage their use, and of deterrents against large families. During the early, non-coercive stages of India's sterilisation campaign, the emphasis was on rewards. Transistor radios or small sums of money were offered to men who were prepared to co-operate. A less crude approach involving both rewards and deterrents had been described earlier by Professor Richard Titmuss in a scheme designed for use in Mauritius (Titmuss and Abel-Smith, 1968). This scheme, which has been very influential in a number of countries, sought to provide improved support for the family, together with modest incentives for restricting its size. There were also proposals for publicity for family planning, and referral to family planning agencies for those who exceeded the advocated three-child norm. Whether as a result of the success of this policy or not, Mauritius has one of the lowest birth rates in the African region.

China has taken this approach very much further. As part of its very successful population policy – which also includes possibly intimidating pressure by party cadres in the residential neighbourhood and the workplace – it imposed a salary reduction on the parents of more than three children, and denied the third and later children free education and medical care. Parents who restricted themselves to two children, on the other hand, had priority housing, and those with only one child could have 'an apartment that can accommodate four people; a monthly pension on retirement; and for the child, preferential treatment in school admission and job assignment and an adult grain ration. The birth of a second or third child not only negates all benefits given to small families, but the State is to be compensated for previous benefits' (Nortman, 1982, p. 46). There has been some relaxation in this policy since, especially to take account of Chinese concern about the continuation of the family line in the absence of male children.

Incentives and deterrents, located like this within the welfare system, whether they have an impact on reproductive behaviour or not, certainly have serious repercussions on other objectives of social welfare policy. Large families need more support rather than less. To take away from them financial benefits, housing, health services and education is to punish the children as well as their 'recalcitrant' parents. For this reason, incentives for compliance may seem preferable to the imposition of punishments. But even these will lead to inequity in the distribution of benefits. And because welfare resources are very limited in underdeveloped countries the outcome will still be deprivation and suffering for the members of large families.

There may be countries where the population crisis is urgent enough to justify adopting such methods, but it will be necessary to design them very carefully to ensure that their social costs are not too great. The approach through community education may be less dramatic, but it does at least operate through improving the understanding and self-determination of the people, which should be a central social policy objective anyway.

Such short cuts (if short cuts they really prove to be) have another drawback. They hamper development, not only by the inequitable distribution of the means of personal development, but also by distorting a country's growth-motivated investment in human capital. The larger implications of this need to be soberly considered; but even when measured only against the criterion of population control, such methods may be counterproductive in the long run. The theory of the 'demographic transition' suggests that it is development – the decline in traditionalism, better health and education (especially of women), the wish to protect a higher standard of life – which causes people to seek to limit the sizes of their families.

This certainly seems to have been what happened in the North. The experience of Singapore, Hong Kong, Taiwan and South Korea suggests that it is equally applicable to the countries of the South. Side by side with their economic success the four 'baby tigers' have achieved a remarkable decline in fertility – greater than that of any of the other Third World countries for whom the World Bank has given figures (World Bank, 1988, p. 231; Reynolds, 1985, p. 173).

It was suggested earlier that a population policy could advance the process of development. The present suggestion is that development could help to make such a policy successful. This pattern – of reciprocal causation – is now a familiar one. It remains only to complete the circle by pointing out that a successful population policy is also part of what is meant by development.

Summary

Although demographic conditions vary widely between different countries, general population trends in the Third World are still steeply upwards. This is because mortality is declining faster than fertility. As a result, improvements in GNP or in the proportion of children enrolled in education are swallowed up by the increase in the absolute numbers to be provided for. The Malthusian fear of a food shortage is also looking more credible than some seem willing to admit.

For many families this means even more poverty, and for some, perhaps, hunger. The consequences for women are particularly severe. Constant pregnancies sap their health and vitality. Education and employment are out of their reach. Their chances of improving their status and the quality of their lives becomes increasingly remote.

If real development can be set in train this process of immiseration may be slowed up. But by itself this will not be enough to deal with the immediate or the long-term problem. It needs to be accompanied by a population policy, combining education on birth control with the availability of suitable devices.

Religious opposition is still powerful but is no longer as united as it used to be. Some countries have made use of welfare privileges to persuade families to co-operate in such a policy, but it is difficult to think of any such incentives which will not run counter to the principle of meeting human needs, on which welfare programmes ought to be based. The best incentive is rational choice, strengthened as it would be by a rising standard of life.

13

Government and Misgovernment

Political Power

The right of people to share in the decisions which affect their lives has been seen throughout this book as part of the definition of development. The implication is that political freedom and self-determination are values in themselves, on a par with having enough food, shelter, education and health care. They are also the only way of ensuring that the decisions made are in the interest of the population at large rather than that of a powerful minority.

Few underdeveloped countries have yet made enough progress towards sharing power in the state this way. Dictatorships and electoral gerrymandering abound, and where honest elections are held it is often in a one-party system. Behind the panoply of government, moreover, there are not infrequently *éminences grises*, 'powers behind the throne' who are the real beneficiaries of any action the government takes. These may be multinational corporations, local capitalists, the educated elite, or even a dominant ethnic group.

There is no suggestion that multi-party representative government on the Northern model, adopted by countries like India, is the only desirable form which power sharing can take. It has its own serious defects, not least that it disfranchises minorities, and gives effective control over the government, even for the majority, only at election time.

Although no one would offer military majority dictatorships or governments based on fraudulent elections as alternatives, what is

259

to be said about one-party politics? In countries where so much needs to be done, and to be done quickly, the one-party system has obvious attractions. This may exist in a variety of forms. One may be merely a facade for a military oligarchy – really a non-party rather than a one-party system. Or it may be a provision in the law or the constitution which permits only the one party to operate. This need not mean voting docilely for the only candidate put forward by the governing party; it is possible, as in countries like Zambia and Kenya, for contenders bearing the same label to compete with one another at the hustings. That these elections are not merely formalities is shown by, for example, the fact that 'between 40–50% of Kenyan M.P.s are turfed out at each election, a far higher proportion than in Western democracies' (Hague and Harrop, 1987, p. 103). Where multiple candidates do not exist, the political situation is, of course, no different from that of the military-backed no-party system.

In addition to *de jure* one-party states like these, there are others which purport to have a multiple party system, but in which opposition groups are barred from office, either by the overwhelming prestige of the party in power, or by its use of intimidation or fraud (these are not mutually exclusive). A good example of the latter, until recently, was Guyana. There is also the practice of rewarding supporters through political patronage, what is known as 'clientelism' (discussed in more detail below), but this is too widespread to distinguish one Third World government from another. As a result of the operation of these various factors, there have been few Third World countries since the war in which the party in power has been displaced in an election – and none at all in the whole of Africa.

Where (clientelism apart) honest elections between such individual aspirants do take place, it might be argued that one-party systems do have certain advantages. Voters can choose on the basis of personal qualities, thus preventing unsatisfactory candidates from riding in on the coat-tails of a popular party. What a one-party system also does, on the other hand, is to eliminate from consideration those major differences of principle which find their expression in party affiliation. Instead the election focuses on local grievances and issues, and on which of the candidates can attract most government help to the area in the form of employment, roads, schools and so on. The influence which the various candidates can claim to have within the clientelist system looms large here.

Behind such a system is the assumption that there is no argument about policy, about the big issues: only about how to carry them out. Some would say that this is unavoidable in an underdeveloped country where the government are seeking to bring about a social and economic revolution against a background of ethnic and tribal rivalries and fear of change. Nyerere, President of Tanzania, expressed this view very frankly when he remarked that contending political parties were like football teams, engaged in sterile conflict instead of confronting important national problems.

The 'national mission' would be proclaimed by a single or dominant party, often personified by a charismatic national leader. Examples include Nyerere himself, Kenyatta and later Moi in Kenya, Kuanda in Zambia, Banda in Malawi, Benazir Bhutto in Pakistan and Aquino in the Philippines, Lee in Singapore, Mao and then Deng in China, and Burnham, Prime Minister of Guyana for so many years. Such leaders may be supported or even controlled by party obligarchies or by powerful economic or foreign interests, but they and their popular appeal hold the key to power.

There is great danger in this situation. Lord Acton's much quoted adage, 'Power tends to corrupt, and absolute power corrupts absolutely' is only too relevant. The overcentralisation and lack of criticism which it often implies can also enable very costly errors of judgement to remain uncorrected. Nevertheless such rulers often become impatient of any resistance to their will. It is often suggested that they are constrained by the many other centres of power in the society: the civil service, trade unions, industry or commerce (especially TNCs), regional or ethnic interests and religious groupings. Where these really do have power, however, they will often be co-opted by the rewards in the form of patronage which the government can bestow on them or their leaders if they are prepared to become its clients.

The ultimate check on a single party, or even a military dictator, is its need to secure co-operation in the villages. In underdeveloped countries where the population is often widely dispersed, communications poor, and administration inefficient, life can go on much as it always has done, irrespective of the views of the government. Peasants also need a good deal of persuasion. They may not be the rigid and purblind reactionaries that they have often been painted, but they (often rightly) believe they have good reasons for what they do (see Chapter 3).

But this applies as much to the bringing about of improvements in agricultural methods, hygiene and diet, family planning and the rest as to less desirable impositions by the government, such as the furthering of vested interests. This underlines the importance of having village workers in these various fields as well as a community development programme. Community development, in particular, has the potential for serving a wider, specifically democratic function in a country in which the seat of government is geographically far away and psychologically even more remote. Unfortunately governments which are impatient for results, or concerned more with strengthening their authority, are very likely to downgrade the element of participation involved in it, turning it into a mere instrument of government policy (see Chapter 10). Local cadres in China often seemed, for example, in the family planning campaign, to have abandoned even the aim of persuasion in favour of pressure sometimes amounting to social coercion.

Other aspects of government which call for examination are the planning process; the role of the bureaucracy; and the effect of clientelism and of the wider corruption which it encourages.

Planning

Given the general value orientation of a government, the next step is to select the policy options most likely to make a reality of that orientation, bearing in mind the financial and human resources available. However, a government never starts with a clean sheet. There will be traditional ways of doing things which have to be accommodated. In addition, earlier policy decisions will have established vested interests, some of them able to place great pressure on the government, as well as public expectations and familiar institutional procedures.

Secondly, the factual information on which a plan must be based is anything but 'hard data'. Consider the problems of formulating a national plan in a country in which the government cannot even be sure about the size, age and sex structure and geographical distribution of the population. Its freedom to pursue a rational or 'synoptic' solution (Simon, 1983) will be drastically curtailed by such factors.

There is also the difficulty of holding to a policy once it has been formulated. Changes in circumstances are a particular hazard for the underdeveloped country, which can often be blown off course by occurrences over which it has no control, especially in the world economy. Another 'change' may be strong public opposition to a particular development, forcing the government to vary or even abandon its plans. An example would be the Chinese government's modification of its 'one child' family planning policy because of the resistance to it of country people. Such problems could result from lack of adequate consultation, but, whether or not this is the case, the government of a developing country has to face the possibility of resistance from a population which rates local and traditional concerns more highly than those of a remote and possibly modernising national government.

The opportunity also has to be available of learning by experience. To persist with a programme, even when it is seen to be not working, simply because it has been included in a plan, would obviously be foolish. Even a successful policy, through its very success, may change the situation in a way which brings about that policy's own obsolescence.

Because of such difficulties as these, a plan may end up less as a serious programme for development than as a public relations or international fund-raising exercise. Meanwhile the policies actually followed will be governed by the exigencies of the moment – responses to the more powerful continuing pressures or the more urgent problems. In other words they will be 'incremental' (Lindblom, 1979) rather than 'synoptic'. The objectives of policy being thus lost sight of, it is not surprising that they are so rarely attained.

There is no gainsaying the very real difficulties confronting planners: the pure synoptic model is an unrealisable ideal. Nevertheless just 'swimming with the current', which is all that pure incrementalism offers, means abandoning any attempt to set targets and to try rationally to achieve them. The long-term aim of 'growth with social justice' would become a meaningless platitude if policies for land reform, agricultural development, city environmental and housing programmes, health, education and social welfare were jettisoned when the going became rough.

Notwithstanding what has been said above, there are some favourable indications. Advances are being made in planning technology (see, for example, Chenery, 1981). And not all changes in circumstances have the effect of making a plan less tenable. For example, a country may have taken more control over its internal economy, or through the adoption of measures advocated by the Brandt Commission and other sympathetic commentators, may find itself facing fewer uncertainties in the global market place.

There is also a half way house to be found in some form of what Etzioni (1976, pp. 90ff) has called a 'mixed scanning' approach. Elements in a plan which are considered crucial to government intentions would be planned in detail and protected against pressures which might weaken them – at least until it was clear that they were no longer tenable. Less central elements could be more provisional, 'markers' to indicate policy aspirations. They would not therefore become expendable. Timetables and the strategies for achieving them might have to be changed, but if for good reason they had to be given up entirely this would be a public act, open to general scrutiny.

Departmental Co-ordination

An important aspect of any plan is its cohesion. What happens in one sector has implications for all others. Failure in co-operation between departments of government can therefore be very damaging to effectiveness. Governments will establish their priorities at the budgetary stage, but rarely treat as seriously as they should the further repercussions of one aspect of policy on another.

This may be the result of ignorance or administrative incompetence, but sometimes it is owing to the competing ambitions of politicians. Achieving a co-ordinated policy may require ministers to reduce their range of responsibilities, and therefore their importance or their ability to offer patronage to their constituents, neither of which they will do very willingly. Third World politicians can also be very opportunist, offering sops where political gain is likely to accrue, and yielding where political pressure is greatest. Such self-serving incrementalism can be very damaging to co-ordinated policy making.

Among the policy interrelationships which make co-ordination necessary, is that between urban development and the flight from the countryside, with its consequence of a decline in the traditional welfare system. They are inseparable, but are rarely seen in this light.

Then there are the wider ramifications of improved health and nutrition. They have already led in most countries to an increase in population, and made an active population policy imperative. And because the increase in numbers is among children and the elderly, the pressure on a faltering pattern of traditional support for dependants is mounting. Multi-generational families, also a familiar part of the traditional scene, will become even more common, with an important bearing on the size of dwellings. Housing policy, particularly in the countryside, must allow for this; it is no use aiming to revitalise the extended family as a welfare resource if the living space made available cannot accommodate the larger group.

Although many welfare needs can be met within the community in this way, the traditional care-givers will require some state help in the form of social work, and specialised geriatric and child and infant welfare services. Pressure on the health services will increase as the number of infants and old people increases. Pressure on educational services will mount as the growing number of infants reach school age.

Two major areas of possible conflict are in the division of financial and other scarce resources between town and country, and in the competition for land. The festering social problems of the towns, and the political muscle which large aggregations of people and urban commercial and professional interests can bring to bear, have caused in the past and may still cause the problems of the villages to receive less than their share of attention. In a number of countries land for subsistence agriculture is now becoming scarcer, and governments may have to make difficult choices between agriculture on the one hand, and land for improved housing and communications on the other.

As far as land allocated to agriculture is concerned there is also the competition between large and small units, capital- and labour-intensive cultivation, and between export crops and food consumed locally. Conditions in different countries of the Third World vary a great deal, but for many the revival of the countryside, the prevention of famine, and the preservation of the traditional mutual aid network will depend on the competition for land being resolved in each case in favour of the second alternative.

Sometimes, however, the achievement of one objective may actually bring another closer to attainment. This is the assumption on which the policy of investing in human capital rests. The inverse relationship between education and poverty is one example. A more egalitarian structure of educational opportunity, especially when, as 'basic education', it is defined very broadly, can help to relieve the many social problems which beset the poor. This is partly through its overall impact on GNP, and partly more directly through improvements in 'life chances', health, nutrition, family planning and so on. At the same time the reduction of poverty and its various social consequences can make education itself a more practicable and fruitful proposition for the less privileged sections of the population, especially in the rural areas.

Skeet (1978, pp. 65–6) describes attempts in Indonesia to utilise a programme for better health more explicitly as an instrument of economic growth. Such a combination should be readily attainable in the light of the obvious economic value of a healthy population. That it did not work out in this case was attributed to too much interference from outside the community concerned, and the need for a more gradual introduction of such sweeping changes, but mostly to failure to encourage participation on the part of the villagers themselves. In the reverse direction, the improvements in the indices of health in China are attributable not only to the health programmes themselves, but also to gains made in education, the status of women and improvements in the work environment (Rohde, 1983, p. 14).

These are only a few of the ways in which different aspects of social policy impinge upon one another, but they may perhaps serve to demonstrate how the failure to evolve (and carry out) an overall plan, and to achieve co-operation between the ministries responsible may lead to policy frustration and failure.

Integrated Rural Development

At the local level – the 'sharp end' as far as the implementation of policies is concerned – the discussion about co-ordination has centred on what has been called 'integrated rural development' (Ruttan, 1984). Mehta (1984, p. 68) has blamed the failure of development plans in India partly on inadequacies in this respect.

There have been many local experiments of this kind (Ruttan, 1984, p. 396). The earlier schemes concentrated on the co-ordination of activities connected with agriculture, such as the supply of credit, agricultural inputs like water and fertilisers, transport, markets and training. In more recent years, under the influence of 'basic needs' thinking, these projects have gradually widened their scope to include health and family planning, schools, religion and other cultural elements, and social work. There is an obvious need in these programmes for the establishment of good team work between village health and education workers, family planners and social work aides. As already indicated, there may be scope for the uniting of some of these functions in a single person.

But it is the responsibility of the professionals also to involve local residents, and to help them to decide how they want their local services to be integrated. Finding ways of achieving this is the responsibility of the community development worker. In a traditional world, in which people are very responsive to the views of their fellows, a high level of participation in discussion will make for agreement on acceptable solutions. In the process, the bearing of a policy decision in one field on that in another will be speedily brought to light. Community development workers have an important role here. They can exercise pressure to ensure wide participation, and be an important influence towards achieving integrated solutions to the problems of the community. And if they act, as they should, as a channel of communication between the village and the government, the national implications of such discoveries will be brought to the attention of those with the power to do something about them.

Community work in one form or another is the crossroads where many aspects of social policy meet. Here they can be subjected to the acid test of local experience, both with regard to their individual effectiveness and their consistency with one another (Ruttan, 1984, p. 398).

The Bureaucracy

Public officials often have considerable power. This derives partly from their permanence. Even though both the party in power and its leader may remain unchanged for long periods, particular legislators and even ministers often have a less secure tenure of office. Government reshuffles are often a way in which the national leader is able to shift the responsibility and thus preserve his own position.

As a result of their permanence bureaucrats often know more about what is going on than the politicians, and have more control over the actual machinery of government. It is not surprising, therefore, that the leader finds it necessary to develop a close relationship with them. In the process the distinction made in the North between the political and the administrative levels of government may be blurred or even eliminated, as in countries such as Zambia (Tordoff, 1988) and Tanzania (Dore and Mars, 1981, p. 142). In Guyana the party flag flies over government offices.

Members of the civil service may become, to all intents and purposes, party *apparatchiks*. They may sometimes even move directly into the political arena, becoming ministers. All of which increases the patronage at the disposal of the leader, and therefore his dominance, and also tends to increase the technocratic element in the government at the expense of the political and the ideological. This does not represent a breach with the traditional Weberian view about the 'legal rational' role of the civil service so much as apparently to enthrone that concept within the political field, placing the emphasis on pragmatic solutions.

These have their part to play in social welfare planning but as earlier chapters have shown, the importance of the ideological element should not be underestimated. Whatever the claims made that the position taken by a government is 'dictated by the facts', there is no doubt that value biases, conscious or unconscious, are often much more important as determinants of action. It is therefore important to recognise the value biases of bureaucrats. Like most politicians they belong to the elite. They are well educated, exercise power, and are well paid compared with the rest of the population (though sometimes less so when the extent of their responsibilities is considered). Having a stake in the maintenance of a *status quo* which provides them with such rewards, they are not likely to be friendly to proposals for the radical reordering of society (Mehta, 1984, p. 69). Even the sharing of power through community development may be seen as

a threat (ibid., p. 76–7). Usually urban-based and with a modernised life-style and commitment, they have difficulty in understanding the problems of the rural masses and little confidence in
traditional solutions to those problems (Chambers, 1985, p. 76).

Most former colonial territories carried over into independence
the bureaucratic machinery which they inherited from the days of
empire. There were important differences, however. Previously
local staff had operated under the direction of senior officials
imported by the colonial power, and in accordance with traditions
which were not their own. Now they were confronted by their own
people and their own culture, and they had no choice but to come
to terms with this. Also, until now, they had rarely been allowed to
occupy the most senior posts, or to make the more important decisions. They lacked experience for assuming these responsibilities.

Their relationships with ministers, their political masters, were
also different in many cases. The dependence of the latter upon
them has already been mentioned. Ministers for their part were
not content, like their imperial predecessors, to confine themselves to general issues, leaving individual cases to be dealt with by
their officials. A civil servant might, for example, find a minister
bending the pension rules, or warning off the police for the sake of
one of his constituents or somebody who had a call on him within
the 'economy of affection'.

These circumstances do not make for efficient or consistent
administration. Nor was it very surprising, in spite of their
preference for a modernised society, if bureaucrats like the
politicians, also temporised with or exploited the powerful demands emanating from the 'economy of affection'. The borderline
here between corruption and legitimate cultural obligations, both
for politicians and bureaucrats, is a fine one. It is not surprising
that it is so frequently crossed.

Clientelism

One of the bridges across this borderline is political patronage. As
will be seen, this is not unknown in the North (consider the
notorious 'pork barrel' system in the United States), but it is
widespread throughout the Third World, where it takes the form
of 'clientelism'. This, as it occurs in Jamaica, has been defined by

Stone (1983, p. 95) as: 'personal loyalty to individual political actors who have or are perceived to have a high capability to allocate divisible material and social benefits, as well as indivisible sectoral, class or communal benefits'. He estimates that '51% of the electorate [in Jamaica] are clientistic in their party loyalty patterns' (ibid., p. 96).

These benefits are usually passed on through intermediaries or 'brokers' – influential members of parliament, traditional leaders, local party bosses, trade unions and so on – who are also themselves beneficiaries of the system. It is a quasi-feudal network in which the broker is enabled by the government to reward the loyalty of his retainers, and is rewarded in his turn for delivering that loyalty to the government. It is an essentially personal bond, which accounts among other things for the direct involvement of legislators or ministers in the individual cases of their supporters and relatives instead of leaving these to the civil servants concerned.

It should not be assumed that clientelism is confined to the more reactionary regimes. In Jamaica it has been well established for over thirty years (ibid., p. 107). In Zambia the slogan 'It pays to belong to UNIP' (Zambia's governing party) has been openly used in elections (Tordoff, 1988; Cammack *et al.*, 1988, p. 92). Hyden (1980) points out that, in Tanzania, the government offers incentives to conformity which are little short of bribes. In India, according to Mehta (1984, p. 77), politicians in both central and local government offer 'inducements' to local leaders simply in order to maintain their authority, contributing substantially to corruption in the country in the process.

There may be some evidence from Latin America that, where parties do have to compete for power, they may come eventually to realise that they cannot go on indefinitely outbidding each other in this way (Cammack *et al.*, p. 101). Also the rewards available to governments for distribution as patronage among their supporters have become much more limited with the decline in growth since the halcyon years of the fifties and sixties (Tordoff, 1988, p. 24) – though increased poverty cannot be seen as a satisfactory solution to clientelism or anything else. On the contrary, it is poverty and inequality which make possible this subornation of the 'have nots' by the 'haves' (Hague and Harrop, 1987, p. 99; Stone, 1983, pp. 96–7).

Meanwhile, so long as the government of a country is prepared to use its prerogative quite openly to 'buy' support, functionaries at all levels either in the public services or private business, if they have a permit, a contract or some other privilege to sell, will feel justified in following suit, particularly when (as will be seen) this appears to be sanctioned by customary values. This latter is one of the problems overlooked by Clapham when he suggests (Clapham, 1985, p. 51) that a solution can be found simply in increasing the public accountability of those concerned.

Corruption

Because corruption in government is so common, the practical effect of government policies (as distinct from what those policies are said to be) cannot be understood without taking it into account. Andreski (1968, 1979) talks of 'Kleptocracy as a System of Government in Africa'. And as an example of how much it is 'ingrained into the system' in Nigeria, Cohen (1979, p. 295) writes:

> My students at the University spoke of a ... job in the public service that provides an opportunity for rapid promotion, an access to public resources that may be used for the betterment of oneself, one's friends, relatives, and others that can claim an obligation on one or become part of one's retinue in a faction within the service.

This problem is not confined to the underdeveloped countries, of course. Eighty years ago, in the United States, Lincoln Steffens (1904) wrote of 'the shame of the cities', and some American city governments are still bedevilled by 'pork barrel' politics (Scott, 1979b). There is no reason to believe that the penetration of the police and even the courts in the United States by organised crime has ceased since Kefauver (1951) wrote his celebrated report on *Crime in America*. In Britain, revelations about the bribing of officers of the much-vaunted Criminal Investigation Department of New Scotland Yard tell a similar story.

Banfield (1979) describes corruption in the United States, as it occurs in business as well as government. In both Britain and the United States, the giving of presents to the purchasing officers of large companies is common. This may not usually be in anticipation of a direct *quid pro quo* in the form of orders, but is certainly aimed at maintaining an agreeable attitude on the part of the person who allocates them. Familial nepotism is also common in business in Britain, and no doubt in other countries too. Recent scandals in the City of London over 'insider dealing' or shady company take-overs are probably only the tip of an iceberg of corruption in the most famous financial market in the world.

Third World corruption, then, does not stand alone, but it is more blatant and there is more of it (Wraith and Simpkins, 1963). A minister may initiate developments which favour his own area or ethnic group (Hanley, 1975), or give jobs to his political supporters. A politician seeking election may give beer or food for votes in a way reminiscent of the Eatanswills of Britain before the electoral reforms of the nineteenth century. Senior officials (and indeed ministers) may expect a 'commission' before placing a contract or granting, say, an import licence.

Transnational corporations are often willing to pay bribes, but such giants are not the only foreigners to be drawn into this process. Humbler petitioners may find that a tip lubricates the administrative machinery and increases the zeal of the minor functionaries with whom they have to negotiate. Customs officers in some countries are notorious for this, but all who issue licences or permits are in a position to demand their own 'sweeteners'.

A number of writers (in Ekpo, 1979a) have argued that such practices are not necessarily a bad thing, that corruption may actually help to further the process of development. Thus, for Tilman, it is a way of allocating scarce resources, and Leff argues that it reduces uncertainty and makes competition effective. Scott sees it as a means by which ethnic and other minorities who are excluded from legislative influence may be able to obtain some compensation for this by bending the administration of the law in their direction. Nye comes out in favour of its positive value in assisting capital formation – making the system work by, for example, cutting red tape and encouraging enterprise.

Some may feel that this is taking the neo-classical devotion to the market to the level of absurdity. It is difficult to see how corruption among politicians and bureaucrats can do anything but harm to the development of a poor country. Quite apart from the damage to its image abroad, and the cynicism about government, democracy and 'the nation' which it engenders at home, it replaces the criterion of efficiency by that of pandering to those with the deepest purses. Administration becomes unpredictable and chaotic, and often self-defeating; and planning becomes meaningless when plans are so often not carried out 'on the ground'. From the viewpoint of development in the sense of progress towards social justice, it gives all the advantages to the rich. Social policy is intended to make good the deficiencies of a market system, not to capitulate to it.

Countries vary a good deal in the amount of corruption with which they are burdened. Andreski believes that 'free Asia' and some of the Latin American dictatorships are the most corrupt (Andreski, 1979, pp. 278–80). In other countries, such as Tanzania, China or Cuba, one would have expected the collective ideology of the country to provide an inhospitable environment for gross venality of this kind, though this is not the case, it seems, with its more discreet forms. In Poland 'the act of passing a bribe has been nicknamed "a socialist handshake"' (ibid).

If one rejects the *laisser-faire* orientation of the apologists for corruption and seeks to control it, it must first be understood. It certainly is not enough to see it solely in moral terms: as due simply to the exceptional greed and dishonesty of those implicated, or to the incompetence or naivety of their governments. These have their part to play, as in the developed countries of the North, but in the South it is modernisation which makes the exploitation of office both tempting and easy. Four factors in particular are open to exploitation in a modernising country: the role of the 'big man', the custom of gift-giving, one's obligation to one's kin, village or tribe, and the low salaries sometimes paid to lower-grade officials, who nevertheless have considerable responsibility and deal with matters involving large sums of money.

The 'big man' – the chief, the head of a family or village, or the man with more cattle or pigs than anybody else – has prestige and sometimes power, but with these advantages go duties: to look after his people in preference to all others. This is not so different from the obligations of the lord to his serfs and tenants in the feudal system of mediaeval Europe.

In a modernising Third World society, the big man may be a politician, a civil servant, or somebody with the power to 'hire and fire'. The concept of *noblesse oblige* requires him to offer to his faithful follower whatever licence, contract or job he has at his disposal. Indeed he would be failing in his traditional obligations if he did not do so. It would also be perfectly proper for the recipient of his favour, as a mark of respect, to give something in return.

Within the framework of a clientelist system this would mean political loyalty, but under other circumstances it could take the form of a gift, which in a cash economy would not be a traditional gift like livestock, food or cloth, but money. The Latin American *cacique*, whom land reform has put into the place of the great landowner as a source of favours, is not alone in sometimes exacting a cash pay-off as well as votes (Esman, 1978, p. 16). Gifts are not only given in this way, as a mark of deference, but also between equals: as a gesture of friendship, hospitality or social solidarity. Sometimes a gift is made in order to score over the recipient, by placing him under an obligation.

Then there is, in traditional societies, the special responsibility imposed upon those who have done well in life to make provision for their less fortunate kinsmen. This is an aspect of the 'economy of affection' which we have seen to play such an important part in providing food, shelter and protection for those in need. Seen in this light, the giving of a job or other opportunity to a relative, even if he is less well qualified than other candidates, is misunderstood if it is interpreted as no more than nepotism.

The effect of the low salaries paid by some governments to their public servants has to be understood in the light of these customs. To their relatives and friends they have now become 'big men', well able to provide financial assistance to their needy kinsmen. To plead that they cannot means a considerable loss of face. The contrast between their incomes and those of the business men and others with whom they deal, and the ready availability of bribes from these individuals, adds to the temptation.

In a modernising society in which the use of one's assets for self-enrichment becomes the rule, it is not easy for politicians or civil servants to see why the power and resources placed at their disposal should not be utilised by them for their own purposes when such use is legitimised by the traditions of the country.

There is no suggestion that they are always naive in doing this, only that they find themselves in the happy position of operating a market economy within a traditional collective moral climate and, in accordance with the best principles of market behaviour, seek to

***Exhibit* 13.1   Traditions and corruption**

In Chinese culture, Lee (1981) points to the importance attributed to good personal relations in Confucian thinking, and
therefore in Chinese life. The 'dominance of Chinese folk
norms over legal codes' has caused the individual discrimination which they demanded to prevail in the Chinese bureaucracy
over the official policy of treating everybody alike. It is these
widespread traditional practices, according to Lee, which has
facilitated the growth of corruption in Hong Kong. He reports
on a survey which confirms that 'The higher the degree of
Chinese traditionalism, the greater the acceptance of corruption as a way of life' (ibid., p. 84).

These customs can lead to behaviour which appears corrupt
to Northern eyes, even though it may be permissible or even
obligatory in local terms. They may also be used to provide a
spurious legitimacy for acts which are corrupt. Thus Taub
(1969) points out that the word 'dash', which many European
and American visitors to Nigeria learn to translate into 'bribe',
really means any tip given, say to a taxi driver or a waiter, in
order 'to keep the machinery oiled'. Ekpo (1979b, p. 171) dis-
cusses how the use of the words 'drink' or 'road money' (given
by road-users to the police) implies that the payment is
ethically justifiable, even if it is to further some illegal purpose.
The word 'drink' is probably particularly significant, because of
the moral obligation to give sustenance to the wayfarer. A
parallel is the use of the words 'tea money' in Hong Kong, to
refer to bribes given to the police in that country during its
period of widespread corruption in the seventies.

maximise those advantages. When First World visitors or business
organisations offer a bribe, even if it is called a 'commission', they
are in collusion with them in this. To focus all the attention on
corrupt officials, then, is like the equally hypocritical practice of
blaming the prostitute and ignoring the responsibility of her client.

Scott (1972, pp. 88ff; 1979a) has made a distinction between
what he calls 'parochial' and 'market' corruption, the former
relating to actions which are solely concerned with the meeting of
traditional obligations, and the latter to corruption for personal

profit. It is not easy to draw this distinction in practice, except in the more extreme examples of both forms. It relates to motives, and although some will be quite disinterested in their pursuit of customary objectives, and others will be equally clear that they are in it for the money, there will undoubtedly be, in the middle, a good deal of rationalisation.

The accumulation of bureaucratic regulations multiplies the opportunities for corruption, as do protectionist trade policies, for both create opportunities for favouritism. As Myrdal puts it: 'Individuals who might have performed useful tasks in the economic development of their country become idle hangers-on, watching for loopholes in the decrees, and dishonesty in their implementation' (Myrdal, 1956).

A state welfare system offers similar scope for illicit preferences, whether paid for or not. Who is to get the house, the pension, the scholarship, the medical treatment, will, under the conditions of acute scarcity which exists in many Third World countries, depend on village, family or political contacts. In a few countries it will depend on who can scrape together the money to pay a bribe.

Stories also surface from time to time about food, clothing or medical supplies sent by international aid organisations being misappropriated. As the supplies in question are usually intended to meet desperate human need – famine, a natural disaster, refugees from war or persecution – this kind of corruption is particularly reprehensible, and very damaging to the image of international aid as a whole.

Corruption in the social policy field will always be at the expense of the 'have nots'. Whether it involves the allocation of contracts, the engagement of staff, or the distribution of welfare benefits, it will usually result in the direct transfer of resources from the poor to the rich. Meanwhile social policy itself is distorted, making a mockery of the humane objectives which it professes.

Corruption is nevertheless a highly intractable problem, as experience in Nigeria over many years has shown. One regime has followed another, corruption usually being the main justification for change. But, whether the government was military or civil, it has never been long before allegations of graft were being made all over again. It is a problem of social change: how to reduce poverty and inequality through a process of development in which the transitional normative ambiguity, of which much corruption is a symptom, is minimised. Dysfunctional modernisation and commercial corruption from abroad are important elements in this. Here as elsewhere, dependent underdevelopment has much to answer for.

In the meantime, there are no simple solutions. Foreign governments should treat as criminals any of their citizens or home-based companies who engage in these practices. There has been some sign in recent years of the United States, at least, taking these responsibilities more seriously. International agencies, also, should introduce measures to prevent intended recipients of their aid from being robbed of it. And the international community should also rally in support of reforming administrations, and encourage them to go further than merely the condemnation and punishment of corrupt members of a previous regime.

Anti-corruption measures should be given teeth. A state anti-corruption organisation, perhaps an Ombudsman's Department, might be set up with members appointed and removable only by the Supreme Court. Experience in a number of countries has demonstrated the powerlessness against corrupt politicians of an Ombudsman who is himself the creature of the government. Such a department would initiate its own enquiries, or investigate complaints made by other people, would issue reports regularly and, unlike many Ombudsmen, should have the power to prosecute where sufficient evidence of corruption existed.

Politicians, civil servants or businessmen found guilty would be required to pay over their illicit gains to the state (even if this meant that they were bankrupted) and they would be debarred from public life or business for a period prescribed by the law. To protect anti-corruption provisions from legislative erosion, they should be incorporated into the constitution. The Leadership Code of Papua New Guinea is an example of how this might be done (Papua New Guinea, 1973).

All of this sounds very drastic, but experience in Nigeria, Asia, Latin America shows that anything less would be unlikely to reduce corruption. Even then it will not be eradicated. Its persistence in Europe, and also in the USSR and Eastern Europe, proves that. What cannot be tolerated is a situation in which it poisons the whole climate of government and business, and not only represents a serious obstacle to economic growth, but also to any progress towards social justice.

Summary

To discuss social and development policies without examining the activities of the politicians and administrators responsible for them would be unrealistic. Regimes are of many kinds: military dictatorships, governments based on electoral fraud and one-party states, as well as representative democracies on the Northern model. Under all these types of regime, political patronage or clientelism is to be found. The power and charisma of a national leader are almost always the main unifying factor, though behind him and his government (as in the industrialised world also) there are usually powerful vested interests.

The one-party state does not necessarily limit the choice of candidates, but it does limit the choice of policies. The emphasis shifts from 'Why?' to 'How?' – to technocratic rather than political solutions. It also reduces the possibility of a change in the national leadership. Whatever the system, however, poor communications and an independently-minded peasantry condition the influence of government over the daily lives of the population. In such circumstances participation in decision making by local residents is not only a precondition for real democracy, but also for decisions which can be carried out.

Such local views have to be reconciled with one another within the framework of a national plan, but the plan itself has to be flexible – within the limits set by its long-term aims. In other words a compromise has to be found between the rigidity of a synoptic model, and the incrementalism to which governments often succumb.

As part of such a plan it is necessary to ensure that different sectors of the economy or the public services do not frustrate each other's aims. Achieving such co-ordination at the national level means tempering the competing ambitions and opportunities of departmental ministers, as well as their vulnerability to pressures from the 'economy of affection'. At the local level co-ordination could be attempted through 'integrated rural development' schemes.

Civil servants who have to administer the policies face problems not known to the colonial civil servants whom they succeeded. Though they lack experience and confidence, they are often more permanent and therefore more influential than their ministers.

This strengthens still further the technocratic element, as against the political, in government, as does the identification sometimes of the civil service with the party, and the appointment of civil servants to ministerial posts. Another beneficiary of all this is that other permanent figure, the 'maximum leader', who controls the machinery of government and is thus able to reinforce his own position.

The education, the role and class interests of civil servants make them modernisers, and yet they have often to deal with situations where modernisation is no solution. Indeed they have to come to terms with an 'economy of affection' which even makes its demands on them. Clientelism, and much of what is called Third World corruption, have their starting points in the same 'economy of affection' – in the quite legitimate traditional obligations of 'big men', or one's duty towards one's kinsfolk or other dependants. Obligations of hospitality or of gift-giving also play their part. But it is only too easy in a modernising society, where the functions of the state are proliferating and governments have valuable privileges in their gift, for these traditions to become the rationalisation for more blatantly corrupt behaviour.

The industrialised countries cannot pretend to any superiority. Not only do they have their own forms of corruption, but they play an important part in advancing the process among their poorer neighbours. It is Northern multinationals who are prepared to subvert governments or pay 'commissions' in order to gain profitable concessions or contracts. Their home governments appear to frown on these activities, but seem prepared to benefit from the employment and other economic advantages which such contracts bring.

Clientelism and corruption hamper development, and in the field of social welfare distort the distribution of benefits, preventing them reaching those who need them most. They flourish under conditions of extreme inequality, and in the no man's land which exists between a traditional and a modernised society. But this in itself is no argument for more rapid modernisation, as corruption in the Northern countries amply demonstrates.

A solution has to be found within the framework of a society which is engaged in an organic and controlled process of development. This requires Third World governments to work for the kind

of social and economic change required to achieve growth combined with greater equality, but in a way which ensures that that
process does not cause what Scott called 'parochial' corruption to
become 'market' corruption. Those guilty of the latter should be
treated as the criminals that they are.

14

Social Welfare in Development

The achievement of social welfare means, first and foremost, the alleviation of poverty in its many manifestations. This cannot be solely a matter of redistributing more fairly what wealth there already is, but requires in poor countries that redistribution be incorporated within a policy for economic growth. In other words it depends on the achievement of development in the fullest sense of that word.

Economists of the neo-classical school argue that development will occur only if countries liberate their economies from the trammels of government intervention in order that the mutual advantages of a free market may be realised. In contesting this view the structuralists point to the many inflexibilities which exist in the real economy. As a result, the adjustments towards economic equilibrium, on which the neo-classicists rely, take place in the real world either too late or not at all.

In fact close examination of the requirements for growth and for an effective social policy makes it clear that government intervention is unavoidable, and that it calls for planning in which these two aspects are closely integrated. This is disputed by some Marxists who see welfare services as an obstacle to development, as much in the industrialised as in the Third World.

The Pessimists

These Marxists argue that social services are palliatives, softening the rigours of an exploitative capitalism. Such 'sops' divert attention from radical solutions, which would involve the reconstruction of the economic system itself, into the safer channels of social reform (Pritchard and Taylor, 1978). The Welfare State ideal becomes a kind of 'false consciousness', in which its true nature as a prop of the capitalist system is concealed behind a veneer of social justice.

Others place more stress on the class struggle (Gough, 1982, pp. 64ff). They see the social services as a concession extracted from unwilling capitalist governments by trade union pressure. The vicissitudes of those services in a country like Britain give some support to such a view. They have tended to advance when the working-class movements have been in a powerful bargaining position, as during the periods of prosperity and labour shortage during and after the war. They have been forced into retreat at times like the present, when recession and mass unemployment have coincided with a pro-employer government with a consistent anti-welfare ideology and a large parliamentary majority.

In the first of these two views, welfare is seen as a sham, used by the ruling class as a smoke-screen. In the second, it is envisaged as a potential source of genuine benefit to the workers, and recognised as such by them – though it may sometimes be so structured that its benefits are more apparent than real. Both agree, however, in regarding the state as an instrument of class domination in the classical Leninist mould (Lenin, 1918).

According to the 'false consciousness' formulation, therefore, the state will rein back the Welfare State when it appears that its costs to the capitalist economy exceed its advantages as a supportive ideology. The 'class struggle' theory implies that this will happen when the balance of power between the antagonists in that struggle moves against the workers. These occurrences will tend to coincide with one another at times of economic crisis.

Gough (1982, pp. 39ff), although accepting that the state is under pressure to minister to the needs of the capitalist system, believes that it has more independence than many who espouse these views would allow. In the developed countries it has evolved a philosophy and practice of representative democracy which limits the extent to which it can engage in partisan activities. This is probably a realistic picture of the ambiguous position of the modern democratic state. But on his assumptions, no less than those discussed previously, the welfare concessions made by the state would never go so far as to threaten the viability of the capitalist system itself.

It has been left to Bill Warren (1980, pp. 224–35), a Marxist of unimpeachable credentials, to deny that capitalism prevents advances in welfare in the Third World. This is somewhat unexpected in the light of his thesis that, when capitalism has run its full course, socialism will follow. For it is the widespread social misery, which the internal contradictions of capitalism are alleged to cause, that is expected eventually to precipitate the revolution. Any amelioration of social conditions by means of the social services would presumably delay that outcome. This is the basis for the argument that, as a palliative, the social services have a counter-revolutionary effect.

Much of the Marxist analysis can be accepted. Earlier chapters of this book have shown that social progress is limited by dependent underdevelopment, which is the main way in which capitalism manifests itself in the Third World. As such it generates social problems and limits the capacity of a country to provide the social services necessary to counter them.

The bias of the state itself within this framework is also evident. Even the more socialistically inclined Third World governments feel impelled by economic imperatives to favour the exploitative transnationals operating within their boundaries. There is also undoubtedly a conflict of interests between social classes, a struggle in which labour, in surplus and unorganised, is very weak. All these factors are reflected in the amount of welfare provision, and the form it takes.

The elimination of dependent underdevelopment is therefore a priority; and bringing about that desirable objective may in some countries mean a change in the power structure which amounts to revolution. But, while we await the revolution, widespread deprivation remains unrelieved. To suggest that, unless everything can be gained at once, nothing is worth having, is not only illogical: it shows callousness in the face of suffering.

How much can we expect to achieve within the limits imposed by underdevelopment? Because we cannot know the answer to this we should exert pressure on those limits all the time. Gains made as a result of this will bring with them new kinds of established expectations and, eventually, changed attitudes. The redistribution of both resources and power can thus proceed from

successive new baselines, the new dispensation becoming legitimated by new attitudes at each stage.

This is at least realistic as an immediate programme for action.
It also casts doubt on the idea of social justice as a millennium, to
be attained by a sudden, convulsive turn of events at some
moment in the future, leaving the developing aspirations of the
people out of account. For social reforms themselves change the
terms of the argument, and social justice becomes an elusive aim
to be pursued afresh in each generation.

Growth and Welfare

This does not mean abandoning more fundamental aims but it
does imply that progress towards these might be made in the same
stepwise fashion. At the forefront must be the campaign for a new
World Economic Order, to make know-how, capital and markets
available to the underdeveloped countries.

There needs also to be more recognition of the contribution to
underdevelopment of international capital, through the creation of
limited enclaves of development within vast deserts of neglect.
Ways have to be found, with international support, of taming the
predatory transnationals which are responsible for this state of
affairs. Alternatively they have to be indigenised. One way of
achieving this would be through nationalisation. Another would
be that chosen by countries like Malaysia, which have insisted on a
majority of the shares being in local hands.

A result of the enclave pattern of development, for which the
transnationals are mainly responsible, is the phenomenal rate of
city growth in many countries, bringing with it such serious
problems as unhygienic and sordid living conditions and mass
unemployment. Housing, sewerage and the provision of a pure
water supply are therefore all important urban priorities, for
reasons of growth as well as health and the quality of life.
Industrial and commercial development, but of a more balanced
kind, can play its part, on condition that it is not at the expense of
the rural majority.

The informal sectors both in employment (street traders and the
rest) and in housing (the squatter settlements) have their limited
contributions to make. The modernising tendencies of governments

and local elites should not be allowed to stand in the way of such growing points. That is, on condition that they are truly autonomous, and not merely a subtler way of manipulating and exploiting the poor.

So long as rural–urban migration continues at its present rate, however, it is difficult to see how the problems of the cities can be brought under control. Unemployment will be even more intractable. Real progress on both fronts will depend on a more widely distributed process of development, to help to stem the stampede from the countryside.

For enclave development and the urban bias which it embodies have had a particularly destructive impact on the rural majority. The hazards of nature can be devastating enough to the subsistence farmer with no reserves to fall back on. They could be tempered by providing sufficient investment in irrigation and other agricultural improvements, but the urban bias of overseas investors, and the lack of other sources of capital, ensure that this does not happen. Other forms of infrastructural investment – in roads, access to markets and so on – are also inadequate.

Where development has taken place it is often more damaging than the neglect which preceded it. Traditional land is alienated to form large, highly capitalised farms, turning independent peasants into landless and, to a large extent, unemployed labourers. This has often been an unanticipated consequence of the so-called 'green revolution'.

There is no reason to believe that small-scale, intensive farming *per se* is necessarily the less productive, but constant subdivision under the pressure of a rapidly rising population has sometimes produced holdings which are too small to be effectively worked, or even to produce enough food to maintain the family dependent on them. Land reform, involving the distribution of large estates (such as the *latifundia* of South America) among the peasants has been seen as one solution, enabling these minuscule holdings to be enlarged, and land to be provided for the landless. This is a direct threat to powerful interests, which have been able, in some countries, to nullify its effects. Political reform may therefore have to precede land reform in some cases.

Where land is plentiful, the colonisation of new areas is also possible, but good virgin land is becoming scarcer, and the infrastructure and irrigation often required are expensive. There may also be ecological costs, some of which (like deforestation in the Amazon basin) may be global in their impact.

Land reform also opens up the possibility of a new kind of 'green revolution' which could be to the advantage of the rural poor, and not merely of agricultural capitalists. Improved agricultural methods do not have to involve too great a break with traditional practices. Indeed the rigid disciplines and high costs of modern chemical husbandry may not be either culturally or economically viable among the peasants of the South. There is plenty of scope instead for improving customary practices. Even the much-despised 'slash and burn' method can be made very productive in countries with sufficient land. Combine improvements of this kind with the personal commitment and family support of the small peasant, and the potential high productivity of the small farm can become a reality.

With the reinvigoration of peasant agriculture it would also become possible to revive the flagging system of mutual support which has been such a central feature of traditional rural society – the so-called 'economy of affection'. This still has an important part to play in poor countries whose governments confront a poverty problem which it will be beyond their resources to tackle for a very long time.

However, as GNP rises, redistribution through the social services also becomes a possibility. Once primed and the process of social advancement begun, there is reason to believe that a more fully employed, better educated and housed, better fed and healthier population will be more creative, energetic and productive. The World Bank speaks of investment in human capital. That such investment will more than pay for itself is supported both by theory and research. The returns to expenditure on education, especially primary education, have received most research attention, but economic gains from, for example, investment in health, nutrition and the advancement of the position of women seems almost as well established.

Social Policy

In the development of these social services, the key requirement seems to be the use of what is now often called 'appropriate technology'. A number of factors combine to make Northern social welfare approaches unsuitable for use in many Third World countries. Low GNP is important among these factors, indicating a need to concentrate on preventive rather than remedial services.

Thus poverty has to be attacked through the pursuit of growth, and a more equitable distribution of resources, like land, capital and a healthy environment, rather than through income mainten-ance services on the Northern model. Against such a background it is possible to envisage a reviving kinship and community support system, through which financial assistance from the state could be channelled. There will remain some for whom traditional support does not exist, especially in areas where the sense of communal obligation has been destroyed by alienation from its basis in a collective system of land holding. Where this has happened, the responsibility of the state is to provide support as a 'right', that is, without the stigma which such 'uncovenanted relief' has often carried with it in the past.

In the field of health, the need to give priority to prevention is even more apparent. Low GNP is a central factor here also; curative services – hospitals, doctors, drugs and so on – are very costly. Lack of financial resources is reinforced by the lack also of enough professionals in curative medicine. The number of doctors and even of nurses and other paramedicals, is too few to provide the cover required, especially in the sparsely populated country-side. Training more is bound to be a slow business, and again very expensive.

These considerations might seem decisive enough by them-selves, but they are massively reinforced by the fact that the most serious causes of morbidity and mortality are diseases of environ-mental origin. Malnutrition, a polluted or germ-infested water supply, lack of proper sewerage or refuse disposal, housing which is overcrowded or provides inadequate protection from the ex-treme weather conditions of the tropics and of course poverty itself, which underlies so many other forms of deprivation – attention to factors like these will do more to improve the general state of health than the entrenchment of a rich and powerful, and inevitably urban-based, medical elite.

There is no suggestion that Third World countries do not need a curative health service. It is a question only of where priorities should lie in countries where resources are so seriously limited.

But it is also generally acknowledged now that such treatment as is provided should be organised differently from that which is familiar in the industrialised countries. A village health worker, a local resident with a basic medical training, would be at the heart of such an 'appropriate technology'. Such a person might be a 'witch doctor', a herbalist, a female birth-attendant or other traditional practitioner, or might even function as a health worker in time available from work on the land or as a housewife.

The village worker would have the support of an area health centre staffed by trained medical auxiliaries, and of qualified medical staff working in an even more remote district hospital, but would deal personally with most of the village's health problems. The national hospital, practising scientific medicine up to the frontiers of knowledge, would have to exist, but would have a much lower profile than in the industrialised countries. The principle of progressive care would be applied, avoiding unnecessary hospitalisation and maximising community care.

The preventive and remedial aspects would come together at the local level, for the health worker would also have the duty of giving advice on personal hygiene and alerting neighbours to the need for dietary improvement and a healthy environment. The health centre would give advice on this, and also act as a channel of communication with the central government. It would promote the government's policies for health, and also ensure that it was well informed about local conditions which might have a bearing on the formation of policy.

Family planning is necessary for both the relief of poverty and the improvement of health. Giving birth control advice could be the responsibility of the village health worker or even a social worker, but it is probably better for it to be provided by bodies which have the specialised expertise and access to the necessary appliances – perhaps the area health centre. But people have to be motivated to go for advice. A national campaign of persuasion will be necessary, and experience in countries such as China shows that the co-operation of the local community is also required.

Apart from the family planning aspect of birth control, which is concerned with the need of families to gain control over the number and spacing of their children, there is the government's interest in having a population policy. The problem in many countries is that, although births are increasing at a slower rate (if at all), an even greater decline in deaths, resulting from the introduction of Northern medicine and improved hygiene, means that the rate of natural increase is still going up. In some countries there is already a land shortage, food shortages are becoming endemic in certain parts of the world, and the rise in population is sometimes enough to cancel out any benefit from a rise in GNP.

Surveys show that there is still reluctance on the part of some governments, either on religious or traditional grounds, to countenance birth control for other than family reasons, but if a population policy is to be made effective it must be through educational work at the grass-roots level. Although some would argue that Chinese policies have been too intimidatory, they have been highly successful, and this is the result of linking state regulation, propaganda and incentive with personal education and pressure in the neighbourhood and the workplace.

One important gain from family planning must be in the lives and status of women. Annual pregnancies and the burden involved in caring for very large families preoccupy and sap the vitality of many women in underdeveloped countries. Control over pregnancy makes it more realistic to aim at advancing their education, which in its turn increases their willingness to adopt birth control measures. Also, when they are no longer continuously either pregnant or nursing infants, it is possible for them to take what opportunities exist for gainful employment. Education and outside work, between them, can do more than anything else to improve their position.

But it is not enough for the government to be convinced of the need to bring about such an improvement. Deeply ingrained traditional attitudes stand in the way of justice for women: attitudes which underlie both the resistance to family planning and to equality in education between the sexes. The removal of such resistances must take place in the villages, and in Third World society, the task includes the persuasion of traditional authority figures – the chiefs, headmen, heads of families and so on.

It is not only women, of course, who stand to benefit by a more equitable distribution of educational opportunities. Most Third World governments still spend most of their education budgets on secondary and higher education, which are largely monopolised by the better-off. There is also a bias in favour of urban areas, even at the primary level, and this worsens still further the relative position of a poor who are mainly to be found in the decaying countryside. The indications for policy are a shift of expenditure to primary education and into rural education. But equity is not the only argument. There is reason to believe that such changes would at the present time be the best investment also for the country.

Both the cost and the shortage of trained teachers may make it necessary to replace them in thinly populated areas with community education workers analogous to the community health workers already mentioned. Though not fully-qualified, they could provide much of what is required at the primary level, especially if supported by well-designed 'distance teaching' material in the form of correspondence, radio lessons and so on.

The raising of levels of literacy among the adult population is also necessary, on economic as well as social grounds. The maintenance of literacy among children who have had a few years of primary schooling would also be assisted by the presence of other literate persons in their households. A 'functional' approach, emphasising the value of literacy in daily life and work, can increase motivation. As with so many other things, it is necessary to combine such a national campaign with work at village level. In particular, it is no use mounting a national literacy programme if well-organised local facilities for making it a reality do not exist.

The value of the 'functional' approach is not confined to adult literacy campaigns. It can justify education in the minds of children and their parents, both of whom have to be convinced that the expenditure of time and money is justified. It is part of the wider concept of non-formal education, which in its turn is linked to recent proposals for providing a broad 'basic education' for all, rather than a high level of education for the fortunate few and little or nothing for the rest.

With a curriculum aimed at meeting the immediate, perceived needs of the population, and non-formal methods of instruction with their advantages of flexibility and familiarity, a 'basic education' programme has the potential for reaching many of those who had previously missed out on school. Among these would be adults, particularly women, poor farming families for whom the direct and opportunity costs of school were prohibitive, others living far from the nearest schools, school drop-outs, and unemployed young people in need of occupation and vocational training.

Even then universal 'basic education' would, according to some, still suffer from the fatal disadvantage of leading nowhere. As Foster has reminded us, people have to feel that education will improve their life chances, which for the rural population, or the unemployed in the urban enclave, will only occur if the new educational opportunities are accompanied by some evidence of economic revival.

The importance of secondary and higher education has been exaggerated. Post-primary education needs to be better related to a country's ability to utilise educated manpower. The question of who should receive these very limited opportunities then arises, with profound significance for the future distribution of power and wealth in a country. Selection according to ability to pay is no longer defensible. Selection on the basis of academic examinations is also known to incorporate the effect of existing social inequalities, and would greatly disadvantage those educated in the nonformal system. Perhaps the Third World will show how to select in a more defensible way.

There remain the 'human faces of welfare' in the shape of social work and community development. It is almost a cliché to say that social casework, based on direct work with individuals and families in need, is inappropriate for the countries of the underdeveloped South, and that it needs to be replaced by something called 'community work'. There is no doubt that work in 'communities' needs to be a feature of many aspects of social welfare. This has been seen to be the case in land reform and agricultural improvement, in urban development, education and the support of the needy, in health, the improvement of nutrition and family planning, and in achieving greater participation in decision making by the population at large.

This does not mean that the more personalised approach of social workers can be dispensed with, for they have a responsibility for relieving deprivation and suffering over a wide field. But they also must draw on the resources available in the kin-group and the village – the 'economy of affection'. These resources have been depleted by the inroads made upon traditional loyalties and obligations as a result of the private acquisition of traditional land, and the related migration into the towns.

Fortunately there is now more interest in preserving and utilising these customary assets. Without them, widows and orphans, the elderly and the handicapped will be increasingly neglected. A poor country cannot be expected to provide adequately for them through the public services. In seeking solutions to their problems through the community, the social worker will be helping that institution itself back to health, like a disused muscle at last subjected to exercise.

This can only happen, of course, if more basic requirements for the reinvigoration of traditional community life, associated with the revival of peasant agriculture and rural life, are met. This is a further reminder of the link between economic policy and social welfare.

A charge often laid against social work is that it is a form of social control, aiming to persuade individuals to accept existing social injustices. This is no more true than it is of the other social services, such as education and health, and it has become less true in recent years as social reform ideas have gained ground among social workers. Social work is probably less open to challenge on this ground than what goes by the name of community development. This is often an instrument of government policy in nation building, or encouraging self-help in the building-up of the physical infrastructure – constructing roads, sinking wells, erecting schoolrooms and so on. It may also be used to create a local public opinion favourable to government policies for improving local hygiene and dietary practices, popularising family planning or raising the status and education of women.

The danger arises when it is used to bolster up support for a particular political regime. In spite of the ideology of self-determination which surrounds much of the discussion about community development, community workers are rarely in a position to act in these matters in any other way than as agents of the government which employs them. It is within these limits imposed by government policy and the realities of the local power structure that the community development worker must try to realise his objective of enabling people to participate in the making of the decisions which control their lives. It is still an important aim. Moreover sound decisions can only be made on the basis of reliable information. Decisions in which everybody participates will be better decisions because they are better informed. This is one of the ways in which the individual can contribute from his personal assets to the common store of welfare, and enrich his own personality in the process.

The community worker can also take responsibility for co-ordinating that revival of community life which has been seen to be so important for economic growth and social progress. The alternative may be piecemeal and competitive demands by a variety of government departments and other agencies upon the already attenuated energies of these communities.

A major community problem for many governments is what they see as the threat to public order represented by the presence in the towns of large numbers of unemployed young people. They responded at first with party youth movements, and camps organised on military lines. Later and more realistic organisations were those which also provided vocational training, especially where these were developed in partnership with the villages and provided training which could improve methods of husbandry. The problem for an underdeveloped economy remains one of finding employment for the young people after they have completed their training. We have returned full circle to that ultimate limitation which hampers progress in so many ways.

The limitations within which both community workers and social workers must operate are underlined by the ways in which underdeveloped countries are governed. Some are ruled by military or other forms of dictatorship, often representing powerful economic or social oligarchies. Many of the rest permit only one party to offer itself for election. This does not necessarily preclude a choice between different candidates, but it does limit choice as far as the national leadership or major government policies are concerned.

This may be unavoidable where the fissiparous tendencies arising from tribal, cultural or racial influences are still powerful, but it brings with it other hazards. As experience has frequently shown, a politician whose position is unchallengeable may become impatient of opposition or even criticism, and is also exposed to the danger of corruption. Corruption is a widespread scourge in the Third World, and endemic in some countries, such as Nigeria.

It is not as straightforward a matter as it may seem when viewed from the very different cultural situation of the developed country. It is complicated by a web of customary obligations, forming part of the 'economy of affection', the potentially valuable mutual aid system on which some stress has been laid in this book. But these obligations to followers, relatives and so on, though legitimate in themselves, easily become a rationalisation for exploiting a position of power or authority. One form of this, clientelism, in which material inducements are offered in exchange for political support, is common and widely accepted as a political practice.

But office-holders can also use their positions for personal enrichment. Officials and politicians are encouraged in this by foreigners, especially foreign commercial interests, who want to buy privileges or contracts for themselves. The corrupt functionary's fellow-countrymen are the real victim. Such practices are difficult to control. As a start a clearer distinction could be drawn between permissible mutual aid and venal corruption, treating those who engage in the latter as criminals.

Social and economic progress will have to be brought about in the face of hard-headed scepticism among the peasants who constitute the greater part of the population of Third World countries. In such circumstances, participation is not merely a desirable principle of democratic government, but a necessity if they are to be convinced that change is in their interest. Policies, in other words, have to be 'bottom-up'.

But they must also be 'top-down'. There are many divisions – tribal, racial, linguistic, religious – within the population, often embedded in a traditional way of life and sanctioned by custom. These divisions are frequently reinforced by what are perceived as (and indeed sometimes may be) divergent economic interests. By comparison, an integrated plan for development, even if it has been drawn up after widespread consultation, may still seem remote from the urgent pressures of daily life. Countries like China and Cuba have shown that such groups, living far from the centres of political power, can be seized and united by powerful ideas which give meaning to what is happening to them in a changing world. Such a master philosophy (or ideology, according to taste) can also be a unifying force in another sense, presenting a set of ideals as a touchstone for the evaluation of policies of all kinds, and for bringing them into relationship with one another.

The examples given have been of countries which have taken socialism as their guiding philosophy, and this would be congenial to many of the so-called emergent nations. In others the idea of the nation provides a similar source of inspiration and unification, especially if the ethnic and tribal differences can be seen as a source of strength to the nation, rather than as divisive influences to be ruthlessly stamped out. Unfortunately, in too many Third World countries, they are more likely to be seen as divisive. Underdeveloped countries cannot afford the loss of creative diversity which this perception involves.

References and Author Index

Note: Page numbers *in italics* at end of references provide an index of authors' names.

Abel-Smith, B. (1978) *Value for Money in Health Services* (London: Heinemann). *137, 142, 143*

Abel-Smith, B. and A. Leiserson (1978) *Poverty, Development and Health Policy* (Geneva: World Health Organisation). *106, 120, 132, 146*

Abercrombie, K. (1972) 'Agricultural mechanisation and employment in Latin America' *International Labour Review*, April 1972, pp. 315ff. *68*

Acker, S. (ed.) (1984a) *Education and Women, Year Book of Education, 1984* (New York: Kogan Page). *166*

Acker, S. (1984b) 'Sociology, gender and education', in S. Acker (ed.) (1984) *Education and Women, Year Book of Education, 1984* (New York: Kogan Page). *231*

Acosta, C. J. (1976) 'Columbian elites and the underdevelopment of the social welfare system', in D. Thursz and J. Vigilante (eds) (1976) *Meeting Human Needs 2: Additional Perspectives from Thirteen Countries* (Beverley Hills: Sage). *197, 202*

Adelman, I. and C. Morris (1973) *Economic Growth and Social Equity in Developing Countries* (Stanford: Stanford University Press). *5*

Ahluwalia, M. S. (1976) 'Inequality, poverty and development', *Journal of Development Economics*, 3, pp. 307–42. *245*

Ahluwalia, M. S. and N. G. Carter (1981) 'Growth and Poverty in developing countries', in H. B. Chenery *Structural Change and Development Policy* (Oxford: Oxford University Press). *1, 5, 42, 53, 125, 159*

Amis, P. (1984) 'Squatters or tenants: the commercialisation of unauthorised housing in Nairobi, *World Development*, 12, pp. 87–96. *92*

Anderson, J. E. (1971) *The Village Polytechnic Movement* (Nairobi: Institute of Development Studies). *176*

Anderson, J. E. (1973) 'The formalization of non-formal education: village polytechnics and pre-vocational training Kenya', in P. Foster and J. R. Sheffield (eds) *Education and Rural Development, World Year Book of Education, 1974*, pp. 283–301 (London: Evans Bros). *176*

Andresky, S. (1968) *The African Predicament: a Study in the Pathology of Modernisation* (London: Michael Joseph). *271*

Andresky, S. (1979) 'Kleptocracy as a system of government', in M. U. Ekpo (ed.) (1979a) *Bureaucratic Corruption in Sub-Saharan Africa* (Washington D.C.: University Press of America). *271, 273*

Arnon, I. (1981) *Modernization of Agriculture in Developing Countries* (Chichester: John Wiley). *66*

Aziz, S. (1980) *Rural Development: Learning from China* (London: Macmillan). *55, 60, 62, 63, 212*

Bader, M. B. (1980) 'Breast-feeding: the role of multinational corporations in Latin America', in K. Kumar (ed.) *Transnational Corporations: Their Impact on Third World Societies and Cultures* (Boulder, Colorado: Westview Press). *126*

Baer, W. (1965) *Industrialisation and Economic Development in Brazil* (Homewood, Illinois: Irwin). *54*

Baer, W. and M. E. A. Hervé (1978) 'Employment and industrialisation in developing countries', in S. P. Singh (ed.) *Underdevelopment to Developing Economies* (Oxford: Oxford University Press). *84*

Bairoch, P. (1973) *Urban Unemployment in Developing Countries*, (Geneva: International Labour Office). *63*

Banfield, E. C. (1979) 'Corruption as a feature of governmental organisation', in M. U. Ekpo (ed.) (1979a) *Bureaucratic Corruption in Sub-Saharan Africa* (Washington DC: University Press of America). *271*

Barraclough, S. (1973) *Agrarian Structure in Latin America* (Lexington, Mass.: Lexington Books).

Beneria, L. (ed.) (1982a) *Women and Development* (New York: Praeger).

Beneria, L. (1982b) 'Accounting for women's work', in L. Beneria (ed.) (1982) *Women and Development* (New York: Praeger). *223*

Benston, M. (1969) 'Political economy of women's liberation', *Monthly Review*, 21, pp. 13–27. *222, 231*

Berry, A. R. and W. R. Cline (1979) *Agrarian Structure and Productivity in Developing Countries* (Baltimore: Johns Hopkins University). *69*

Bettenhausen, K. (1971) 'Approaches to employment problems of Asian youth', in Commonwealth Secretariat, *Youth and Development in Asia and the Pacific* (Kuala Lumpur: Commonwealth Secretariat). *219*

Blaug, M. (1973) *Education and the Employment Problems in Developing Countries* (Geneva: International and Labour Office).

Blaug, M., R. Layard and M. Woodhally (1969) *The Causes and Consequences of Graduate Unemployment in India* (London: Penguin). *156*

Bondestam, L. (1980) 'The political ideology of population control', in L. Bondestam and S. Bergstrom, *Poverty and Population Control* (London: Academic Press). *246*

Bondestam, L. and S. Bergstrom (1980), *Poverty and Population Control* (London: Academic Press). *246*

Bose, A. (1983) 'The Community Health Scheme: an Indian experiment', in D. Morley, J. Rhode and G. Williams (eds) *Practising Health for All* (Oxford: Oxford University Press). *133*

Bradley, D. J. (1977) 'Improvement of rural domestic supplies', in

298   *References and Author Index*

D. A. J. Tyrrell *et al.* (ed.) *Technologies for Rural Health* (London: The Royal Society). *127*

Brandt, W. (chairman) (1980) *North–South: a Programme for Survival*, (the *Brandt Report*) (London: Pan Books). *3*

Brandt, W. (chairman) (1983) *Common Crisis: North–South Co-operation for World Recovery* (London: Pan Books). *3*

Brehm, J. W. and A. R. Cohen (1962) *Explorations in Cognitive Dissonance* (New York: John Wiley). *240*

Brett, E. A. (1985) *The World Economy since the War: the Politics of Uneven Development* (Basingstoke: Macmillan). *18, 19, 25, 28*

Brett, S. (1974) 'Low income urban settlements in Latin America', in E. De Kadt and G. Williams (eds) *Sociology and Development* (London: Routledge & Kegan Paul).

Bruton, H. J. (1978) 'The two-gap approach to aid and development', in S. P. Singh *Underdevelopment to Development Economics* (Oxford: Oxford University Press. *18*

Bryceson, A. D. M. (1977) 'Rehydration in cholera and other diarrhoeal diseases', in D. A. J. Tyrrell *et al.* (ed) *Technologies for Rural Health* (London: The Royal Society). *139*

Buckles, R. G. (1980) 'It is appropriate to create new pharmaceutical products within developing countries', in D. A. J. Tyrrell *et al.* (eds) *More Technologies for Rural Health* (London: The Royal Society). *121*

Budihardjo, E. (1985) 'The role of non-government organisation in housing the non-citizen urban poor: the case of Semarang, Indonesia', in S. M. Romaya, and G. H. Franklin (eds) *Shelter, Services and the Urban Poor. Report of the Third World Planning Seminar* (Cardiff: University of Wales Institute of Science and Technology). *94*

Bullivant, B. (1981) *The Pluralist Dilemma in Education: Six Case Studies* (London: George Allen & Unwin). *169, 170*

Caldwell, J. C. (1982) *Theory of Fertility Decline* (London: Academic Press).

Cammack, P., D. Pool and W. Tordoff (1988) *Third World Politics: a Comparative Introduction* (Basingstoke: Macmillan). *228, 235, 270*

Carnoy, M. (1975) 'The role of education in a strategy of social change', *Comparative Education Review*, 19, pp. 393ff. *172*

Carrin, G. (1984) *Economic Evaluation of Health* (London: Croom Helm). *126*

Carron, G. and T. N. Chau (1980) *Regional Disparities in Educational Development: Diagnosis and Policies for Reduction* (Paris: UNESCO).

Casanova, P. J. (1964) 'Internal colonisation and national development', *Studies in Comparative Development*, 4, pp. 27–37. *27*

Castells, M. (1977) *The Urban Question* (London: Arnold). *93*

Caston, D. (1982) *Low Cost Aids* (London: AHRTAG). *206*

Cathie, J. (1982) *The Political Economy of Food Aid* (New York: St. Martin's Press). *74*

Chambers, R. (1985) *Rural Development: Putting the Last First* (London: Longman). *38, 67, 68, 119, 269*

Chan, G. H. (1984) 'A Comparative Study of the Development of Social

Welfare Services in the Developing Countries, with Special Reference to Three Chinese Societies: Hong Kong, Singapore and Taiwan', unpublished PhD thesis, University College, Cardiff. *44*

Charvet, J. (1982) *Feminism* (London: Dent). *225, 226*

Chenery, H. B. (1975) 'The structuralist approach to development policy', *American Economic Review 5, Supplement: Papers and Proceedings of the American Economic Association*, p. 310–16. *18*

Chenery, H. B. (1981) *Structural Change and Development Policy* (Oxford: Oxford University Press). *19*

Chenery, H. B. and A. MacEwan (1981) 'Optimal patterns of growth and aid: the case of Pakistan', in H. B. Chenery *Structural Change and Development Policy* (Oxford: Oxford University Press). *20*

Chenery, H. B. and W. J. Raduchel (1981) 'Substitution and structural change', in H. B. Chenery *Structural Change and Development Policy* (Oxford: Oxford University Press). *19, 264*

Chenery, H. B. and A. Strout (1966) 'Foreign assistance and economic development', *American Economic Review*, 56, pp. 679–732. *18*

Chin, F. K. (1984) 'An Evaluation of the Social Insurance Schemes in Malaysia', unpublished MEc(PA) thesis, University of Malaysia. *44*

Chodorov, N. (1979) 'Mothering, male dominance and capitalism', in Z. R. Eisenstein (ed.) *Capitalist Patriarchy and the Case for Socialist Feminism* (New York: Monthly Review Press). *227*

Chodorov, N. (1983) 'Family structure and feminine personality', in M. Z. Rosaldo, and L. Lamphere (eds) *Woman, Culture and Society* Stanford: Stanford University Press). *226*

Chow, N. W. S., A. Y. M. Tang and T. F. Chan (1985) *A Study of the Values, Leisure Behaviour and Misbehaviour of the Youths in Tsuen Wan and Kwai Tuna* (Hong Kong: Tsuen Wan District Board). *186*

Clapham, C. (1985) *Third World Politics: An Introduction* (London: Croom Helm). *271*

Clark, C. and M. Haswell (1971) *The Economics of Subsistence Agriculture* (London: Macmillan). *67*

Clinard, M. B. and D. J. Abbott (1973) *Crime in Developing Countries* (Chichester: John Wiley). *214*

Cochrane, S. (1977) *Can Education Reduce Fertility?* (Washington D.C.: World Bank). *166, 237*

Cochrane S., D. J. O'Hara and J. Leslie. (1980) *The Effects of Education on Health* (Washington D.C.: World Bank). *117, 118*

Coe, R. L. (1973) *The Kenya National Youth Service: a Governmental Response to Young Political Activists* (Ohio: University Centre for International Studies). *216*

Cohen, R. (1979) 'Corruption in Nigeria: a structural approach', in M. U. Ekpo (ed.) (1979a) *Bureaucratic Corruption in Sub-Saharan Africa* (Washington D.C.: University Press of America). *271*

Colclough, C. (1982) 'The impact of primary schooling on economic development: a review of the evidence', *World Development*, 10, pp. 167–85. *152*

Collins, R. (1975) 'A conflict theory of sexual stratification', in H. P.

Dreitze (ed.) *Conflict Sociology* (New York: Academic Press). *228*

Comparative Education Review (1980) 24, Special number on the education of women and related issues. *166*

Conyers, D. (1982) *An Introduction to Social Planning in the Third World* (Chichester: John Wiley). *79*

Coombs, P. H. (1985) *The World Crisis in Education: the View from the Eighties* (Oxford: Oxford University Press). *160, 161, 165, 182, 184, 228*

Cornia, G. A. (1985) 'Farm size, land yield and the agricultural production function: an analysis for fifteen developing countries', *World Development*, 13, pp. 513–34. *69*

Council of Europe (1978) *Population Decline in Europe* (London: Arnold). *246*

Coward, N. (1983) *Patriarchial Precedents* (London: Routledge & Kegan Paul). *225, 229*

Craig, G., N. Derricourt and M. Loney (eds) (1982) *Community Work and the State: Towards a Radical Practice* (London: Routledge & Kegan Paul). *209*

Crooke, P. (1983) 'Popular housing supports', in R. J. Skinner and M. J. Rodell (eds) *Poverty, People and Shelter: Problems of Self-Help Housing in the Third World* (London: Methuen). *101*

Cumper. G. (1983) 'Economic development, health services and health', in K. Lee and A. Mills (eds) *The Economics of Health in Developing Countries* (Oxford: Oxford University Press). *108, 120, 129, 144*

Cumper, G. (1984) *Determinants of Health Levels in Developing Countries* (Letchworth: Research Studies Press).

Cutler, P. (1984) 'The measurement of poverty: a review of attempts to quantify the poor, with special reference to India', *World Development*, 12, pp. 1119–30. *36*

Dahlberg, K. A. (1979) *Beyond the Green Revolution: the Economics and Politics of Global Agricultural Development* (New York: Plenum). *71*

Dakhil, F. H., O. Ural and M. F. Tewfik (1978) *Housing Problems in Developing Countries* (Chichester: John Wiley). *95*

Desai, M. M. and M. D. Khetani (1979) 'Intervention strategies for the aged in India', in M. I. Teicher, U. Thursz and J. L. Vigilante (eds) *Reaching the Aged: Social Services in Forty-four Countries* (Beverley Hills: Sage). *202*

Despres, L. (1967) *Cultural Pluralism and Nationalist Politics in British Guiana* (Chicago: Rand McNally).

Dilnot, A. W., J. A. Kay and C. N. Morris (1984) *The Reform of Social Security* (Oxford: Oxford University Press). *50*

Dix, G. B. (1985) 'The place of shelter in national development', in S. M. Romaya and G. H. Franklin (eds) *Shelter, Services and the Urban Poor. Report of the Third World Planning Seminar* (Cardiff: University of Wales Institute of Science and Technology). *98*

Djamour, J. (1959) *Malay Kinship and Marriage in Singapore*, cited in Binte Abdul Rahman Shamsiah (1981) 'Socialisation of a Malay Child with reference to Child Care Services', unpublished MSc Econ.thesis, University College Cardiff. *189*

Djukanovic, V. and E. P. Mach (1975) *Alternative Approaches to Meeting Basic Health Needs in Developing Countries* (Geneva: World Health Organisation). *130, 131*

Dlamini, N. (1984) 'The Student Guidance Service in the University of Zululand', unpublished MScEcon thesis, University College Cardiff. *189*

Dore, R. (1976) *The Diploma Disease* (Berkeley: University of California Press). *161*

Dore, R. and Z. Mars (eds) (1981) *Community Development* (London: Croom Helm). *208, 212, 268*

Doyal, L. (1979) *The Political Economy of Health* (London: Pluto Press). *146*

Doyal, L. (1983) 'Poverty and disability in the Third World: the crippling effects of underdevelopment', in O. Shirley (ed) *A Cry for Health: Poverty and Disability in the Third World* (Frome: Third World Group for Disabled People). *146, 205*

Drakakis-Smith, D. (1979) 'Low-cost housing provision in the Third World: some theoretical and practical alternatives', in H. G. Murison and J. P. Lea (eds) *Housing in Third World Countries* (London: Macmillan). *87, 93*

Dunhill, P. (1980) 'The provision of pharmaceuticals by appropriate technology', in D. A. J. Tyrrell *et al.* (eds) *More Techniques for Rural Health* (London: Royal Society). *121*

Dunning, J. H. (1981) *International Production and the Multinational Enterprise* (London: Allen & Unwin). *25*

Dwyer, D. J. (1974) 'Attitudes towards spontaneous settlement in Third World cities', in D. J. Dwyer (ed) *The City in The Third World* (London: Macmillan). *89, 90*

Dwyer, D. J. (1975) *People and Housing in Third World Cities* (London: Longman). *93*

Ebrahim, G. J. (1983) 'Nutrition and the prevention of disability', in D. Shirley (ed.) *A Cry for Health: Poverty and Disability in the Third World* (Frome: Third World Group). *127*

Economist Intelligence Unit, (1981) 'Multinationals and world trade', in *Multinational Business*, 4, p. 20. *26*

Egero, B. (1970) 'People and underdevelopment – the example of Tanzania', in L. Bondestam and S. Bergestrom (eds) *Poverty and Population Control* (London: Academic Press). *247*

Eisenstein, Z. (ed.) (1979) *Capitalist Patriarchy and the Case of Socialist Feminism* (New York: Monthly Review Press). *225*

Ekpo, M. U. (ed.) (1979a) *Bureaucratic Corruption in Sub-Saharan Africa* (Washington D.C.: University Press of America). *272*

Ekpo, M. U. (1979b) 'Gift-giving and bureaucratic corruption in Nigeria', in M. U. Ekpo (ed.) (1979a) *Bureaucratic Corruption in Sub-Saharan Africa* (Washington D.C.: University Press of America). *275*

Elliott, C. (1975) *Patterns of Poverty in the Third World* (New York: Praeger). *68, 82*

El Shakhs, S. (1972) 'Development, primacy and systems of cities', *Journal of Developing Areas*, 7, pp. 11–36. *81*

Engels, F. (1884) *The Family, Private Property and the State* (reprinted London: Lawrence & Wishart, 1972). *227*

Epstein, T. S. (1982) *Urban Food Marketing and Third World Rural Development: the Structure of Producer–Seller Markets* (London: Croom Helm). *71*

Esman, M. J. (1978) *Landlessness and Near-Landlessness in Developing Countries* (Ithaca, New York: Cornell University Press). *62, 63, 69, 70, 274*

Etzioni, A. (1976) *Social Problems* (Englewood Cliffs: Prentice Hall). *264*

Evans, D. R. (1981) *The Planning of Non-Formal Education* (Paris: UNESCO). *163, 164, 175*

Evens, P. (1977) *Community Work: Theory and Practice* (Oxford: Alastair Sharnach). *208*

Fanon, F. (1980) *The Wretched of the Earth* (Harmondsworth: Penguin). *102, 171*

Fawcett, J. T., S.-E. Khoo and Smith (1984) *Women in the Cities of Asia: Migration and Urban Adaptation* (Boulder, Colorado: Westview Press). *168, 235, 236*

Feder, E. (1970) 'Counterreform', in R. Stavenhagen (ed.) *Agrarian Problems and Peasant Movements in Latin-America* (New York: Doubleday, Anchor Books). *62*

Fei, J. C. H., G. Ranis and W. Y. K. Shirley (1980) *Growth with Equity: the Taiwan Case* (Oxford: Oxford University Press). *65*

Fiji, Government of (1969) *Report of the Social Welfare Department* (Suva: Social Welfare Department, Government of Fiji). *191*

Fiji, Government of (1980) *Eighth Development Plan Vol. 1* (Suva: Central Planning Office, Government of Fiji). *167, 192*

Firestone, S. (1971) *The Dialect of Sex* (New York: Bantam Books). *225*

Foster, P. (1965) *Education and Social Change in Ghana* (London: Routledge & Kegan Paul). *180*

Foster, P. (1966) 'The vocational school fallacy in development policy', in C. A. Anderson and M. J. Bowman (eds) *Education and Economic Development* (London: Tavistock). *178*

Foster, P. (1975) 'Dilemmas of educational development', *Comparative Education Review*, 19, pp. 375ff *172, 181, 185, 186*

Foster, P. and Sheffield, J. R. (1973) general introduction to P. Foster and J. R. Sheffield (eds) *Education and Rural Development: World Yearbook of Education 1974*, p. 7 (London: Evans Bros). *178*

Freedman, R. (1971) *Marx on Economics*, (Harmondsworth: Penguin).

Freire, P. (1972) *Pedagogy of the Oppressed* (London: Sheen and Ward). *171, 172*

Friedan, B. (1965) *The Feminine Mystique* (Harmondsworth: Penguin). *225, 226*

Gershenberg, I. (1987) 'The training and spread of managerial know-how, a comparative analysis of multinational and other firms in Kenya', *World Development*, 15, pp. 931–9. *29*

Gilbert, A. (1977) *Latin American Development: a Geographical Perspective* (London: Penguin). *58, 59, 61, 62*

Gilbert, A. and P. Ward (1984) 'Community action by the urban poor:

democratic involvement, community self-help, or a means of social control', *World Development*, 12, pp. 769–82. *209*

Gilbert, A. and P. M. Ward (1985) *Housing, the State and the Poor: Practice in Three Latin American Cities* (Cambridge: Cambridge University Press). *91, 92, 101, 102*

Gish, O. (1975) *Planning the Health Sector: the Tanzanian Experience* (London: Croom Helm). *145*

Golladay F. L. and C. K. Koch-Weser (1977) 'New policies for rural health', in D. A. J. Tyrrell *et al.* (ed.) *Technologies for Rural Health* (London: The Royal Society). *143*

Goode, J. William (1968) 'The role of the family in industrialization', in R. F. Winch and L. W. Goodman (eds) *Selected Studies in Marriage and the Family* (New York: Holt, Rinehart & Winston). *38*

Gotip, G. E. (1983) 'Patterns of Family Structure and Function in Britain and Nigeria with reference to social work and non-social work management of family problems', unpublished MScEcon thesis, University College Cardiff. *202*

Gough, I. (1982) *The Political Economy of the Welfare State* (London: Macmillan). *282*

Graaf, J. F. de V. (1982) *Youth Movements in Developing Countries* (Manchester: Manchester Monographs). *216, 217, 218*

Gramsci, A. (1979) *Letters from Prison* (London: Quartet).

Greenland, D. J. (1975) 'Bringing the Green Revolution to the shifting cultivator', *Science*, 190, pp. 841ff. *67*

Griffin, K. (1981) *Land Concentration and Rural Poverty* (London: Macmillan). *59*

Griffin, K. and A. R. Khan (1982) 'Poverty in the Third World: ugly facts and fancy models', in H. Alavi and T. Shanin (eds) *Sociology of Developing Societies* (London: Macmillan). *5, 36*

Griffiths, A. and M. Mills (1983) 'Health sector financing and expenditure surveys', in K. Lee and A. Mills (eds) *The Economics of Health in Developing Countries* (Oxford: Oxford University Press). *145*

Guhr, I. (1983) 'Co-operatives in state housing programmes – an alternative for low income groups', in R. J. Skinner and M. J. Rodell (eds) *Poverty, People and Shelter: Problems of Self-Help Housing in the Third World* (London: Methuen). *97*

Hague, R. and M. Harrop (1987) *Comparative Government and Politics: An Introduction* (Basingstoke: Macmillan). *260, 270*

Hakim, C. (1982) 'The social consequences of high unemployment', *Journal of Social Policy*, 11, pp. 433–67.

Hall, B. and A. Dodds (1974) *Voices For Development: Tanzania Radio Study Group Campaigns* (Cambridge: International Extension College). *164*

Hammond, D. and A. Jablow (1976) *Women in Cultures of the World* (Menlo Park, California: Cummings Publications). *230*

Hanley, E. R. (1975) 'Rice, politics and development in Guyana', in I. Oxaal *et al.* (eds) *Beyond the Sociology of Development* (London: Routledge & Kegan Paul). *272*

Hardiman, M. and J. Midgley (1982) *The Social Dimensions of Development* (Chichester: John Wiley).

Hardoy, J. E. and D. Satterthwaite (1981) *Shelter: Need and Response* (Chichester: John Wiley). *56, 86*

Harpham, T., P. Vaughan and S. Rifkin (1985) *Health and the Urban Poor* (London: Evaluation & Planning Centre, London School of Hygiene & Tropical Medicine). *118, 135*

Henderson, P., D. Jones and D. Thomas (1980) *The Boundaries of Change in Community Work* (London: Allen & Unwin). *208*

Hereford, B. (n.d.) *Food Production and Agriculture in Africa: Information Pack on the Brandt Report* (Oxford: Oxfam). *68*

Heyzer, N. (1982) 'From rural subsistence to an industrial peripheral work force: an examination of female Malaysian migrants and capital accumulation in Singapore', in L. Beneria (ed.) *Women in Development* (New York: Praeger).

HMSO (1967) *Children and Their Primary Schools (Plowden Report)* (London: HMSO). *156*

Hogg, C. (1983) 'Self-reliance through appropriate technology', in O. Shirley (ed.) *A Cry for Health: Poverty and Disability in the Third World* (Frome: Third World Group for Disabled People). *206*

Hoogvelt, A. M. M. (1983) *The Third World in Global Development* (London: Macmillan). *26*

Huque, A. (1982) *The Myth of Self-Help Housing* (Stockholm: Royal Institute of Technology). *89, 90, 91, 93*

Hutton, C. and R. Cohen (1975) 'African peasants and resistance to change', in A. Oxaal, T. Barnett and D. Booth (1975) *Beyond the Sociology of Development* (London: Routledge & Kegan Paul). *66*

Hyden, G. (1980) *Beyond Ujaama in Tanzania* (London: Heinemann). *57, 66, 68, 82, 192, 208, 210, 270*

Illich, I. (1971) *Deschooling Society* (London: Calder & Boyars). *175*

International Labour Office (1984) *World Labour Report, Vol. 1* (1985) *Vol. 2* (Geneva: ILO). *224, 234*

Jelliffe, D. (1970) 'Paediatrics', in M. King (ed.) *Medical Care in Developing Countries* (Oxford: Oxford University Press). *112*

Jenkins, M. (1981) 'Social security trends in the English-speaking Caribbean', *International Labour Review*, 120, pp. 631ff. *43, 48*

Jere, H. (1984) 'Lisaka: local participation in planning and decision-making', in G. K. Payne (ed.) *Low Income Housing in the Developing World* (Chichester: John Wiley). *96*

Johnston, M. (1983) 'The ant and the elephant: voluntary agencies and government health programmes in Indonesia', in D. Morley, J. Rohde and G. Williams (eds) *Practising Health for All* (Oxford: Oxford University Press). *141*

Jolly, R. (1982) 'The development decades: promises, performance and proposals', in A. Jennings and T. G. Weiss (eds) *The Challenge of Development in the Eighties: Our Response* (Oxford: Pergamon).

Jolly, R. *et al* (1970) 'The economy of a District Hospital', in M. King (ed.) *Medical Care in Developing Countries* (Oxford: Oxford University Press). *137, 138*

Jolly, R. and M. King (1970) 'The organisation of health services', in M. King (ed.) *Medical Care in Developing Countries* (Oxford: Oxford University Press). *141*

Jones, E. (1966) *Towns and Cities* (Oxford: Oxford University Press). *81*

Jones, H. (1965) 'Punishment and social values', in T. Grygier, H. Jones and J.C. Spencer (eds) *Criminology in Transition* (London: Tavistock). *40*

Jones, H. (1981) *Crime, Race and Culture: a Study in a Developing Country* (Chichester: John Wiley). *40, 83, 169*

Joseph, Sir K. (1972) 'The cycle of deprivation', in E. Butterworth and R. Holman (eds) (1977) *Social Welfare in Modern Britain* (London: Fontana). *41*

Kadzamira, E. J. (1975) 'Traditional and Modern Patterns of Welfare in Malawi', unpublished MscEcon thesis, University College Cardiff. *190, 198*

Kahama, C. G., L. Matiyamkono and S. Wells (1986) *The Challenge for Tanzania's Economy* (London: James Curry). *57*

Kaim-Caudle, P. (1983) *Social Insurance in Taiwan and the Federal Republic of Germany: a Comparative Study* (Taipei: National Insurance Association of Republic of China). *44*

Kaplan, F. M. and J. M. Sobin (1982) *Encyclopedia of China Today* (London: Macmillan). *133, 239*

Kaye, B. (1974) 'Some residents of Upper Nankin Street, Singapore', in D.J. Dwyer (ed.) *The City in the Third World* (London: Macmillan). *86*

Kefauver E. (1951) *Crime in America* (New York: Doubleday). *271*

Kelly, G. (1984) 'Women's access to education in the Third World', in S. Acker (ed.) *Women and Education. Year Book of Education, 1984* (London: Kogan Page). *238*

Kennedy, R. E. Jr (1973) *The Irish* (London: University of California Press). *250*

Kenya, Government of (1971) *How to Start a Village Polytechnic* (Nairobi: Ministry of Cooperatives & Social Services). *176*

Keohane, N. O., M. Z. Rosaldo and B. C. Gelpi (eds) (1982) *Feminist Theory: a Critique of Ideology* (Brighton: Harvester Press).

Killick, T. (1981) *Policy Economics* (London: Heinemann). *249*

King, M. (ed.) (1970) *Medical Care in Developing Countries* (Oxford: Oxford University Press).

Kirke, J. (1985) 'Urban services and infrastructure for shelter', in S.M. Romaya and G. H. Franklin (eds) *Shelter, Services and the Urban Poor. Report of the Third World Planning Seminar* (Cardiff: University of Wales Institute of Science and Technology). *95, 97*

Klouda, A. (1983) ' "Prevention" is more costly than "cure": health problems for Tanzania, 1971–1981', in D. Morley, J. Rohde and G. Williams (eds) *Practising Health for All* (Oxford: Oxford University Press). *125, 142*

Koedt, A. de, E. Levine and A. Rapone (1973a) *Radical Feminism* (New York: Quadrangle). *225*

Koedt, A. de, (1973b) 'Lesbianism and feminism', in A. de Koedt, E. Levine and A. Rapone (eds) (1973a) *Radical Feminism* (New York: Quadrangle). *229*

Kosinski, L. (1970) *The Population of Europe* (London: Longman). *242*

Kumar, K. (ed.) (1980) *Transnational Corporations: Their Impact on Third World Societies and Cultures* (Boulder, Colorado: Westview Press). *25*

Lall, S. (1980) *The Multinational Corporation* (London: Macmillan). *29*

Lambo, A. (1970) 'The Village of Aro', in M. King (ed.) *Medical Care in Developing Countries* (Oxford: Oxford University Press). *139*

Lappé, F. M. and J. Collins (1979) *Food First: Beyond the Myth of Scarcity* (New York: Ballantine Books). *72, 73, 125*

Lea, J. (1979) 'Self-help and autonomy in housing: theoretical critics and empirical investigators', in H. S. Murison and J. P. Lea (eds) *Housing in Third World Countries* (London: Macmillan). *94*

Lee, K. (1983a) 'Resources and costs in primary health care', in K. Lee and A. Mills (eds) *The Economics of Health in Developing Countries* (Oxford: Oxford University Press). *131, 143*

Lee, K. and A. Mills (eds) (1983) *The Economics of Health in Developing Countries* (Oxford: Oxford University Press).

Lee, R. P. L. (1981) 'Incongruence of legal codes and folk norms', in R. P. L. Lee (ed.) (1981) *Corruption and its Control in Hong Kong* (Hong Kong: Chinese University). *275*

Lee, V. (1973) *Social Relations and Language* (London: Open University). *180*

Leeds, A. (1981) 'Lower-income urban settlement types: processes, structures, policies', in UN Centre for Human Settlements (Habitat), *The Residential Circumstances of the Urban Poor in Developing Countries* (New York: Praeger). *102*

Leiner, M. (1975) 'Cuba: combining schooling with practical experience', in M. Ahmed and P.H. Combs (ed.) *Education for Rural Development: Case Studies for Planners* (New York: Praeger). *176*

Lele, U. (1975) *The Design of Rural Development: Lessons from Africa* (Baltimore: Johns Hopkins University Press). *67*

Lenin, V. I. (1918) *State and Revolution* (reprinted London: Lawrence & Wishart, 1941). *282*

Leslie, J. and D. I. Jamison (1980) 'Policy implications of instructional technology: cost and effectiveness', in J. Simmons (ed.) *The Education Dilemma: Policy Issues for Developing Countries in the 1980s* (Oxford: Pergamon Press). *162, 164*

Lewis, O. (1967) *La Vida* (London: Secker & Warburg). *40, 101*

Lewis, W. A. (1954) 'Capital accumulation and growth. Economic development with unlimited supplies of labour', *Manchester School of Economic and Social Studies*, 22, pp. 139–91. *12*

Lindblom, C. (1979) 'Still muddling, not yet through', *Public Administration Review*, 39, pp. 517–26. *263*

Linsky, A. S. (1969) 'Some generalisations concerning Primate Cities', in G. Breese (ed.) *The City in Newly Developing Countries* (Englewood Cliffs: Prentice Hall). *81*

Lipsey, R. G. and K. Lancaster (1956–7) 'The general theory of second-best', *Review of Economic Studies*, 24, pp. 11–32. *17*

Lipton, M. (1977) *Why Poor People Stay Poor: A Study of Urban Bias in World Development* (London: Temple Smith). *142*

Little, I. M. D. (1982) *Economic Development* (New York: Basic Books). *3, 25, 35, 63, 69, 84*

Little, V. C. (1979) 'For the elderly: an overview of services in industrially developed and developing countries', in M. I. Teicher, D. Thursz and J. L. Vigilante (eds) *Reaching the Aged: Social Services in Forty-Four Countries* (Berkeley Hills: Sage). *202, 203*

Lowie, R. H. (1953) *Primitive Society* (London: Routledge & Kegan Paul). *250*

Mabogunje, A. L. (1980) *The Development Process* (London: Hutchinson). *27, 57, 81, 85*

Mabogunje, A. L., J. E. Hardoy and R. P. Misra (1978) *Shelter Provision in Developing Countries* (Chichester: John Wiley). *56, 85, 86, 95*

McKinlay, J. B. (ed.) (1984) *Issues in the Political Economy of Health Care* (London: Tavistock). *146*

MacKinnon, C. A. (1982) 'Feminism, Marxist method and the state: an agenda for theory', in N. O. Keohane, M. Z. Rosaldo and B. C. Gelpi (eds) *Feminist Theory: a Critique of Ideology* (Brighton: Harvester Press). *226*

McLachlan, G. and A. Maynard (eds) (1982) *The Public/Private Mix for Health* (London: Nuffield Provincial Hospitals Trust). *144*

McPherson, S. (1982) *Social Policy in the Third World* (Brighton: Wheatsheaf Books).

McPherson, S. and J. Midgley (1987) *Comparative Social Policy and the Third World* (Brighton: Wheatsheaf Books).

Malthus, T. R. (1798) *Essay on the Principles of Population* (reprinted London: Macmillan, 1968). *72, 242, 243, 245, 257*

Marnham, P. (1979) *Nomads of the Sahel* (London: Minority Rights Group). *73*

Marris, P. H. (1981) 'Meaning of slums, and patterns of change', in United Nations Centre for Human Settlements (1981) *The Residential Circumstances of the Urban Poor in Developing Countries* (New York: Praeger). *89, 99*

Marris, P. H. and A. Somerset (1971) *African Businessmen: a Study of Entrepreneurship and Development* (London: Routledge & Kegan Paul). *99*

Martin, R. J. (1983) 'Upgrading', in R. J. Skinner and M. J. Rodell (eds) *People, Poverty and Shelter: Problems of Self-Help housing in the Third World* (London: Methuen). *95*

Marx, K. (1852) *The Eighteenth Brumaire of Louis Bonaparte*, reprinted 1979, in *Collected Works of Marx and Engels*, Vol. 11, pp. 99ff (London: Lawrence & Wishart). *60*

Marx, K. (1859) Preface to: *A Contribution to the Critique of Political Economy*, reprinted 1918 (Chicago: C. H. Kerr & Co). *226*

Marx, K. (1867) *Capital Vol. 1*, reprinted 1976 (Harmondsworth: Penguin). *231*

Marx, K. and F. Engels (1846) *The German Ideology*, reprinted 1976, in *Collected Works of Marx and Engels*, Vol. 5, p. 52 (London: Lawrence & Wishart). *215*

Marx, K. and F. Engels (1888) *Manifesto of the Communist Party*, reprinted in L. S. Feuer (ed.) (1969) *Marx and Engels: Basic Writings* (Harmondsworth: Penguin). *22, 31*

Maxwell, S. J. and H. W. Singer (1978) 'Food aid and developing countries: a survey', *World Development*, 7, pp. 225–47. *73, 74*

Mayer, A. *et al.* (1958) *Pilot Project, India* (Berkeley: University of California Press). *211*

Medawar, C. (1979) *Insult or Injury* (London: Social Audit). *120, 127*

Medawar, C. (1983) 'The disabled consumer: how multinational corporations affect the Third World', in O. Shirley (ed.) *A Cry for Health: Poverty and Disability in the Third World* (Frome: Third World Group for Disabled People). *120, 121*

Mehta, S. R. (1984) *Rural Development: Policies and Programmes* (New Delhi: Sage). *63, 65, 66, 69, 210, 266, 268, 270*

Mencher, S. (1967) 'The problem of measuring poverty', reprinted in J. L. and J. K. Roach (eds) (1972) *Poverty* (Harmondsworth: Penguin). *36, 37*

Midgley, J. (1981) *Professional Imperialism: Social Work in the Third World* (London: Heinemann). *194, 211*

Midgley, J. (1984) *Social Security, Inequality and the Third World* (Chichester: John Wiley). *43*

Millet, K. (1971) *Sexual Politics* (New York: Avon Books). *225*

Mills, A. (1983) 'Economic aspects of health insurance', in K. Lee and A. Mills (eds) *The Economics of Health in Developing Countries* (Oxford: Oxford University Press). *143, 144*

Mishra, R. (1973) 'Welfare and industrial man: a study of welfare in Western industrial societies', *Sociological Review*, 21, pp. 535–60. *7*

Mishra, R. (1976) 'Convergence theory and social change: the development of welfare in Britain and the Soviet Union', *Comparative Studies in Sociology and History*, 18, pp. 28–63. *7*

Molyneux, M. (1984) 'Strategies for the emancipation of women in Third World socialist countries', in S. Acker (ed.) *Education and Women, Year Book of Education, 1984* (New York: Kogan Page). *239*

Moore, B. (1967) *Social Origins of Dictatorship and Democracy* (London: Allen Lane). *210*

Morgan, L. H. (1877) *Ancient Society* (London: Macmillan, reprinted 1978, Palo Alto: New York Labor News). *227*

Morley, D., J. Rohde and G. Williams (eds) (1983) *Practising Health for All* (Oxford: Oxford University Press). *107, 130, 133*

Morley, P. and R. Wallis (eds) (1978) *Culture and Curing* (London: Peter Owen). *133*

Morrison, D. (1976) *Education and Politics in Africa: the Tanzanian Case* (London: Hurst). *218*

Morrow, R. H. (1983) 'A P.H.C. policy for Ghana', in D. Morley, J. Rohde and G. Williams (1983) *Practising Health for all* (Oxford: Oxford University Press). *112*

Mouton, P. (1975) *Social Security in Africa* (Geneva: International Labour Office). *47*

Muller, M. (1982) *The Health of Nations* (London: Faber & Faber). *120*

Mutziwa-Mangiza, N. D. (1985) 'Post-independence low-income policies in Zimbabwe: a preliminary appraisal of affordability', in S. M. Romaya and G. H. Franklin (eds) *Shelter, Services and the Urban Poor. Report of the Third World Planning Seminar* (Cardiff: University of Wales Institute of Science and Technology). *97, 98*

Myrdal, G. (1956) cited in I. M. D. Little (1982) *Economic Development* (New York: Basic Books) p. 73. *276*

Navarro, V. (1982a) *Imperialism, Health and Medicine* (London: Pluto Press).

Navarro V. (1982b) 'The underdevelopment of health, or the health of underdevelopment', in V. Navarro (1982a) *Imperialism, Health and Medicine* (London: Pluto Press). *122*

Nelson, G. O. (1981a) 'Improving the effectiveness of food aid', in G. O. Nelson *et al.* (1981) *Food Aid and Development* (New York: Agricultural Development Council). *74*

Nelson, G. O. (1981b) 'Macro-economic dimensions of food aid', in G. O. Nelson *et al.* (1981) *Food Aid and Development* (New York: Agricultural Development Council). *74*

Nelson, G. O. *et al.* (1981c) *Food Aid and Development* (New York: Agricultural Development Council).

Nelson, J. M. (1979) *Access to Power*, (Princeton, N.J., Princeton University Press). *90*

Newell, K. W. (1975) *Health by the People* (Geneva: World Health Organisation). *130, 132*

Noor, A. (1981) *Education and Basic Human Needs*, World Bank Staff Working Paper No. 450 (Washington: World Bank). *173, 177, 182*

Nortman, D. L. (1982) *Population and Family Planning Programmes: a Compendium of Data through 1981* (New York: The Population Council). *248, 249, 256*

Nortman, D. L. (1985) *Population and Family Planning Programmes: a Compendium of Data through 1983* (New York: The Population Council). *247, 248, 249*

Nyerere, J. K. (1968) *Freedom and Socialism: Uhuru na Ujaama* (Nairobi: Oxford University Press). *57*

Nyerere, J. K. (1977) *The Arusha Declaration: the Years After* (Dar es Salaam: The Government Printer). *57*

Odongo, J. (1979) 'Housing deficit in cities of the Third World: fact or fiction?' in H. S. Murison and J. P. Lea (eds) *Housing in Third World Countries* (London: Macmillan). *87*

O'Kelly, C. G. (1980) *Women and Men in Society* (New York: Van Nostrand). *232*

O'Laughlin, B. (1983) 'Mediation of contradiction: why Mbum women do not eat chicken', in M. Z. Rosaldo and L. Lamphers (eds) *Woman, Culture and Society* (Stamford: Stamford University Press). *232*

Oram, P., J. Zapata, G. Alibaruhu and R. Shyamal (1979) *Investment and Input Requirements for Accelerating Food Production in Low Income Countries by 1990* (Washington DC: International Food Policy Research Institute). *72, 76*

Park, S. I. (1988) 'Labour issues in Korea's future', *World Development*, 16, pp. 99–119. *153*

Parthasarati, S. (1978) 'Social Security as a mobilizer of savings: the experience of Malaysia', *International Social Security Association Review*, 19. *47*

Payne, G. K. (ed.) (1984) *Low Income Housing in the Developing World* (Chichester: John Wiley). *96*

Pearson, G. (1973) 'Social work as the privatised solution of public ills', *British Journal of Social Work*, 3, pp. 209–27. *190*

Pearson, G. P. (1974) 'Brigades in Botswana, their national impact', in J. R. C. Sheffield (ed.) *Road to the Village* (New York: African American Institute). *218*

Plaschaert, S. R. F. (1979) *Transfer Pricing and Multinational Corporations* (Farnborough, Hants.: Saxon House). *29*

PNG (Papua New Guinea) (1973) *Organic Law on the Duties and Responsibilities of Leadership*, revised edition of the *Laws of Papua New Guinea*, Chapter 1, pp. 161–75. *277*

Polger, S. and J. F. Marshall (1978) The search for culturally acceptable fertility regulation methods', in M. H. Logan and E. E. Hunt Jr (eds) *Health and the Human Condition: Perspectives on Medical Anthropology*, (N. Scitnate, Mass.: Duxbury Press). *254*

Portes, A., S. Blitzer and J. Curtis (1986) 'The urban informal sector in Uruguay: its external structure, characteristics and effects', *World Development*, 14, pp. 727–41. *99*

Preston, R. (1984) 'Dependency perspectives on the impact of education on family livelihood strategies in rural areas of Andean America', in K. Watson (ed.) *Dependence and Interdependence in Education* (London: Croom Helm). *158*

Pritchard, C. and R. Taylor (1978) *Social Work: Reform or Revolution* (London: Routledge & Kegan Paul). *282*

Psacharopoulos, G. (1973) *Returns to Education: an International Comparison* (Amsterdam: Elsevier Scientific Publishing Co). *153, 155*

Psacharopoulos, G. (1980) *Higher Education in Developing Countries: a Cost-Benefit Analysis* (Washington D.C.: World Bank). *153*

Psacharopoulos, G. (1981) 'Returns to education: an updated international comparison', *Comparative Education Review*, 17, pp. 321–41. *154, 155, 159, 163*

Psacharopoulos, G. (1982) 'The economics of higher education in developing countries', *Comparative Education Review*, 26, pp. 139–59. *154*

Psacharopoulos, G. and Sanyal, B. C. (1981) *Higher Education and Employment: the IIEP Experience in Five Less Developed Countries* (Paris: UNESCO). *162*

Quibria, M. G. (1982) 'An analytical defence of basic needs: the optimal savings perspective', *World Development*, 10, pp. 285–91. *7*

Randall, V. (ed.) (1988) *Political Parties in the Third World* (London: Sage).

Ratcliffe, J. (1983) 'Social justice and the demographic transition lessons from India's Kerala state', in D. Morley, J. Rohde and G. Williams. (eds) *Practising Health for All* (Oxford: Oxford University Press). *108*

Redfield, R. and Singer, M. B. (1954) *The Cultural Role of Cities* (New York: Bobbs-Merrill). *79*

Reimer, E. (1971) *School is Dead: an Essay on Alternatives in Education* (Harmondsworth: Penguin). *175*

Reviglio, F. (1967) 'Social Security, a means of saving mobilisation for economic development', *I.M.F. Staff Papers* (Washington: I.M.F.) cited in P. Mouton (1975) *Social Security in Africa* (Geneva: International Labour Office) p.104.

Reynolds, L. G. (1985) *Economic Growth in the Third World, 1850–1980* (New Haven: Yale University Press). *17, 53, 63, 153, 257*

Rich, A. (1981) *Compulsory Heterosexuality and Lesbian Existence* (London: Onlywoman Press). *229*

Richards, P. and M. Leonor (1981) *Education and Income Distribution in Asia* (London: Croom Helm). *155, 156, 163*

Richmond, M. (1917) *Social Diagnosis* (New York: Russell Sage). *192*

Rimlinger, G. V. (1971) *Welfare Policy and Industrialisation in Europe, America and Russia* (Chichester: John Wiley). *7*

Roberts, B. (1982) 'Cities in developing societies', in H. Alavi and T. Shanin (eds) *Sociology of 'Developing Societies'* (London: Macmillan). *22, 82, 102, 103*

Rodell, M. J. (1983) 'Upgrading', in R. J. Skinner and M. J. Rodell (eds) *Poverty, People and Shelter: Problems of Self-Help Housing in the Third World* (London: Methuen). *96, 97*

Rogers, B. (1980) *The Domestication of Women* (London: Kogan Page). *66, 223, 234, 237, 238, 253*

Rohde, J. (1983) 'Health for all in China: principles and relevance for other countries', in D. Morley, J. Rohde and G. Williams (eds) *Practising Health for All* (Oxford: Oxford University Press). *133, 134, 266*

Roosens, E. (1979) *Mental Patients in Town Life. Geel – Europe's First Therapeutic Community* (Beverley Hills, California: Sage). *140*

Rosaldo, M.Z. (1983) 'Woman, culture and society: an overview', in M. Z. Rosaldo and L. Lamphere (eds) *Woman, Culture and Society* (Stanford: Stanford University Press). *226, 227*

Rosaldo, M. Z. and L. Lamphere (eds) (1983) *Woman, Culture and Society* (Stanford: Stanford University Press).

Rowntree, B. S. (1901) *Poverty: a Study of Town Life* (London: Macmillan). *36*

Rowntree, B. S. (1918) *Human Needs of Labour* (reprinted 1937, London: Longmans Green). *36*

Roxborough, I. (1979) *Theories of Underdevelopment* (London: Macmillan). *23, 31*

312   *References and Author Index*

Ruttan, W. D. (1984) 'Integrated rural development programmes: a historical perspective', *World Development*, 12, pp. 393–401. *54, 211, 266, 267*

Sacks, K. (1983) 'Engels revisited: women, the organisation of production and private property', in M. Z. Rosaldo and L. Lamphere (eds) *Woman, Culture and Society* (Stanford: Stanford University Press). *223, 231*

Salloway, J. C. (1982) *Health Care Delivery Systems* (Boulder, Colorado: Westview Press). *142, 143, 144*

Sanday, P. (1983) 'Female status in the public domain', in M. Z. Rosaldo and L. Lamphere (eds) *Woman, Culture and Society* (Stanford: Stanford University Press). *227*

Sanders, D. (1985) *The Struggle for Health: Medicine and the politics of Underdevelopment* (London: Macmillan). *111, 121*

Schuh, C. E. (1981) 'Food aid and human capital formation', in G. O. Nelson *et al.* (1981c) *Food Aid and Development* (New York: Agricultural Development Council). *74*

Schwerdtfeger, F. W. (1982) *Housing in African Cities* (Chichester: John Wiley). *87*

Scott, J. C. (1972) *Comparative Political Corruption* (Englewood Cliffs: Prentice Hall). *275*

Scott, J. C. (1979a) 'Analysis of corruption in developing nations', in M. U. Ekpo (ed.) (1979a) *Bureaucratic Corruption in Sub-Saharan Africa* (Washington DC: University Press of America). *275*

Scott, J. C. (1979b) 'Corruption, machine politics and social change', in M. U. Ekpo (1979a) *Bureaucratic Corruption in Sub-Saharan Africa* (Washington DC: University Press of America). *271*

Scott W. (1981) *Concepts and Measurement of Poverty* (Geneva: United Nations Research Institute of Social Development). *36*

Seers D. (1969) 'The meaning of development', *International Development Review*, 2–6. *3*

Shah, K. (1984) 'People's participation in housing action: meaning, scope and strategy', in G. K. Payne (ed.) *Low Income Housing in the Developing World* (Chichester: John Wiley). *96*

Shamsiah, A. R. (1981) 'Socialisation of a Malay Child, with reference to Child Care Services', unpublished MScEcon thesis, University College Cardiff. *126, 189, 198*

Shepperdson, M. (1985) *The Political Ecomomy of Health in India* (Swansea: University College Centre for Development Studies). *121, 133, 146*

Shorter, A. (1974) *East African Society* (London: Routledge & Kegan Paul). *250*

Sidel, V. W. and R. (1975) 'The health care delivery system of the People's Republic of China', in K. W. Newell (ed.) *Health by the People* (Geneva: World Health Organisation). *133*

Simpkins, T. (1977) *Non-Formal Education and Development* (Manchester: Manchester Monographs). *175, 183*

Simmons, J. (ed.) (1980) *The Education Dilemma: Policy Issues for Developing Countries in the 1980s* (Oxford: Pergamon Press). *185*

Simmons J. and L. Alexander (1980) 'Factors which produce school achievement in developing countries: a review of the research', in J. Simmons (ed.) *The Education Dilemma: Policy Issues for Developing Countries in the 1980s* (Oxford: Pergamon Press). *163*

Simon, H. (1983) *Reason in Human Affairs* (Oxford: Blackwell). *263*

Singh, S. P. (1978) *Underdevelopment to Developing Economies* (Oxford: Oxford University Press). *12*

Skeet, M. (1978) 'The experience of the Third World', in M. Skeet and K. Elliott (eds) *Health Auxiliaries and the Health Team* (London: Croom Helm). *134, 266*

Skeet, M. and K. Elliott (eds) (1978) *Health Auxiliaries and the Health Team* (London: Croom Helm). *132*

Smith, M. G. (1960) 'Social and cultural pluralism', in V. Rubin (ed.) *Social and Cultural Pluralism in the West Indies: Annals of the New York Academy of Science*, 83, pp. 753–77.

Standing G. (1981) 'The notion of voluntary unemployment', *International Labour Review*, 120, pp. 563ff. *39, 47, 99*

Steffens, J. L. (1904) *The Shame of the Cities* (New York: McClure and Philips). *271*

Stewart, F. (1985) *Planning to Meet Basic Needs* (London: Macmillan).

Stokes, C. J. (1962) 'A theory of slums', *Land Economics*, 38, pp. 187–97. *85*

Stone, C. (1983) *Democracy and Clientelism in Jamaica* (New Brunswick: Transaction Books). *270*

Streeten, P. *et al.* (1981) *First Things First: Meeting Basic Human Needs in Developing Countries* (Oxford: Oxford University Press). *7*

Streeten, P. (1984) 'Basic needs: some unsettled questions', *World Development*, 12, pp. 937ff.

Sudaprasert, K., V. Tunsiri and T. N. Chau (1980) 'Regional disparities in the development of education in Thailand', in G. Carron and T. N. Chau (eds) *Regional Disparities in Educational Development: Diagnosis and Policies for Reduction* (Paris: UNESCO). *159*

Superlan, P. and H. Sigit (1980) *Culture and Fertility: the Case of Indonesia* (Singapore: Institute of S.E. Asian Studies). *237*

Taub, R. P. (1969) *Bureaucrats under Stress: Administrators and Administration in an Indian State* (Berkeley: University of California). *275*

Tawney, R. H. *Equality* (London: George Allen & Unwin). *156*

Taylor, A. (1981) 'Mass education North–South – where next?', in Roger M. Garrett (ed.) *North–South Debate: the Educational Implications of the Brandt Report* (Windsor: NFER–Nelson). *160*

Taylor, P. (1984) *The Smoke Ring* (London: Bodley Head). *116*

Thrasher, F. M. (1937) *The Gang* (Chicago: Chicago University Press). *170*

Titmuss, R. M. (1963) *Essays on the Welfare State* (London: George Allen & Unwin).

Titmuss, R. M. (1968) *Commitment to Welfare* (London: George Allen & Unwin). *143*

Titmuss, R. M. and B. Abel-Smith (1968) *Social Policies and Population Growth in Mauritius* (London: Case). *255*

314   *References and Author Index*

Tordoff, W. (1988) 'Political parties in Zambia', in V. Randall (ed.) *Political Parties in the Third World* (London: Sage) pp. 7ff. *268, 270*
Townsend, P. (1979) *Poverty in the United Kingdom* (Harmondsworth: Penguin). *37*
Turner, J. F. C. (1967) 'Barriers and channels for housing development in modernising countries', *Journal American Institute of Planners*, 33, pp. 167–81. *85*
Turner, J. F. C. (1968a) 'Housing priorities, settlement patterns and urban development in modernising countries', *Journal American Institute of Planners*, 34, pp. 354–63. *91*
Turner, J. F. C. (1968b) 'The squatter settlement: architecture that works', *Architectural Design*, 38, pp. 335–60. *95, 96*
Turner, J. F. C. (1969) 'Uncontrolled urban settlement problems and policies', in G. Breese (eds) *The City in Newly Developing Countries* (Englewood Cliffs: Prentice-Hall). *90, 95*
Turner, J. F. C. (1976) *Housing by People, Towards Autonomy in Building Environments* (Salem, N.H.: Marion Boyars).
Turner, J. F. C. (1982) 'Issues in self-help and self-management housing', in P. M. Ward (ed.) *Self-Help Housing: a Critique* (London: Mansell Publishing Co).
Tym, R. (1985) 'The financing and affordability of shelter', in S.M. Romaya and G. H. Franklin (eds) *Shelter, Services and the Urban Poor, Report of the Third World Planning Seminar* (Cardiff: University of Wales Institute of Science and Technology). *98*
UNCTAD (United Nations Conference on Trade and Development (1985) *The Least Developed Countries: 1985 Report* (Geneva: UNCTAD) *25*
UNESCO/UNDP (1976) *The Experimental World Literacy Programme: a Critical Assessment* (Paris: UNESCO). *178, 179*
UNESCO (1977) *Development of School Enrolment: World and Regional Statistical Trends and Projections* (Paris: UNESCO). *151*
UNESCO (1978) *Estimates and Projections of Illiteracy* (Paris: UNESCO).
UNESCO (1980) *Literacy 1972–6* (Paris: UNESCO). *178*
UNESCO (1982) *Employment-Orientated National Youth Programmes in Africa* (Paris: UNESCO). *219*
UNESCO (1983) *Trends and Projections of Enrolment by Level of Education and by Age: 1960–2000 (as assessed in 1982)* (Paris: UNESCO). *150, 151, 161*
UNESCO (1984a) *Women in the Villages, Men in the Towns* (Paris: UNESCO). *83*
UNESCO (1984b, 1986, 1987, 1988) *Statistical Year Book* (Paris: UNESCO). *165*
United Nations (1976) *Report of Habitat: United Nations Conference on Human Settlements* (New York: United Nations). *90, 96, 98*
United Nations (1980) *World Population Trends and Policies: 1979 Monitoring Report, Vol. II* (New York: United Nations). *249*
United Nations (1981) *Report of the U.N. Conference on the Least Developed Countries* (Paris: United Nations).

United Nations (1982a) *World Population Trends and Policies: 1981 Monitoring Report Vol. I* (New York: United Nations). *78, 81, 117, 118*

United Nations (1982b) *Demographic Indicators of Countries: Estimates and Projections as Assessed in 1980* (New York: United Nations).

United Nations (1982c) *Levels and Trends of Mortality since 1950: a Joint Study by the United Nations and the World Health Organisation* (New York: United Nations).

United Nations (1985a) *Strategies Document: Conference on the Decade of Women* (Nairobi: United Nations). *223, 229, 238*

United Nations (1985b) *World Population Trends and Policies, Population and Development Interrelations: 1983 Monitoring Report vol.I* (New York: United Nations). *55, 80, 81, 166, 253, 254*

United Nations (1986a) 'International Youth Year', *United Nations Chronicle*, January 1986, XXIII pp. 23–42. *214, 219, 251*

United Nations (1986b), *World Population Prospects: Estimates and Projections as Assessed in 1984* (New York: United Nations). *243, 244, 248, 252*

United Nations (1988) *State of World Population, 1988*, a Press Kit produced for the UN by *The New Internationalist* (New York: United Nations Population Fund). *64, 75, 76, 151, 254*

US Department of Health, Education and Welfare (1981) *Social Security Programs Throughout the World* (Washington DC: Department of Health Education and Welfare). *43*

Urzua, R. (1978) *Social Science Research on Population and Development in Latin America* (Mexico City: International Review Group, Social Science Research on Population and Development, El Colegio de Mexico). *248*

Van der Berghe, P. L. (1969) 'Pluralism and the polity', in L. Kuper and M.G. Smith (eds) *Pluralism in Africa* (Berkeley: University of California).

Van Rensburg, P. (1967) *Education and Development in an Emerging Country* (Uppsala: Scandinavian Institute of African Studies). *218*

Vaughan, P., A. Mills and D. Smith (1984) *District Health Planning and Management* (London: Evaluation and Planning Centre, London School of Hygiene and Tropical Medicine). *130*

Vuori, H. (1982) 'The World Health Organisation and traditional medicine', *Community Medicine* 4, pp. 129–37. *133*

Wade, R. (1988) 'Village Republics', *Economic Conditions for Collective Action in South India* (London: Cambridge University Press). *66*

Walton, R. G. (1975) 'Welfare rights and social work: ambivalence in action', in H. Jones (ed.) *Towards a New Social Work* (London: Routledge & Kegan Paul). *48*

Ward, P. M. (1982) 'The Practice and potential of self-help housing in Mexico City', in P. M. Ward (ed.) *Self-help Housing: a Critique* (London: Mansell Publishing House). *103*

Ward, P. M. (1984) 'Mexico: beyond Sites and Services', in G.M. Payne (ed.) *Low Income Housing in the Developing World* (Chichester: John Wiley). *91, 97*

Warren, W. (1973) 'Imperialism and capitalist industrialisation', *New Left Review* 81, pp. 3–4. *31, 32, 33*

Warren, W. (1980) *Imperialism: Pioneer of Capitalism* (London: Verso). *31, 32, 33, 283*

Watson, K. (1982) 'Educational neo-colonialism – the continuing colonial legacy', in K. Watson (ed.) *Education in the Third World* (London: Croom Helm). *159, 179*

Weber, M. (1962) *The Protestant Ethic and the Spirit of Capitalism* (London: George Allen & Unwin). *22*

Weisbrod, B. *et al.* (1973) 'Disease and Economic Development: the Impact of Parasitic Disease in St. Lucia (University of Minnesota)' *cited* in L. A. H. Msukwa (1981) *Meeting the Basic Health Needs of Rural Malawi* (Swansea: University College Centre for Development Studies). *106*

Weiss, T. G. (1982) 'The Third World's views of the New International Development Strategy for the Third U.N. Development Decade', in A. Jennings and T. G. Weiss (eds) *The Challenge of Development in the Eighties: Our Response* (Oxford: Pergamon). *25*

Weiss, T. G. and A. Jennings (1983) *More for the Least: Prospects for the Poorest Countries in the Eighties* (Lexington, Mass.: Lexington Books).

Werner, D. (1979) *Where There is No Doctor* (London: Macmillan). *139*

Werner, D. (1983) 'Health care in Cuba: a model service or a means of control?' in D. Morley, J. Rohde and G. Williams (eds) *Practising Health for All* (Oxford: Oxford University Press). *120*

Whitehead, R. G. (1977) 'Some quantitative considerations of importance to the improvement of the nutritional status of rural children', in D. A. J. Tyrrell *et al.*, *Technologies for Rural Health* (London: The Royal Society). *111, 126*

Whyte, M. K. (1978) *The Status of Women in Pre-Industrial Societies* (Princeton: Princeton University Press). *228*

Williams, E. and P. 'Progressive patient care', in M. King (ed.) *Medical Care in Developing Countries* (Oxford: Oxford University Press). *134, 138*

Williams, G. (1987) *Third World Political Organizations* (Basingstoke: Macmillan). *35*

Women's Studies Group (1978) (Centre for Contemporary Cultural Studies, University of Birmingham) *Women Take Issue* (London: Hutchinson). *225*

Wood, A. W. (1970) 'Training Malawi's Young Pioneers', *Community Development Journal*, 5, pp. 130–8.

World Bank (1975) *Rural Development Sector Policy Paper* (Washington D.C.: World Bank).

World Bank (1979, 1980b, annually 1981–8) *World Development Report* (New York: Oxford University Press). *3, 4, 10, 11, 14, 19, 24, 25, 33, 36, 42, 66, 68, 73, 107, 108, 109, 129, 130, 137, 143, 149, 152, 154, 155, 157, 158, 159, 160, 164, 166, 172, 184, 185, 186, 187, 202, 257*

World Bank (1980a) *Education Sector Policy Paper* (Washington D.C.: World Bank). *41, 150, 186*

World Health Organisation (1977) *The Primary Health Worker* (Geneva: World Health Organisation). *128, 131, 132*

World Health Organisation (1979) *Formulating Strategies for Health For All by the Year 2000* (Geneva: World Health Organisation). *131*

World Health Organisation (1980) *Sixth Report on the World Health Situation Part 1: Global Analysis* (Geneva: World Health Organisation). *111, 112, 113, 114, 116, 117, 126, 129*

World Health Organisation (1983a) *World Health Statistics Annual 1983* (Geneva: World Health Organisation). *129*

World Health Organisation (1983b) *Integrated Vector Control*, Technical Report Series No. 688, p. 7 (Geneva: World Health Organisation). *113, 116*

World Health Organisation (1987) *Evaluation of the Strategy for Health for All by the Year 2000, Seventh Report on the World Health Situation, Vol. 1: Global Review* (Geneva: World Health Organisation). *110, 111, 112, 113, 114, 115, 116, 124, 125, 126, 131, 136, 144, 150, 164, 222, 252*

World Health Organisation and UN Children's Fund (1978) *Primary Health Care* (Geneva: World Health Organisation). *131, 138*

Wraith, R. E. and E. Simpkins (1963) *Corruption in Developing Countries* (London: George Allen & Unwin). *272*

Yasas, F. M. (1974) cited in R. J. Burge (1975) 'A Study of Social Work Developments in Botswana', unpublished MScEcon thesis, University College, Cardiff. *201*

Young, K., W. C. F. Bussink and P. Hasan (1980a) *Malaysia: Growth and Equity in a Multiracial Society* (Baltimore: Johns Hopkins University). *161*

Young, M., H. Perraton and T. Dodds (1980b) *Distance Teaching for the Third World* (London: Routledge & Kegan Paul). *164*

Zachariah, M. (1973) 'Positive discrimination in education for Indian scheduled castes: a review of the problems, 1950–70', in Commonwealth Secretariat (eds) *Education in Developing Countries of the Commonwealth: Reports of Research in Education No. 6* (London: Commonwealth Secretariat). *156*

Subject Index